# YOU LOSE YOURSELF,
# YOU REAPPEAR

# YOU LOSE YOURSELF, YOU REAPPEAR

## BOB DYLAN AND THE VOICES OF A LIFETIME

PAUL MORLEY

**SIMON &
SCHUSTER**

London · New York · Sydney · Toronto · New Delhi

First published in Great Britain by Simon & Schuster UK Ltd, 2021

Copyright © Paul Morley, 2021

The right of Paul Morley to be identified as the author of this work has been
asserted in accordance with the Copyright, Designs and Patents Act, 1988.

1 3 5 7 9 10 8 6 4 2

Simon & Schuster UK Ltd
1st Floor
222 Gray's Inn Road
London WC1X 8HB

www.simonandschuster.co.uk
www.simonandschuster.com.au
www.simonandschuster.co.in

Simon & Schuster Australia, Sydney
Simon & Schuster India, New Delhi

The author and publishers have made all reasonable efforts to contact
copyright-holders for permission, and apologise for any omissions or errors in the form
of credits given. Corrections may be made to future printings.

A CIP catalogue record for this book
is available from the British Library

Hardback ISBN: 978-1-4711-9514-3
Trade Paperback ISBN: 978-1-4711-9515-0
eBook ISBN: 978-1-4711-9516-7

Typeset in Bembo by M Rules
Printed in the UK by CPI Group (UK) Ltd, Croydon, CR0 4YY

MIX
Paper from
responsible sources
FSC
www.fsc.org  FSC® C020471

e.s.p.

*Who has set me here? By whose order and design have this place and time been destined for me?*

—Blaise Pascal (1623–1662)

# CONTENTS

# ONE

## A STRANGER CALLS

Because of how things change, this book does not begin as I once intended it to; this was not going to be the opening line. I wasn't completely sure what the opening line was going to be in the first weeks of 2020 as I planned the initial few pages, but it would have been the start of a different kind of book. 2020 was at the time a vastly different kind of year from the testing, fretful one it became.

There were a few possible first lines I could use to set up my introduction to a certain book making some statements and speculations about where Bob Dylan was, in his mind, in my mind, and in the mind of a world that had a lot of preoccupations – but that was before time and history, and just your basic domestic life, seemed to split apart and all those possible first lines were now not going to work. Not necessarily because the world had stopped, but actually because Bob Dylan hadn't. It was a good job I hadn't planned the ending of the book but decided to let that take care of itself, once the Dylan in this biography had turned up, made his presence felt and in his own way taken over.

Before the world fell apart following a ruthless revision by nature, fate or whatever you want to call the powers of the universe, back when twentieth-century momentum seemed to be continuing into the twenty-first without any outrageous signs of absolute disruption – just the usual warnings, complaints and apprehensions, the unthinkable shapes and forms of climate change and global warming, the accelerating problems with social media, systemic racism and Mark Zuckerberg, a riotous, poisonous, surely doomed, unreality television president and various new kinds of accelerating generation and gender gaps – this was going to be a Bob Dylan book written when it seemed he might well have produced his final album of original songs.

His album discography seemed to have stopped in 2012 with *Tempest*, his longest ever studio album, released a tidy fifty years after his debut album, plainly called *Bob Dylan* because he then needed to be clearly, unambiguously introduced; he hadn't yet paid his dues and earned his spurs as artist, star or even much more than a minor local cult. That first record didn't sink like a stone or disappear without trace, but the world was unprepared for it. Bob Dylan needed a little getting used to. His odds at the time to win the Nobel Prize in Literature within sixty years would have been astronomical, if some Las Vegas betting shop had cared to take the bet. Revered, all-conquering Americans like O'Neill, Faulkner, Hemingway, Steinbeck and Bellow, the Big Dogs, became Nobel Laureates, not someone who mostly sang his words, apparently cheapening their effect through performance.

Pop albums at the time weren't yet works with their own innate, abstract significance deserving to be titled like novels or films. Solo singers didn't have the power or even the motivation to title their own albums as though they were something other than commercial song collections. Dylan was soon working on both things, which over time would start to reduce those Nobel odds.

Fifty-eight years after Bob Dylan and *Bob Dylan* with little fanfare began a series of records unequalled in recording history for their artistry, adventure and ravishing ambition, Dylanologists – one of the main consequences of those records – logging in at the beginning of 2020 for an annual preview of events reluctantly accepted that as a new decade dawned they were unlikely to be hearing any new music from their man. It seemed this part of his discography was a settled fact, and there would be no follow-up to *Tempest*. His pilgrimage towards some form of nirvana was over. Songs didn't come to him like they once did. He wasn't able to boast, to tap into volatility, and reveal his soul, in quite the same way. He wasn't even so sure what had caused those songs in the first place. There was nothing he could do about it; it was bound to happen sooner or later. His thoughts were drifting elsewhere. In time, even stars burn out.

*Tempest* was, or so it seemed to me, a harrowing, heartbreaking last-gasp batch of buoyant pessimism, sublime divination, opaque self-reflexivity, transcendent nostalgia, stray thoughts, frayed nerves, unscheduled appointments, disaster stories, shipwrecked dreams, unpunctual adventures, tantalising elusiveness, exaggerated thought, from a place where nothing is what it seems and a chill wind is always blowing through, a place where the history of pop music goes from William Blake to John Lennon, and from Bob Dylan to Bob Dylan. On the side it gave us a few lessons in humour, even as he was still using his talents to destroy or correct the structures of world history as we know them.

3

As always he was everywhere present in his work, starring in his own stories, but nowhere apparent, rummaging through his memories, acting his age but a number of others as well. There was still no sign that he was ridding himself of the need to continually decipher his own life, no sense he had given up on singing the meaning of things. You seem to know what's going to happen in each and every song even before you hear it, and this sense of 'what's going to happen' foreshadows impending doom, which has been there since he started recording albums.

Dylan, drawn to the unknown, up to no good in a good way, put forward his latest concerns which were more or less always his concerns: the world has gone wrong, time to change names and hide out somewhere, love's there for the losing, our hearts break, accidents happen, what's done is done, it was fun while it lasted, it's the best I could do, the best I could be, careful what you wish for, grit your teeth, the night's playing tricks, time to make amends, all things have run their course, ancient footprints are everywhere, let's sit tight, let's just move on. Whatever happens, make sure you come back alive. You never know, his heart might have been at peace. Songs emerged out of dreams nursed in darkness, there was a pervading sense of danger, a certain sort of strength was being concentrated and preserved. Stories emerged quickly and often disappeared into themselves, becoming other stories, which got replaced by others, often in the space of one song. He freely mixes the serious and the comic, the sacred and profane, the eminent and the ordinary.

The singer with more past, more biography, debate, discussion and analysis devoted to him than any other musician or artist of recent times was still coming forward like the man without a past, unwilling to settle down, wandering into town as though for the first time, on *Tempest*. Sometimes casually because the sun is shining or seeming wary because the weather is grim and unruly, the dogs are barking and something dark is approaching; sometimes like he's lost, or like he's in exactly the right place; sometimes bringing strange, wonderful news, sometimes passing the time of day. Now and then like he's being watched, shadowed, judged, pestered, or like he's entered a ghost town and he can do what he wants, he can build himself a home and stare at the sky as if he's looking into his soul. All of this was contained in his voice as much as anything else, which might remind you of the voice he had when he was seen to be a spiky, gawky protest singer, or a sunken-cheeked seminal po-faced rebel star in all black, or a fire-breathing disciple of Jesus Christ, or a soulful, transcendent balladeer, or a cranky, argumentative drifter, but that's because there were a lot of voices he was keeping track of in his head, and this latest one, a little drained of energy but as meticulous as ever, had found new ways to sing about how you have to move into darkness to find real beauty.

*Tempest* contained nothing he hadn't noted and promoted before, but was nothing like anything he'd ever done before – familiar, for Dylan, but showing us the world in a way that was fresh, appreciative and alive, this endlessly ricocheting fusion of intellectual culture, mass culture and folk culture, this awareness of the melodic messages of medieval minstrels and the sacred rhythms of Christianity and Judaism, this balancing on a blues-based, country-slanted, jazzed-up knife edge between chaos and order, using the endlessly rearranged loose-limbed free-style rock and roll music to grasp the ungraspable and experience the impossible, taking in and then recirculating tradition, inhaling and exhaling, connecting ancient tunes to a live wire. And, of course, he was in his own self-certified way a poet, one of those beings who've got nothing to lose, living a kind of detachment that leads to all sorts of truth.

He was then over seventy, and with all that was now behind him, all that artistic and religious history he was always finding and processing, he was still thinking forward, still tapping into the energetic, enigmatic nature of reality. Drawing upon a wild assortment of sources, he went back and beyond to the Bible, to serving and preserving Cicero, Ovid, Virgil and Homer, the worlds of ancient Greece and Rome, to Norse legend, back and beyond to the broadsheet ballads, carols and epic laments of the sixteenth century and the troubadours of southern France, to the healing properties of ancient Siberian shamans – 'one who knows' – to the birth of cinema and the first record by Bessie Smith, 'The Downhearted Blues', who made up her own melodies to fit the poetry of her song. All his best ideas had been stolen by the ancients. Sometimes he seemed to be emptying paradise into a song, sometimes just random stuff he found in his pocket that he'd picked up along the way.

It could easily have been the end of what he felt he needed to say, even as it seemed to stop half-way through, with no particular conclusion, definitely no resolution. There was no fatal drop of energy, and the death stuck in the records grooves had let's face it been tossed into his songs for fifty years – almost as soon as he changed his name to Bob Dylan, deeply attuned to moods and impressions, to verbal acts, to the handling of secrets, to the turnover of history, he was considering the idea of death as the destroyer of worlds, where no-one ever died of natural causes.

In one junkyard scrap of a song written when he was coming up to twenty, he was already acting like he'd come to the end of his life, like he'd done enough, he was doomed – already in one of his songs he's using a pack of cards, a straight symbol of the unpredictable adventure of life, and his grave is being dug with a silver spade, and twenty years have gone, and he'll never reach twenty-one. Perhaps he was so afraid of dying because he hadn't yet lived, and he'd been thinking he'd got a lot of things to do, already aware of a tremendous world he had inside him, one he needed to get out. A fear of dying was a fear of having already failed, a dread of being no good.

But since 2012, as the years passed by, and he became the furtive showman elegantly ravaged by time, the seventy-something surrealist crooner, possibly part of the plan since he was a teenager, it did seem *Tempest* was becoming the final Dylan album of songs he had written. It wasn't that he had given up caring or stopping going against the grain, he hadn't lost the strength to carry on; he was still putting up a fight, but the terms of the fight, the rules and regulations, were being revised. And there were many different ways to continue being epic to follow how he moved through decades of drama, deflection and reflection from 'Man of Constant Sorrow' to 'High Water (for Charley Patton)', from 'All Along The Watchtower' to 'Not Dark Yet', from one end of life to another in an order and with a range, depth and detail no other composer-performer has come anywhere near matching.

And of course he was a singer that kept on singing, wherever his voice took him, whatever happened to it, however much he disappeared little by little into his own abbreviated time; a voice that, however old he was, however young, however not one

7

thing or the other, clearly never stopped laughing, loving and most of all living. A voice that started hoarding wisdom when he was a teenager, a kid, and which, whatever he was doing with it, sounded like wisdom, whether he used it to shout, plead, complain, adore, celebrate, seduce, dismiss, apologise, resent, command, retreat. A voice that eventually would become as comfortably, uncomfortably eccentric as everyone more or less always expected it to be; a voice battling the ravages of time and getting sharpened by ageing. A voice that had always seemed to say, at whatever stage of attack or defence, at whatever point of contact with fame or a peaceful life, at whatever stage of his contemplation of human fortune and misfortune: it's time. Time tells him what he is. He changes and he is the same.

*Tempest* was a follow-up to *Together Through Life* three years before, which itself was a follow-up to *Modern Times* three years before that. Both were contenders for a while to be Dylan's final studio album of original songs, and in their own ways not doing much to deny it, with the rattled, woozy, grim and bitching furies of *Together Through Life* – when you're up to your neck in shit, there's nothing left to do but sing – and the hunted, delirious eloquence of *Modern Times*, where he sounds a little used up, but living deeply, still on call, deadpan and funny, and then frightening and not funny, still heading out into a future of unknowable change as he watches over his past.

The idea that Dylan might be finished in some form or another seemed to have been going on for a quarter of a century; in a way it might all have started back in the 1960s, as soon as there was a gap between albums of longer than a few months. As much as he did, as much as he got done, he still seemed to spend a lot of time in exile, starting over in some new place, a little frozen in time. Once he released *Time Out of Mind* in 1997, the beginning of a so-called 'modern era', seen as a return to form as a maker of records after fifteen years of hedging and sidestepping, from then on – he was fifty-six, he'd had serious heart trouble, a real life-threatening tipping point – it seems everything pointed towards death, whether it does or not, as if the grave was just around the bend and hovering inside every song, which it is and isn't, just like it always has been. In an interview about the record, he was a little put out that one view was that the record deals with mortality – and his mortality at that – and if he accepted that it might, one way or another amongst other ways, deal with mortality, how come not one critic said that it dealt with *their* mortality?

Dylan has the best weapon when it comes to getting to terms with ageing: words. He doesn't stop being a guide to life, and in the end it turns out he has time to grow old, and what seemed at the time like a possible last statement was just another stop on the road, for some catch-up, and some reviving of the soul.

Shortly before *Modern Times* came out, as a music critic, I was unceremoniously shown into a bare, soulless office room by his then label Sony to hear the album. I wasn't allowed to review the record until it was actually released a few weeks later. I was, though, permitted to write that I had heard it, but I could say no more. It was a little visit into the fenced-off world of Dylan, as though he was being guarded by publicists and his record company like some rare iridescent sea creature, and the great artistic rule breaker was surrounded by rules and regulations and terms and conditions. I did write about the experience of being locked alone in a room with the record, almost chained to a chair, as though I hadn't actually heard it, just looked at it, and it gives a sense of where Dylan was in the world in 2006. As I sat listening in this empty office room feeling a little awkward, I must admit I did wonder once or twice, as one of Dylan's earthy, rasping late voices filled the room, making it seem like it was part of a haunted house, if at any moment Bob Dylan himself might walk into the room. Well, suddenly materialise, and help me out with his own press release for the record, which consisted of a few anagrams of the title; Dire Moments, Mind Meteors, Timed Sermon, Demon Mister, Trod Immense and Monetised Mr.

He didn't turn up, though, except through song, which was spooky enough, and real enough, and this was my report:

I signed a contract, something to do with giving away all my hard-earned privileges and forfeiting my ears if I breathed a word to anyone about what I heard, and this gave me the permission required at this point in history to listen in a darkened room to the new Bob Dylan album, to be released in a few weeks.

According to the contract I signed I'm allowed to tell you that Dylan is a legendary rocker, the album's called *Modern Times*, it has ten tracks, it's his first new release for five years and it unofficially completes the third part of a trilogy begun with *Time Out of Mind* and *"Love and Theft"*, for those old enough to have such a view considered his best albums since *Blood on the Tracks* and *Desire*.

His last album was released on September 11 2001, so I figured it's no wonder they want me to sign a contract before I heard his new one. If Dylan doesn't make as much instant history as he once did, if he seems in some kind of moody exile from everything else that's happening in rock, he remains the one true master at turning up out of the blue/the shadows/his dreams when the time is right, or wrong, and there's a sudden change in the weather only he saw coming.

According to the terms of the contract I signed, I'm not allowed to tell you anything that might give the game away, but I guess I can speculate a little without ruining any secrets. Everything about the album including the title and the cover is thieved from some source or another, even if that source is himself. I imagine the songs are all about love and death, or the mystery of time, or the fear of losing reputation, or the secret to controlling the wind and the rain, or the final empty monotony of the human experience. And how beyond a certain point there is no return.

The songs are probably played on instruments you've heard more than a million times before. He'll be apparently shuffling the same old pack of cards, telling the same crooked story again and again, swinging between cold blooded and warm hearted, singing 'baby' a lot, twanging and twitching in the regular irregular tangled country blues woods. The calmly accrued details, the dialogue trails, the passionate suspicion, the fearful warnings, the sly attempts to win some affection, to shed his confusions, to stake his claims, the splendid cleverness, the thin line between happiness and melancholy, the collisions between seemingly unconnected lines that produce instant meaning, the abrupt way he likes to wander off the edge of a song – at first there will seem nothing new about anything to do with *Modern Times*, and Dylan of course damn well knows it, which is why he gave it the title, unless he was just celebrating seventy years of Charlie Chaplin's film, Chaplin always creating his own ideal image of the world, with the opening title reading 'A story of industry, of individual enterprise, humanity crusading in the pursuit of happiness'. Chaplin's *Modern Times* was a silent movie – his last – made deliberately for the sound era, and Dylan's *Modern Times* is an album of non-electronic music made at a time when most popular music is electronically created.

Apart from the already leaked mention of Alicia Keys – which may or may not become a clue to finding the key to unlocking the bitter-sweet truth about his lies – there'll be little he mentions that couldn't have happened a hundred years ago. Then it will hit you from high above that he's declaring as he always has done that time is not a line; it's a circle, a snake biting its own tail, a figure of eight, or a Gordian knot. He feels things in his bones, the future depends on what you do today, and it comes soon enough. He's always been predicting his future by creating it, and spending a lifetime figuring out how to do it.

Dylan, knowing what he's up to if not where he is, advances menacingly, from the top of a mountain of memory, and quickly withdraws, round the back of his scrolling imagination, singing like he's about to die, or about to be born. All this cliché and familiarity will no doubt rearrange itself into something diabolically unique. The whole damned thing will be disguised as yesterday but really be about today if not tomorrow. Christ, it's almost like I've already heard it.

Already people are talking of the final track where he

12

sounds as old as he has ever done as the greatest final track of all of his albums, which would place it above 'Desolation Row' and 'It Ain't Me Babe' and think about how they redirected the rock song. At this stage he's got more on his mind than just redirecting the course of music, as fun as that was while it lasted. After all, without giving too much away, enough to break the terms of my contract, on this last track, like a post-apocalyptic mythological western written by Samuel Beckett, set in some kind of garden where you can walk forever, because your horse is dead and you're stranded, there's no-one home, the gardener's gone home, the spectral protagonist's carrying a dead man's shield, he's drifting towards a higher state of consciousness, the fire's gone out but the light's never dying and the night turns to day. This might be the afterlife, it might just be another idea Dylan's had about how to write a song about the afterlife, about refusing to be where he clearly seems to be.

Just in case this really is his last complete album of songs, the farewell work, his last silent film, he's no doubt made sure he leaves us with a roguish, indecipherable drama, as if he's been a ghost all along, a floating fragmenting fiction looking for some place to rest for a while more than a prophet, rock star, off-duty legend or mind-bending troubadour. I'm sure that at the end of the song, he'll be walking out of sight, fading into the nearest shadow, taking everything he's ever done with him, rubbing away his tracks, cleaning up his fingerprints, and the last line will be about 'the world's end'.

It's the end of the world every day, for someone.

Six years later, because it wasn't the end after all, there was
more remembering and anticipation to come, and in the years
following *Tempest*, a final farewell framed as a fresh start this
late in the day, there was a series of scrupulous late-life reckon-
ings consisting of unsentimental reflections on and homages to
a certain set of influences and inspirations, versions and interpretations of Tin Pan Alley American standards, jazz classics
and the voice and the less obvious repertoire of Frank Sinatra.

These songs were in themselves so gallantly inimitable they
had the qualities of being original works. But he wasn't singing
his own words, as much as he made them his, and any story of
Bob Dylan is going to be about his words and what they did to
the very idea of what a song is and could be. But then any story
about Bob Dylan is also going to be about how he keeps turning himself into something else, slipping through the cracks,
and using one voice after another sometimes by not singing
songs, just by taking hold of history and shaping his place in it,
appearing on the stage and in the history of the times, leaving
some marks because what else is there to do?

Sometimes a voice or two somehow appeared when he
seemed to disappear for a while, which he was prone to do –
he could drop out like the sun does at sunset, thinking that
people might miss him, perhaps after beginning to take him for
granted. When he reappeared, one way or another, he would
be much loved or at least less ignored.

These records of songs he hadn't written seemed inspired by
the time he turned to sociably presenting his own radio show
between 2006 and 2009, a wired free-thinking combination
of grave disc jockey and good-time guru, rounding up some
musical memories, selected from the collective memory stored

in a central recorded archive, always best listened to as time creeps towards the darkest hour that's just before the dawn. The *Theme Time Radio Hour* for XM Satellite Radio turned the hosting of a show playing records into a relaxed, rapturous art form; he talked about music as if it is down to earth, and out of this world, mostly what you think it is and absolute magic. A cosmically jive-talking Dylan reminded us in this too-easy non-stop randomised streaming era about the important historical, emotional, chronological and social context of popular music. He was unexpectedly warm, but the whole series was a kind of warning. If these songs disappear, their stories and styles forgotten, everyone and everything will disappear. He believed that people would never tire of hearing stories, and stories will be told, and they will be sung, and when you get the pleasure of being sung a story, you get the additional pleasure of the dignity of a voice.

All the spellbinding informative intros he never did live were there in his radio shows as more music led to more music made more special by being introduced and linked by Dylan, welcoming experience from every quarter, and offering his own in return. And the voices on the records he chose and showcased demonstrated how much Dylan is a student, and ultimately a master, of the singing voice, and all that it can achieve, often inside three or four minutes, but eleven or seventeen if necessary, singing for the hell of it, sometimes a voice crying in the wilderness, sometimes a voice of the heart, sometimes a quiet voice of reason chanting words like prayers, slowly making itself heard. Dylan definitely knew his voices, and even if you'd never been sure about his singing, hearing him talk could convince you that he knows how to use his

15

voice, to persuade, to please, to proclaim. To pass the time of day, to pin down chaos. As you listened to him, hanging out in the air, speaking from no known place, cueing another song that makes him feel alive, you could imagine that he was nothing but a voice.

Following trails, curating styles, grouping musical moments into off-beat, funny themes, giving critical shape to whole hordes of musical waifs and strays, treating tracks like holy relics and/or fun for all the family, dislodging music that seemed to have settled once and for all into history, he'd started to think of some songs he should be singing, the kind of songs he seemed to be rebelling against in the early 1960s, but wasn't really. As was often the case, what others read into what he was doing was not necessarily what he was actually doing, as far as he was concerned. He was simply extending the line, accelerating a few musical timelines, coming up with some new forms and genres like it was written in the stars, but not necessarily out of any spite for what the older pre-rock music was, how musty and mild it seemed compared to the new rock and roll, and how it was squarely sung in the years before he turned up, getting himself into some situations, grabbing what he could from the present as much as the past.

He started to sing some of the far-off mid-century songs the radio host he had become might play, making another adjustment to his own history, adding more details, making his time on earth stretch even further. He made it sound as though he might have been around before he was even born, and just as he had done with his radio show, with the kind of talking, an easy, smooth shooting the breeze he hadn't done for decades if ever, he honoured, sometimes exhumed, the greats, the fallen, the neglected, shining light into dark corners, restoring moments dulled by time, and added something extra to the fact and fiction of being Bob Dylan.

Connected to the spirit of the radio show and attaching more elusive detail to the fact and fiction was the first, possibly last, volume of his memoirs, *Chronicles*, published in 2005, which he haunted as much as wrote, hunting himself down all kinds of highways and byways, sending the reader up the occasional blind alley, remembering some things vividly, struggling to recall other moments, in a voice you could make up in your head as you read, a voice that skidded across the surfaces and sensations of memory just as he did, fully aware of the depths. It was an homage to and an extension of the literary lineage he belongs to and enriches, stabilising autobiography running parallel with displaced fiction.

He wondered about the effect that music can have on the mind, and vice versa, and wrote of ten thousand years of culture falling from Johnny Cash's shoulders, Public Enemy hurling horses over cliffs and Hank Williams making movement cease just by singing. It was that kind of true story. He talked of his paternal grandmother's voice possessing a haunting accent – she was a transplanted Jew from Odessa – as though she was an early influence, a voice he'd never forget.

Other voices appeared when he wasn't even singing, writing or talking. A photo of him was a voice, soundless but significant. There were voices in his harmonica playing, his album covers, his one, spidery novel, his bewitching memoirs, his pencil drawings and paintings, his interviews, even his silence to the critics and biographers – especially what they overstated, or missed – voices that stretched so far into the future they could see all the way to the end of time, voices that came from so far in the past they brought with them ghosts that had their own voices. There were the voices where 'there's no telling what can happen' that came when he was portrayed in the 2007 film *I'm Not There* by six different actors of mixed age and gender playing seven different personas, where director Todd Haynes built a Bob Dylan in the same way Dylan often writes a song, stealing discriminately, mixing up yesterday, today, tomorrow, time, lyrics, influences, space, moments, history, pastiche, fable, blending genre, juxtaposing events, challenging facts. There is no actual mention of a 'Bob Dylan'. When, in the very final moments, Dylan himself appears in the film playing the harmonica, as if to fill a few gaps in the story, to encourage further suspension of disbelief, he is no more and no less the real Dylan than any of the other acted, assumed Dylans; he's just another invention, another mythical fake creation taking part in a wild struggle for existence.

There's the straighter but perhaps slippier voice that Martin Scorsese chose to frame in his documentary *No Direction Home* two years earlier; the Haynes and Scorsese voices operate next to his remembering radio voice as a way of showing how he was always moving on even as they all moved through his past, through the ephemeral and the permanent. At the time of these films and documentaries, and his radio show, and his memoirs and official bootlegs, when it could seem Dylan was heading closer to the end of the trail, it seemed a good time to playfully, solemnly resist making out the definitive shape of Dylan, which was a game for fools, by actually making some shapes out of Dylan. Some final words and thoughts about the stranger who never feels at home, who can never belong, who must be a little in love with death.

It turned out there would be at least fourteen years more movement and change as Dylan kept circling the contemporary landscape, finding various craters of his own where he could set up temporary headquarters. Scorsese even had to deliver another documentary to shake up his meaning of Dylan, turning to making up the far-fetched truth about the extravagantly untamed Rolling Thunder tour as a way of sowing some seeds of doubt and drifting a little from the shore of conventional biography, ensuring stable identity and closure are continually deferred.

Each of the characters Dylan imagined or played in his songs, some of whom were places – and those characters he was talking to, which could also seem to be himself, in permanent dialogue with himself – had a voice adding to the overall presence of his voice. The voice of the complete unknown, of the jokerman and the Queen of Spades, of the lover and the thief, Erica Jong and Valentino, Johnny in the basement and Mr Jones, Hollis Brown and Billy the Kid, the Lone Ranger and Saxophone Joe, King Kong and Prince Philip, Charles Darwin and St Augustine, Rasputin and Isis, Jimmy Cagney and John Wesley Hardin, Napoleon in rags and Mr Tambourine Man, the night watchman and the jelly-faced women, Jesse James and Desdemona, Quinn the Eskimo and the Fairy Queen, Adam and Eve and Romeo and Juliet, the savage soldier and the cowboy angel, Walter Cronkite and Captain Kidd, Sherlock Holmes and Judas Priest, Goliath and the Pharaoh, the Statue of Liberty and the Golden Gate Bridge, Little Jack Horner and Dr. Filth, the Lincoln Country Road and Armageddon, Alicia

Keys and Uncle Remus, John the Baptist and Tweedledum and Tweedledee, Tom Paine and Judas Iscariot, Aladdin and his lamp and the flesh-coloured Christs that glow in the dark. All these characters he included in his songs so he could get a chance to meet them, get to know them, even be them, singer and character blurred and melded.

There was the voice he found in the country, on the road, from place to place, in private, and there was the voice he used in the city, a place of recording, performing and broadcasting. There was the voice that was formed from all the voices of those singing Dylan songs, because even though no-one sings Dylan like Dylan, sometimes that means hearing one of his songs being sung in a way that makes it closer to being finished – or at least set up to be finished, with its own surprises and leaps in the dark – than even Dylan imagined. A miscellaneous, volatile Dylan Voice emerges from the hundreds of singers that have covered Dylan whether plodding through the literal motions, fastidiously following the original tune or spelling out their own genius, their particular state of mind, looking for their own voice, their own place in the state of things. He could have just written the songs, never sung them himself, but you would hear the essence of Dylan, a voice of greatness, if you put together Odetta, Maria Muldaur, Joan Baez, the Byrds, John Martyn, Bryan Ferry, Richie Havens, Burl Ives, Nina Simone, Nico, Jimi Hendrix, the Walker Brothers, the Hollies, Van Morrison, Davy Graham, Susan Tedeschi, José Feliciano, Nick Drake, Bobby Bare, Heinz and the Wild Boys, Albert Hammond Jr, Fairport Convention, the Flying Burrito Brothers, Bettina Jonic, Patti Smith, Bobby Darin, Billy Paul, Jackie de Shannon, Sam Cooke, Lou Reed, Frankie Valli and the Four Seasons,

Ian Hunter, Tom Waits, Marianne Faithful, Mountain, Prince, Bill Murray, Loudon Wainwright III, Morrissey, Engelbert Humperdinck, Adele, Emmylou Harris, George Harrison, Solomon Burke, Fotheringay, Willie Nelson, Indigo Girls, Spirit, PJ Harvey, the Persuaders, Madeleine Peyroux, Tom Jones, Johnny Cash, Lucinda Williams, the White Stripes. Cat Power, Beck, Cowboy Junkies, Barb Jungr, Dolly Parton, Thea Gilmore, Yo La Tengo, Noel Harrison, Sufjan Stevens, Rage Against The Machine, Susanna and the Magical Orchestra, the Chicks, Nick Cave, Laura Marling, David Bowie ... all those who took Dylan songs where they should be taken, to the reassembled limits, and sometimes beyond.

There were also, bringing into the centre another kind of shifting, accumulative Dylan voice, an increasing number of official bootleg albums that compiled first takes, outtakes, rough drafts, live shows, rarities and lost other versions, assembling an alternative history of Dylan, a different way of approaching his songs and their chronology. The bootleg voices of Dylan exist in a limbo round the back of what was understood, a series of dead voices, lost sounds, forgotten noises, arcane ceremonies and various vibrations that were perhaps never meant to be heard more than once or twice, or were perhaps as proper, as part of his perceived reality, as the official records. Even if sometimes it sounded as though he was singing under the sea, or as though his phone had been tapped.

The Bootleg Series began in 1991, twenty-two years after what was more or less the very first rock album bootleg (inevitably a Dylan one), *Great White Wonder*, a tantalisingly illegal double album containing a cross-section of unreleased recordings and outtakes from 1961 to 1967. The plain, intriguing shadiness of a Dylan bootleg, the difficulty tracking them down, the sense they were part of some greater lawless cover-up, some scheme, or screen, of misinformation, was always something that added to Dylan's spiky outlying aura.

After years of covert pirate albums, Dylan's record label, Columbia, began to officially release the kind of relentless, rumoured work that had been consistently featured on boot-legs, to fill in the gaps more legally, to satisfy the most ardent, unrepentant Dylan fan's need for completion, to hear discarded ideas, multiple takes, second, third, fourth guesses and songs that were cut from various album releases. The series is part of the constantly whirring mini-industry of Dylan that means, even as the whole point of his action and workings is to never be pinned down, there is so much by and about him that can be used to help pin him down. In the end, perhaps, there's too much material and information to definitively categorise him; so much that it collapses in on itself and he's free to be free, and as invisible as he wants to be even as he is so visible, and so available, and so turned into something again and again that allows him to slip from behind it all.

With the bootlegs it became possible to witness through a completely new lens Dylan as he made a first impression, as he stepped out of obscurity with the look of a cheat and a charmer, and then there he was on the verge of greatness, charging through greatness, spinning out from greatness, rediscovering greatness, reordering greatness, all in all possibly never losing greatness, just moving from moment to moment, but seldom living in the moment, spread-eagled between violent nostalgia and violent anticipation.

The Bootleg Series started to run alongside the regular

Dylan releases, enhancing the weird, warped timing of Dylan's release schedule, dissolving standard opinion structures and adjusting some of the assumptions about a few of his usually less acclaimed, even reviled, periods, especially the extremely arbitrary-seeming, even self-destructive, late-1960s *Self Portrait* and the concerning and unloved born-again years after his late-1970s divorce from wife Sara, both of which turned out to be more misunderstood than useless or unsavoury as was first thought. Sometimes it seemed as though the Bootleg Series made you think you'd got everything wrong about Dylan, and sometimes it confirmed a few hunches.

Hidden inside the series as it unfolded, there were some less familiar Dylan voices, and voices that came and went in the shadows without being fully developed. He's always working out what to do with his voice, and how to sing a certain song, and all those books that make worlds out of his words often fail to notice that none of those words would appear in the way they do, in the order and rhythm they have, if they couldn't be sung as he sees fit. They must work as individual sounds and for how they rhyme and time within the music before any meaning can emerge.

The bootlegs revealed that even if at the time of an original release he sang a song and he seemed to be using one voice, he was using others as well. As for those songs that seemed as great as any at the time, there were sometimes others even better that he'd just left in the cupboard for a while, ready to be slid back into use when the time was right, or there seemed to be a certain public demand. 'Series of Dreams' and 'Dignity' never made it onto the mid-career *Oh Mercy* album after arguments with the producer, Daniel Lanois; 'Caribbean Wind' was left off *Shot of Love*; 'I'll Keep It with Mine' was missing from *Another Side of Bob Dylan* – sometimes as though just on a whim, or for reasons of balance and tone that only Dylan really understood. Down the line, some of them were suddenly remembered, including a song from the album viewed as one of his comeback records, this one a reappearance after three albums of defiantly unambiguous Christian songs.

The *Infidels* album from 1983 took a turn for the secular after his controversial dalliance with Christ, and its original release didn't feature 'Blind Willie McTell', confusing to those hearing it as one of his greatest songs. Dylan would shrug it off whenever it was mentioned to him, claiming it wasn't properly recorded. Maybe he just enjoyed allowing the mystery to grow around the song, letting it be like what had happened to the earliest, evolving blues songs sung in the late nineteenth century, where the singers – like owls – only had the stars in the night sky as their audience. It was as if he had sacrificed the song to achieve the kind of obscurity blues singers like Blind Willie McTell were suffering even a century after the blues emerged out of the terrible tolls of history. Maybe the song needed to exist only as a song, not a seven-inch single, a single act of admission, better never to be heard than be put in the wrong place at the wrong time.

Whatever the reason, it didn't appear in 1983, it appeared eighteen years later, a history lesson in the form of a dream, a dream in the form of a biography of one of the great blues musicians. After a few years of putting his faith in Christ, Dylan made clear his real faith is in the blues, which has everything in it, including Christ, and Satan, and all that is in between. In less than six minutes, with just his piano and some golden chords and the tentative, minimal guitar of the album's producer, Mark Knopfler, Dylan rambles through vast parts of American history, through miles and miles of American land, past significant long-lost scenery. It's a concise, comprehensive and evocative history of the grandeur and horrors of the Civil War-era American South, an explanation and celebration of the cathartic reason the blues exists and needed to exist, a study of power, racism and cold ambition, a meditation on the broad-shouldered Mississippi River, the spiritual home of the blues.

It's also as much as anything a hymn to the voice of McTell, born in Georgia at the very end of the nineteenth century, toiling in obscurity in the first half of the twentieth – as history swells and swings from bad to worse, Dylan wants us to understand that through it all, no-one can sing the blues like McTell – and to the voice of the blues itself, its importance in history, in balancing out history, and its importance to the history of Bob Dylan, as a singer who learnt how to sing whatever he wants, however he wants, because he found it all in the blues – all the way from a kind of resigned optimism to a fierce pessimism, from deep woe to joyous fury. The blues was at the core of a new kind of reliable, trustworthy, adaptable singing style he found, which took him through every style of music he wanted to try, always part of his voice whatever style of music he was singing. He couldn't have sung the songs he liked to sing – never completely sure if he was dreaming his life or it was real, something dreamt by himself or someone else, where fiction and fact merge together seamlessly – if he didn't know the blues, which faced up to reality like no other music.

'Blind Willie McTell' is a song as much as anything about the devastating, disorientating power of a great singing voice, and what it can transmit in a word, a line, a pause, a cry, a whisper – Dylan shows how the singing voice can carry the complicated, tormenting weight of history, convey the terror of racial abuse, the cracking of the whips, underline the beauty of one man's brave, lonely crusade, reach out into the world, work out for yourself the language of liberty and justice, make you feel love and experience real hate. Because it was such a careful, celebratory song about a voice and the voice, it needed a particular voice to sing it that was itself powerful enough to convey the message and cope with the history. No-one could sing the blues like Willie McTell, but then no-one could sing the blues like Bob Dylan; whether he achieved it, or was always trying to, the power of his voice lay in his constant quest to sing the blues – his blues – without sounding inauthentic and lost in sorry, empty white-man imitation. Anyone who feels that Dylan is not a very good singer should hear 'Blind Willie McTell' and hear how seriously he takes the idea that a song about the importance of a great voice, about the purpose of a great voice, needs to be sung with perfect grace, perfect timing and perfect feel.

The history of his own voice is in the song, as he starts out his travels, his travails, quiet and restrained, not sure yet of his destination, and passes through every song he's ever sung, surprised by the sights he sees, the chaos he witnesses, the ghosts he sees, building up almost imperceptibly until he's feeling real pain and despair about a set of circumstances that you might only really understand because of the blues.

A song about the voice – bringing with it all that other bountiful remembrance and homage – is also a song about Bob Dylan's voice, not so much because he can sing like Willie McTell, but because he can sing like Bob Dylan. No-one can sing the blues like Bob Dylan, and maybe initially he hid the song away because at the time he just needed to prove it to himself, especially after all the commotion there'd been about a few years of devotion to Christ. Then again, the bigger way of showing off his own special one-of-a-kind voice was to allow the song to live in the dark for a while, on its own under the stars, so that when it appeared, the song, and the voice about a voice, shined even brighter.

*

Through the various bootlegs you could experience the adjustable originality of his thinking, the processes, procedures and strategies he used to begin and complete a song, to amalgamate disparate experiences. You seemed to spend time inside the recording studio as Dylan felt his way, loosely, fussily, absent minded, deeply focussed, into a mood, a moment, a mystery, even spend time inside his mind as he worked out how to build a world, how to master his material. There was a clear sense of how as he worked on a song he was aware of a great number and variety of elements which could be combined in different ways; the way he mixed different sensations and feelings into a new whole.

These collections from various ages and stages of Bob Dylan didn't exactly reveal what it was he was after as he composed and recorded a song, but they showed you the lengths he would go to in order to get what he wanted. There was nothing explicitly new in the bootleg releases because they were all compilations commenting on the period of time they came from and the albums that belonged there. No new original songs, except for the occasional hidden gem like 'Blind Willie McTell', but X-rays of how his songs were made, snapshots of

YOU LOSE YOURSELF, YOU REAPPEAR

thinking done in various venues, a series of different worlds and histories that the same song came from and ended up in. They proved how much he was a thinker, more than a folk singer, or a rock star, or even a musician, all those things he just happened to be once he'd written his first song – and he constantly saw his actions as experiments and questions, as attempts to find out something about life and death, time and space, dream and memory.

As more exhaustive bootlegs started to appear, keeping the faithful extremely busy, perhaps their function was a clearing up of the past, looking after his affairs, a taking control of the messy past as things wound down, or simply making official and more purposefully organised material that always existed, scattered to the wind, in the outlaw margins, pored over by experts, fanatics, captivated professors, compulsive obsessives, symposiums and serious collectors. These fringe activities now belonged inside the ragged border Dylan had flung around his work.

After *Tempest* there was a lot of mending, managing and modifying archival activity, lots of ways of showing us he was still here and still working, but the fact there was no album of original songs for nearly a decade, for most of his seventies, and no hint of one coming, seemed to suggest that here was one clue to how one strand of the Bob Dylan story was entering an endgame, in many ways a period of waiting after most of the more vital strategies and compelling negotiations had been concluded.

Perhaps, you never know, with *Tempest* finally sealed into place at the end of a sequence, it was time for a relatively settled summary of the life and times, work and themes, the overall progress and stylistic extravagance – as far as I could see, as just one witness in this particular investigation, seeing and hearing things from my place on the street – of an irreplaceable, incomparable, often irritable, for some irritating, artist, vocalist and mesmerising performer. A book following Dylan and the voices he used at various stages of his life as he passed amongst the rest of us who just happened to be alive at the time he was alive. Somehow, I hazarded, the rest of us were becoming shadows in his life as he became more vivid; it was the rest of us that were fading away as he continued his quest, a trail from then to now that featured a cauldron of communications, an obstinacy of false starts, a parade of songs, a cackle of asides, a prickle of disappearances and an exaltation of revelations.

His main regular contemporary work each year during the 2010s continued to be the Never Ending Tour he had been pursuing for over thirty years, officially beginning on 7 June 1988 in Concord, California with the first of seventy-one concerts played in twenty-nine American states and in Canada. By May of 1989, beginning in Sweden, the tour headed out into the world. He figured few if any were doing what he was doing so he might as well keep putting himself out there, quietly hopeful a new audience would discover him. He plays a hundred shows a year, a few months on, a few months off, sixteen songs or so a night, some the same, some different, some regularly, some rarely. The shows become utterly predictable and profoundly surprising.

The tour was also his response to the making of records being a hugely different act in the digital age to what it had been when music was recorded to appear on vinyl. The increasing technological choices made it harder to achieve the kind of sound he preferred, stripped of effects and synthetic atmosphere, taking him away from the spontaneous mood and mystery of music he had been weaned on. Live performance was where he could still be himself, still produce the music he heard in himself. Eventually, after a few years of touring, after making a couple of records filled with other people's songs, clearing his head, he would return to make the sort of records he liked the sound of, intimate marvels filled with wide spaces, protecting himself in the meantime by keeping himself on the road, keeping the engines working. The Never Ending Tour put him back in touch with his roots, even as he kept heading towards unfamiliar quarters.

There had been over three thousand shows between 1988 and 2019, a more or less constant annual tour circling the world again and again which it appeared up to a point could only actually be ended when Dylan himself ended. Even then you had a feeling that somehow the Never Ending Tour would continue in some form, as some mysteriously maintained afterlife artistic circus that kept the songs spinning, the voice measuring and his mind still working. His afterlife would be the great never-ending culmination of the life of someone who seemed in his teens and twenties in such a hurry but then learnt the value of patience, and the patience to wait for the right moment, or for a new audience. Fame is nothing. Openness, patience, receptivity, solitude is everything. Patience ensures victory.

The tour kept rolling, occasionally getting close to where the news was, often just operating in the far fringes of mainstream cultural business, patience incarnate, and even if the new albums stopped coming, the original songs were no more, it seemed as though the Never Ending Tour would take Dylan with it deep into another decade, heading into city after city, night after night, always some lit-up moments to look forward to. He created for himself a schedule, a mock-up of reason and order, some peace among the wreck of time, a way of defending himself against chaos and whim.

I always tried to see Dylan in concert at least once a year as the tour kept its promise to never end through the twenty-first century. Through the official Bob Dylan website it was possible to get special VIP tickets to shows all over Europe, where you could sit, for a price, within a few yards of him, but what price close proximity to such a magician, as he connected with everything he had ever been and ever done, even as he was visibly ageing, coming undone, the night slowly falling, taking with it those songs and his voice, but leaving behind the luminous wisdom?

At some point in his fifties or sixties he'd taken to wearing a deliberately rakish skinny little pencil moustache, which for such a lean throwaway mark on the upper lip needs quite a bit of fussy maintenance, a bit of feminine attention. The moustache had a voice of its own, like Chaplin's did, and Kurt Vonnegut's, George Orwell's and Mark Twain's, saying something about how he deflected attention and demanded attention all at the same time, how he could find a mask with the slimmest of gestures always ready for the next performance. Edgar Allen Poe grew his to disguise the sneer caused by a nervous tic, and it gave him the look of a silent movie star, something Dylan liked the sound of.

Maybe Dylan pilfered the moustache from the Boston Blackie

silent movies where Chester Morris played the reformed jewel thief and safe cracker turned anti-hero detective, 'an enemy to those who make him an enemy, a friend to those who have no friends'. Blackie was always viewed with suspicion whenever there was a crime, and to clear himself, he had to solve the case himself, often wearing disguises. As Jimmy Buffett sang, if you have a pencil-thin moustache, you can solve mysteries too.

The pencil moustache was the mark of the hustler, the spiv, the outlaw, someone trying to elevate themselves above their given class position. It's as though it was Dylan in some previous life that had advised debonair Clark Gable and Errol Flynn to wear one in their black and white movies. Matinee idol John Gilbert had one when he starred opposite Greta Garbo in 1926's *Flesh and the Devil*, followed in the next three years by *Love* and *A Woman of Affairs*, and maybe Dylan drew one on his own famous face a little like Marcel Duchamp scrawled one on the famous face of the Mona Lisa. He'd sung about the Mona Lisa in 'Visions of Johanna', figuring she must have had highway blues, it's clear from the way she smiles.

The 'tache is a little sleazy and puts Dylan in a club of devilish dandies and rogues he'd be happy to be part of with Little Richard, Vincent Price, Robert Donat, Sammy Davis Jr, Ron Mael, John Waters and Prince. It made him very twentieth century but also put him out in the wild zone of cultural timelessness. The club's motto? Confucius says, 'A man without a moustache is a man without a soul.'

At his shows, often in arenas and large theatres, you could get close enough to the manicured hair on his upper lip to stare straight into Dylan's dark, darting eyes and see nothing at all, or something, a sign he was aching to return where he came from, or no such sign at all, just the look of someone happily at work, surrounded by some workmates looking like they'd wandered in from a tall tale and had known a few skid-row hotels in their time.

They'd been wandering for years and years, and Dylan would just start singing at the beginning of the show, as if he was in a roundabout way going to tell you his life story, which turns out to be a mixture of life stories of which only one or two are, vaguely, his. In the end it is perhaps the life story of everyone; if for some cosmic reason you have to choose one artist from the past century and say, this is the definitive summary of the times and all times in all their glory and grotesquery, touching on everything, from the mythic to the slapstick, from a single breath to the entire mystery of the universe, the steady accumulation of small realities, never finishing saying what he had to say, American but also from a place that is placeless, then who else but Bob Dylan?

There were those disappointed with this flickering shadow of a legend, losing something of the lightness of his dreams, whose face had changed so much, whose voice was in time-lashed tatters. Some were offended, even repulsed, by the mild serenity of age taking the place of the riotous blood of youth — although the truth was, really, it was the wild serenity of age, of someone who for a long time had understood he was going to offend some people no matter what. You're offended? Get over it. The blood was still pumping, he still enjoyed the sound of his own voice, he just wasn't moving around the stage as much as he once did.

He tiptoed to his position on the stage, hesitantly facing out towards the audience as if he wouldn't mind if he looked the other way, and then he let his mind do the moving for a couple of hours and a bit, thinking fast enough to keep his slick, quick-witted band on their toes, as they made sure they were heading down the same roads as Dylan, making the turns in time, hitting the exits, spotting the ghosts on the way at the same time as he did.

Some old fans didn't get it: they would say the songs were sung in the wrong order, let alone the wrong key, the high and mighty greatest hits were mostly missing, or were nothing but the bleached bones of what they had once been, and Dylan seemed a little in the distance, and sometimes it seemed like he'd taken one too many punches. Was this a calculated act of a self-conscious living legend, or because he was tired out, or one more self-rebooting artistic refocussing of perspective? Sometimes, especially during those shows where he crouched over a keyboard towards the back of the stage, his hands too arthritically stiff to hold a guitar, for a while as you tried to figure out where he was, it appeared Bob Dylan had failed to turn up for his own show.

It took a few seconds, maybe a little longer, to work out that he was the leader of the six-piece band: he lurked darkly next to the drummer, ignoring the microphone positioned stage centre. He directed the music using winks, glances, gestures, even sniffles, the occasional soft-shoe shuffle, and the songs his zen-blues posse played, some legendary, some undiscovered, were in turn made up of hints, echoes and nudges. He'd wear a dashing hat that made him look dangerous, distinguished and a little seedy. His black shirt would be slashed with a violent red. He could have come from another century – not necessarily the past – or a dream an animal's having about the shape of sound.

After decades of jumpy, secretive Dylan playing electric rhythm guitar at the front of the stage, it took some getting used to seeing him play, sometimes without really playing, this rickety-looking piano tucked to the side. When he fingered the keyboard, he crouched like a question mark, frowned like a whiskered genius, sometimes discreetly dancing on the spot like a nefarious Fred Astaire, aiming scrutinising glances into the mysterious mid-air. His abstract boogie-woogie was sometimes so tentative it couldn't actually be heard, as if the piano was just a prop. He used to punch from inside the music, now he found ways to hide behind himself, and his twisted, sinful stories, as if he was preparing to withdraw altogether. Meanwhile, to add to the effect of disappearance, of covert illusion, his voice seemed to be falling apart, catastrophically collapsing into the void ahead of him that his songs queue up to defy, or delay, or dwell on. He sang like a stranded, mutilated angel who'd traded his holiness for humanity.

He used this blistered, bitter death-voice and floating cubist consciousness to tear his songs apart, to snottily, gutturally shock and shake them into new shapes that reflect the churning strangeness of his imagination. The combination of his wounded voice, the perforated songs and the silent piano means that this psyched-up history of American roots music comes laced with a feverish, surreal force that goes beyond provincial Americana out into the exotic wildness of time and space where you cannot cut corners.

He said nothing between songs, because what on earth could he say that isn't in the songs, which end up explaining, to some extent, everything. He didn't say thank you after a song for the applause, because he wouldn't mean it, it wasn't at the top of his mind. He didn't smile, because that would be too intimate, considering the circumstances. It seemed sometimes he might have ice in his veins, but that makes complete sense considering some of the songs he'd just sung, and he wasn't really there to warm the audience up.

After you had been smoothly transferred into another amazing world, the show would end with soul-shredding abruptness. As became tradition, Dylan would take a last look, out of the corner of his diabolical imagination, at his astonished – or near offer – audience. A teasing trace of a smile that was sort of friendly and wicked, a little mingling with his band, one eyebrow peculiarly raised, and then off to find another stage, wherever he's meant to be.

This was not to the taste of some old-school fans whose memories of life with Dylan had been disturbed, originally hearing those songs at a time when important things were happening in their lives. The memories existed in the first place because of Dylan, and now they've been shaken up, challenged, because of Dylan, which seems to not have been part of the deal.

There were those pleading with him to stop, to end the never-ending, as though he was ruining his own legacy, cruelly sabotaging the accepted transcendent beauty and power of his own songs. They thought he didn't even sound like Bob Dylan anymore. For some he was just coughing up phlegm.

It was as though the Dylan they had loved so much was now betraying them because he was old and weary-seeming, mouth and moustache curling up between sneer and grin, and crankily searching still for elusive perfection; bringing his old songs into the current conditions of his life, within certain limitations, some thought he had turned his hits and classics into unrecognisable, ugly travesties. There were those who just wanted him to sing the songs as they once were, as if time hadn't passed, and he hadn't aged, and they hadn't aged, and they hated what he did to the songs and by implication to them. His death was their death, and they couldn't cope with how he so frankly faced up to extinction, his voice unashamedly acknowledging the span of a life, and the inevitability of what's to come physically and spiritually.

They'd rather he stopped playing live than allow the original life force to seep out of his songs and dare to still sing like an old man with a dry mouth, strangely relishing his age, his voice disappearing into a black hole. There were those wanting to cancel Dylan for the crime of ageing long before cancellation became a more fashionable weapon. It was as though they were the owners of the songs – they had taken them from him, and he had no right to reach back into them and make them something else.

Actually, transformed, remade, as most of his beloved songs became – because the recorded versions were not definitive, just what happened to occur at a given moment, because in the end improvisation was a big part of how Dylan wrote and recorded songs – they still maintained power, original energy still existed, distilled into thrilling new forms. Essentially, even the monumental songs were still forming in his imagination, as he imagined them coming from different musical histories, as if he had discovered 'Blowin' in the Wind' like it was a landmark, a new world waiting to be explored.

He just happened to find it first, before anyone else, and then once he had planted the flag, shown it to the world, given it a name, he would then remember it from different vantage points, from different perspectives and different musical places. It became a memory, or a photograph, or a dream, an anecdote, and the uplifting anthem, fixed in so many minds as one particular of-its-time anti-war protest song – there it is at just the moment the civil rights movement peaks, performed by Peter, Paul and Mary a few hours before Martin Luther King delivered his 'I have a dream' speech – became amongst other things a laid-back honky-tonk song from no time at all. The original 'Blowin' in the Wind' still exists, like a mountain range or a river, but over time, as he travels elsewhere, it becomes something else, reflecting where his mind has gone, not where it once was. What was once topical, and possibly therefore destined to be forever set in amber, is returned by Dylan to wherever it came from, free to be blown anywhere in the wind.

I was constantly enthralled by getting a chance to see Dylan in action at the latest stage of his life, as if it was a chance to see in person Cézanne paint, Gertrude Stein write, Marcel Duchamp play chess, Wittgenstein imagine language as a form of life. It was as though in front of you there was Hamlet, or Keyser Söze, or Atticus Finch, Rick Blaine, Randle McMurphy, Bobby Dupea, Ellen Ripley, Pozzo, the man with no name, living and breathing, enjoying himself in the privacy of his own imagination, starting up his harmonica like he was biting the head off an animal.

It was a way of seeing Dylan close up finish off – or frankly carry on – what he had started over fifty years ago, and what he was doing at the end of his life was just as important as what he did in the so-called golden '60s when rock music was a dream, in the mellow and then uneasy, savage, doubting, doubtless '70s, in the staggered recovery years of the late '90s and early '00s. His latest shows were continuing what he had done as inflamed, savagely original folk hero in his first two or three years, as ringmaster arbitrarily transmitting sheer sneering energy on the electric British tour in 1965, the fierce, grand comeback 1974 Before the Flood tour where The Band had never been bigger, the cockeyed co-operative, hurdy-gurdy utopian Rolling Thunder tour of 1976, the religious tours of the born-again zealot pointing fingers at the faithless around the 1980s, the ones where there was a more obvious disorderly, confrontational quality. One couldn't have happened without the other. One persona stirred another. It's all a part of the history he's made up, and the parts at the end are as important as the parts that came earlier.

The regular live albums released along the way capturing those tours and others summarised changes in style, identity and voice, different stages of an ongoing spiritual battle, existing as records of where he was in between the studio albums, and inevitably some have their fans, and some are seen as aberrations. I happen to love them all, even the ones that traditionally fall at the lower end of the rankings, ones where he seemed to be losing his way, filling in time, trying out some ill-defined artistic rebellion or as much as he ever does found himself going through the motions.

*Hard Rain* represents the life-brightening magical bedlam of the Rolling Thunder Tour at the point it was running out of roll and thunder, so it all got a little pragmatic and it was time to move on; *Live at Budokan*, wiping Rolling Thunder's make-up off his face, was where Dylan appeared to slip through the looking glass into some kind of bizarro Las Vegas and flirt with presenting his songs through a slick, kinky big band revue, which was ironic or sincere or both at the same time; *Dylan and the Dead* was somehow the opposite of being as other-worldly and regally surreal as the partnership promised, but perhaps pointed the way towards the Never Ending Tour; and the *MTV Unplugged* album, which was recorded in 1995 as he was six years into his Never Ending journey but which seemed to cheerfully exist as a pleasing, low-key television special in another dimension, drawing attention to how there was no documenting of the endless tour. And never would be, as though the shows existed on the other side of an impenetrable force field.

Even when he's caught between moods, or trying something out that seemed a little wayward at the time, or deeply counter-intuitive, whether he's in mythic mood or just sounding miffed, you can hear him making his mind up one way or another about where he is and what he's up. You can hear him toy with his voice, make a new discovery, worry at it, throw it all away, and leave it behind for good. All these live Dylans, from profoundly potent and completely himself to a little pale and distracted and outside himself, need to exist to make up the complete picture.

Past live shows did start to appear as part of the Bootleg Series, and as carefully selected re-releases, most closer to being as loved as the top-ranking live record, *Before the Flood*. There were albums from before he was famous, as he was becoming famous, as he was crashing to the other side of fame, as he spent three years turning his shows into a religious service, hailing the fast-approaching return of Jesus, in the business of selling God – so you hear him as he appears full of folky promise in small downtown venues in 1962, as he quickly makes it to the uptown Carnegie Hall in 1963, as he jokes and chats enjoying the spotlight at the Philharmonic in 1964, as he spits fury to the point of infamy at the Manchester Free Trade Hall in 1965 and as he praises the Lord with a keen, grave face between 1979 and 1981.

The Rolling Thunder Revue album is where the roll and thunder was that never made it into *Hard Rain*. It can be seen as the greatest live punk album, the greatest live psychedelic album, the greatest live rock and roll album, the greatest live album of a Bob Dylan musical that never existed, even the greatest Bob Dylan live album, if it's decided that *Before the Flood* was actually Bob Dylan and the Band, and contained Band songs. The Rolling Thunder tour is another interim precursor to the Never Ending Tour, and already, as first displayed on *Before the Flood*, Dylan is taking all sorts of personal liberties with the structure, tone and rhythms of his songs, however beloved, even sometimes revising the words themselves, singing them using different voices, perpetually shifting focus, steadfastly keeping his songs inside the development stage. He's giving them space to breathe, allowing them to hold their breath.

I considered it completely his business what he did with the songs he had written, the idea that they might never actually be finished, how he elongated, shrank or magnified their symbolic and dramatic action, and I loved that sometimes it took the audience a few seconds – for some even longer – to recognise 'Like a Rolling Stone' or 'Tangled Up in Blue'. Once or twice, a pitilessly amended, significantly famous song would come

41

and go with a few not even noticing. It would dawn on them a few songs later, maybe a few weeks later, maybe never. They'd gone to see da Vinci's *Mona Lisa* or Munch's *Scream*, and it had turned into a completely different painting. The fact that his songs could keep changing what they were even as they stayed what they were seemed to be what made them so compelling. There was no one way through them; there were hundreds of different directions to go and Dylan wanted to know them all.

*

For the purpose of beginning this book, I prepared myself to go and see one of the dates being booked into American venues for part of the Never Ending Tour, set to take place from early June 2020. That is how the book would start, and I imagined the opening line would describe me settling into my seat, as close to the front as possible. Ready to hear that first word he sang, reality forgotten but words remembered, so I could work out what kind of shape his voice was in, what kind of mood he was in, how much life he'd got banked up, always on high alert – especially since the death of David Bowie – about how a world without a living, thinking Bob Dylan was going to take some getting used to. Where would his death take the rest of us, and how we remember our own lives? As long as his songs survive, he lives, carried forward by them. He would continue to occupy our thoughts, perhaps as though he'd just travelled abroad somewhere a little off-grid, but there would still be something of a sudden shift in history, the dismantling of a certain world. It would be the end of an era, and it would take some working out how to define that era.

The book might begin with the moment I looked him in the eye, and swore that he looked right back at me, and all sorts of romping wonder filled my brain, as though for a split second I was at one with the universe. I know, I know, at my age as well, but sometimes in a flash you can find yourself in exactly the right place at exactly the right time and reality gets all supernatural on you.

He might actually be sizing me up and wondering if I've got it in me to write a book about him. What kind of fraud am I? – actually, being some kind of fraud is perhaps the qualification he was looking for. A fraud and a fantasist. Or perhaps he's staring a little fiercely at the empty seat beside me – I've seen him do it at some of the shows I've been to – and wondering why the hell it's empty. Who hasn't turned up yet? How dare they, man, but their loss. They may not get another chance to see him in the wild. At some point, not too far away, one of these Never Ending shows will be the last one he ever plays. Imagine turning up late for that, or not bothering to go at all, because in the end you decided there was no chance he was going to play his greatest hits just like they sounded once upon a time.

I fancied seeing him at the Hollywood Bowl. It never occurred to me in February 2020 as I started to plan my trip to Los Angeles later in the year that for the first time in decades there was going to be a postponement of the impending Never Ending shows. There was danger ahead, an erasure of all kinds of eras and routines, of hopes and dreams, but I wasn't paying as much attention as I should have to early news of some suspicious-sounding deaths in a part of China I wasn't too familiar with.

# TWO

## NOTHING BUT A VOICE

I planned for the book to begin with Dylan playing in concert, singing in the voice he now had, settled in its new ways, or settling into something else, and then moving back through all the voices he'd used over sixty years, back to the unknown pre-voice, from his nebulous Midwest middle-of-nowhere prehistory, in the 1950s, before he'd changed his name, and adopted some styles and then some, acting like he'd been on the road since the Great Depression, running away from home at seven years old, travelling with the carnivals, an orphan descendant of the Sioux Nation, learning songs as a kid direct from cowboys and bluesmen, but was also fresh out of the box. How was this 2020 voice, the sound of a crafty, sibylline 79-year-old, still freshly churning, connected to the other voices he had used, found, imitated, shed?

It would be an attempt to understand him and his fishy, implausible ways through his voice and what he could do with it, as an uncanny instrument of expression and an extraordinary carrier for his thoughts. A voice David Bowie described in a *tribute* song as being made of 'sand and glue', author Joyce Carol Oates said was like sandpaper singing, one that Philip Larkin as a possible compliment described as 'cawing and derisive'. It's a sound that traditionally put off the casual listener, even before the splintered, macabre late-life voice, alienated by what they heard as harsh, rough and acrid, a nagging, whining, non-singing voice, a pain rather than a pleasure. A great poet, perhaps, a riveting storyteller, but for many the voice was impossible to listen to.

He never had a single voice, though; there were changing voices, all part of his electrifying masquerade, his bohemian avoidance of resolution, balancing tradition and innovation, the familiarity of the past with the novelty of whatever next, combining conflicting influences to create a living space all of his own. Dylan was not the singer's original name, and he perhaps never used his 'real' voice as he constantly arrived in new lands and told stories about how he got there, how fate obliged him to be constantly in motion. Dylan was always shifting voices. Even if he ever did use his real voice, which one was it? How many voices of Dylan have there been, or is there just the one, always the same, sounding different as time passes, as he ages, as the world around him constantly turns into something else, reflected in that voice, which is many voices, some more familiar and famous than others?

If you say that you do not like Bob Dylan's voice, does that mean you do not like all the voices he has used, or just some of them, or just the idea of his voice, all that disdainful drawling, deranged honking and nasal wailing? The sound of it distracted some from noticing how shaped and incisive it was, how it was at all stages perfect for whatever he was singing and whenever he was singing it.

You do not have to go far to see it written that the genius of Dylan is his words, but it's rarely argued that the genius of Dylan is actually his voice and his constantly fascinating vocal performances. He was a singer with such a love of words, he understood how words are much more than what was set down on paper, how we cannot know what we cannot name, and that it takes the human voice, and a sense of where to place words within and across the spaces of notes and rhythms, to infuse them with a sense of deeper meaning. Nothing in the world has as much power as a word, and Dylan sang each word as if he had spent time like Emily Dickinson looking at a word until it shined. All the time in the world, circling a word until it started to breathe, even share a joke.

Dylan, disciplined and abandoned, would then use his voice to communicate how that word shined. Sometimes as he sang that meant holding on to it for dear life, thinking about it a little longer than seemed right, letting it drift, curling it around his imagination, unloading it with a dismissive sigh, dropping it from a cliff, slicing it open, taking it by the throat, caressing its skin, feeling its sadness, sending it off with quite a flamboyant flourish on a journey all of its own. Sometimes when he'd run out of words or dropped enough clues, there was his harmonica, a different kind of voice with different messages, before the swooping, jolting re-entry back to a singing voice.

He always sang, as a great singer should, with a constantly fascinating voice unmistakably his own, able to sound lovely and weird, sometimes at the same time, the sound of someone shaping fantasies with cool reason, exhilarating precision and a seething brain. Singing, he was making clear, after making it clear in different ways for a few decades, was more about acting and timing than perfect pitch; it was about paying attention to the curious power and magic of words, how even the smallest ones can hurt you and save you, cut you to the core.

Others before him had sung with as much care as Dylan, as much understanding about the life of a word – and the death it contained – but few if any were as passionately in love with language, as mentally alive, keen on using songs to make you question reality, on finding words he never thought to speak, only sing. He sang to make it clear that every mad, sad, lonely word was true, however much he was making up. And just a little pause in what seems the wrong place but turns out to be as right as rain can completely transform the meaning of something.

His voice is where his genius can be really heard and fully felt. His voice is as unique as his lyrics, and in the end the lyrics, all that miraculous latching on to living clamour, need the voice of Dylan to complete them, to fully articulate and contain their complexity, their surprises, disturbances and dramas. He didn't want to simply seduce the listener, he wanted to scandalise them, and completely involve them, make them part of the performance. He used the raw edges, tart bite and fermented musicality of his voice to dispel the softness and easiness of nostalgia, the easy yearning for a safe place, even as he naturally looked to the past for sources, signs and a sense of his own latest beginning, for heroes to emulate and rearrange.

The story of Dylan's voice is also the story of the voice itself in popular music since the 1950s, because Dylan revolution-ised the idea of what a white singing voice could be – it didn't need to be perfect, trained, smooth, simply a case of hitting the right notes and making each word sound clear. The pleasant, stirring, clean-cut voices of the Byrds, Joan Baez, the Beach Boys or Roy Orbison became, after the thrilling, oblique power of Dylan, with all his fighting fear and hope, the tense, nervous, energised voices of Leonard Cohen, Ray Davies, Lou Reed, Grace Slick, Patti Smith, Tom Waits, Bruce Springsteen, Neil Young, Chrissie Hynde, Rickie Lee Jones, Kurt Cobain, Cat Power, Nick Cave, Fiona Apple, PJ Harvey – as well as knocking the Lennons and Jaggers into new directions, some of which involved healthy gloom and doom, some bleak conviction, and somehow in the middle of being a pop star the utter realisation of self.

His influences were often 1950s rock and roll – hard and silly he would call it, with some relish and respect – and gutsy blues, the same as made the hair of the Beatles and the Rolling Stones stand on end, but Dylan found a whole new set of sensations and took things beyond the drawling, shrieking, temperamental volatility of the tortured teenage American originators, adding a confessional urgency, a series of causes, and clauses, a cascade of yearning, a great, more complex and contemplative, even detached, intensity that helped the derivative white blues spin off into its very own capricious, boundary-breaking new forms. The more consciousness, Dylan announced to whom it may concern, the more intensity.

Dylan's impressionistic sense of rhythm and his mischief-making trading of rhymes sneaked from across town into the spaces and stories, the abundant, confrontational, ricocheting oral ammunition of hip hop. The wordy, transactional hip hop rant – eager, grieving, fantastic, dangerous, suspicious, crazed – has roots in Dylan, and his roots in wildfire free verse as much as in the blues, and the singer-songwriter emerges as much from the alert, meta-romantic poetry that Dylan introduced into his songs and singing as from the romantic popular song and the agitating folk tradition, those eternal songs tracking out a true, original course that he raided and remade. A whole new breed of composers and dreamers cut loose by Dylan, who lived a little ahead of everyone, backtracking into the future, started to use voice and melody to see what words can do.

There was a first voice that he'd been polishing, and roughing up, since he revealed himself as Bob Dylan in the late 1950s, and it drove straight through to his debut album, which also got named *Bob Dylan*. He'd been in a hurry for a while, and he recorded his debut in a hurry, songs carried off in a few takes, one or two in just a couple. They were mostly adaptations, arrangements and renovations of traditional songs, filled with phrases that floated through a whole history of folk, blues and country because he'd learnt that to sing songs was to understand how they were written. Maybe it was too early for him to appear writing all his own songs in a world where that just didn't happen, but he took these old songs, written so it seemed by no-one, or Anon, or songs by others, and sang them as though he had thought of them first.

One of only two original compositions on the record, 'Song for Woody', more or less his first recorded original composition, borrowed a Woody Guthrie melody that Guthrie himself adapted from traditional sources. A self-deprecating, world-weary Dylan paid almost passive, reverent tribute to a significant influence, virtually bowing in acknowledgement. He used the song to face up to the uncertainty of life, and work out how to make sense of a 'funny ol' world' even as he revealed his own control over the English language and his ability to create a different kind of setting for a different kind of thinking.

He wasn't yet ready to conceptually and musically race past Guthrie – even if he was ready, after months closely studying his moves, melodies, mannerisms, to announce on his debut that he knew where he had come from and where he had to go next. He sounded like a keen young folk singer deftly acknowledging the work of a master, the one who changed his world, but he was actually demonstrating how he'd learnt that the best sort of songwriters know how to dance above the surface of the world. He knew what had been done – he mentions it in the song, because as well as Woody there are Cisco Houston, Sonny Terry and Lead Belly – and that made him want to find out what had not been done and do that.

He says that he knows that he knows nothing, and he admits as he gets ready to head out on the road that he doesn't know what time he's leaving, or where he's heading, but the way he constructed the song, and sang it, already shows that he knew how to find out things, and how to build a song around his knowledge, and his ability to uncover that knowledge.

He'd had everything ready in his head for a while, and he sounds like he had to get this album out of the way before he could get to the next one, and the one after that, and, more or less, the thirty-seven after that. First, he had to prove something to himself. And often during the next few decades, an album or two, controversially or not, would appear where he would use the songs of others to reinform his songwriting, or to give him a respite from the pummelling demands of his mind, or just because he was in the mood. On his debut album, he's setting himself up, moving through a collection of versions and interpretations into his own writings which he considers a natural extension of those songs.

This 'first voice' was one he found, stole, made up, crafted, a rag-and-bone man-boy and his vigorously strummed guitar, his weapon of choice, plus back-up harmonica, which he blew out of its mind, and as he moved through his life, stealing his way into the night, he changed his voice to suit the music he was making, the pressure of the times, the age he was for real, and the age he felt in his mind. Changing his voice to compel you to listen closer, changing his voice as he kept moving, because moving kept him sane. One voice is for the ordinary; the geniuses have many voices.

Different-enough-looking to stick out above the other Greenwich Village folkies he had started to hang out with, skinny, rough and pale with long fingernails on his right hand to pluck his guitar, scrambling for attention, he quickly became the centre of some talk amongst the crowded, inbred folk scene even if he didn't necessarily stand out musically. You get the feeling that whatever the current music scene had been at the time, centred in Greenwich Village, which was sending music in one direction, he would have been an expert in that. It happened to be ranging, roaming, travelling, talking, protesting folk, and he dressed the part, and claimed to have lived the life. He was already becoming someone mysteriously blank enough, considering all the mental noise and physical presence, that different people could project onto him an idealised version of what they wanted to see. He became a folk hero because enough people decided that's what he was, as if he would never change into anything else.

There's a magnetic and playful, self-surprising power he had on stage that most of the other folkies didn't have, a distinct feeling for syllable and rhythm which meant he invigorated every word he sang. He made friends easily enough amongst the scene's overlapping musicians even if he didn't seem the friendly type. In some biographies it might be noted that a certain social and sexual nervousness was bound up in the edge and tone of his performance, and made it into the early songs he wrote, mixed up with the sophisticated stylist who knew his Dante and Virgil and Ovid as well as his Hank Williams, Elizabeth Cotten and Muddy Waters.

He got to know Texan folk singer Carolyn Hester, who had arrived in New York in 1955, befriended and worked with Buddy Holly, and recorded a couple of albums before she was signed to Columbia Records by John Hammond, the creative talent scout, musicologist, critic and pioneering producer, and above all supreme music lover, looking to find someone to match the current leading female voice of folk, the young soprano Joan Baez.

Hammond's reputation as discoverer of genius was impeccable, especially for finding a singular voice. Much of it was based on coming across a seventeen-year-old Billie Holiday performing in a basement club in Harlem in the early 1930s and recording her when she was eighteen. He was twenty-two and living in Greenwich Village on a Vanderbilt family trust fund, giving him the financial freedom to turn his love for jazz and blues into action – he once said he wanted to do something with his wealth that would make a difference. Jazz especially became his cause, to draw attention to Black music, 'the most effective and constructive form of social protest I could think of'. He organised the 'Spirituals to Swing' concert at Carnegie Hall in December 1938 – 'music nobody knows', the first real African-American showcase for a white audience – featuring black blues, jazz and gospel artists including Sister Rosetta Tharpe, Big Joe Turner, Meade Lux Lewis, the Golden Gate Quartet and Big Bill Broonzy as a replacement for Robert Johnson, who couldn't be tracked down – it turned out he had been murdered in August by a jealous husband in a Mississippi honky-tonk at the age of twenty-seven.

Hammond was enthralled and excited by how Holiday sang like an ingenious, sophisticated improvising instrumentalist, and persuaded the bandleader Benny Goodman, a friend and close colleague, to hire her after encouraging him to use a multi-racial group. He found Count Basie firing up sound in a Kansas City dive and suggested a new sound for the Benny Goodman Sextet in 1939, the amplified electric guitar of Oklahoma City's Charlie Christian, on the cusp between swing and bebop, when the instrument was almost a novelty. Within a few years, led on by how Christian turned riffs into revelations, it would become the basis of the sound of a new America. 'Lights flash, rockets go off,' Hammond said when talking about first hearing Christian, about what he felt when he came across a musician with a sound and a feel like no-one else, who seemed to have dug treasure out of the ground.

After Second World War military duties and time away from Columbia, he returned to the label and, continuing where he left off, tracked down a teenage gospel singer he'd heard of from Detroit, Aretha Franklin, producing her as a jazz singer on her first two albums, which might have been a commercial mistake but definitely wasn't an artistic one.

Supported by Hammond, Carolyn Hester assembled an unusual mixed crew of musicians to work on her Columbia debut, looking to give folk a form of free groove, including the experienced guitarist Bruce Longhorne and Odetta's bassist, Bill Lee. Captivated by Hester and impressed by her closeness to Buddy Holly, Dylan hustled her for gigs, always looking for action, to get a foot in the door, and he asked if he could play on the record. She didn't need a guitarist but could use a harmonica player, so she got him in to play his harp, even though compared to Bruce and Bill he was a little raw. Raw but ready, knowing he was raw, which gave his playing – and, it turned out, his singing – a kind of integral truth that couldn't be denied.

When Hammond came to meet Hester's band at a friend's apartment on West 10th Street in Greenwich Village, Dylan was lurking, eyes darting, finding it hard to sit still, hiding in plain sight. Hammond had heard rumours, of the hungry young singer who wasn't necessarily socially functional but sang like he'd experienced a few lives, and Dylan made one of his more important contacts.

Social activist singer Pete Seeger had already been signed to Columbia by Hammond when no other label would touch him, despite the concern some profit-minded executives inside the label had about working with the blacklisted writer of political anthems. Even if you were a Seeger fan, Dylan seemed like a lighter, lesser model, but Hammond saw straight through Dylan's sound and appearance, his obvious unmilled resemblance to other direct, knowledgeable folk singers, to some essential, more indefinable, originality.

Even by making the album for a commercial label like Columbia, rather than one of the more respected, specialist folk labels like Vanguard or Folkways, Dylan broke a few dogmas of the folk community with its deep suspicion of commercial marketing strategies. Dylan wasn't interested in integrity if it only led to anonymity. He wasn't afraid of modern marketing tactics, wanted to spread the word, not share it amongst a clique, and was impressed that Hammond had the guts and tenacity to sign the uncompromising and, it seemed, deeply uncommercial Seeger.

With his own well-researched sense of musical history, and his bound-for-glory determination, Dylan saw it as inevitable that he should work with someone like John Hammond. It means he immediately walked into the music history Hammond had created, from Billie Holiday and the 'Spirituals to Swing' concerts to Pete Seeger and Aretha Franklin, as well as introducing Robert Johnson to a wider public by releasing his few recordings in 1961 (and later signing Leonard Cohen and Bruce Springsteen). Benny Goodman noted after a few exhausting nights going to obscure gigs with Hammond that to find the rare princes and princesses Hammond had to see an endless number of frogs.

Dylan might have been a bit of an oddball, or hiding in oddball clothing, which has its own oddness, but he had a real sense of where he wanted to belong, and the kind of history he wanted to make. Who better than the scholarly, open-minded music history man John Hammond, the man they say shaped American pop music, with an unparalleled cultural significance, the ultimate A&R man, to be the one who discovered him?

The first album, made for $402, didn't raise much interest beyond the local scene and the emerging cognoscenti, like he belonged on a smaller label after all, and Dylan got labelled as 'Hammond's Folly' inside Columbia. The less music-minded men of the label might easily have dropped him at that point, and Seeger was selling well after all – how many rousing, radical folkies do you need? – but Hammond wasn't the type to drop him. The lights had flashed, the rockets had gone off.

Dylan's first voice is that of an uptight, impressionable, know-it-all kid, fishing around for clues and signs, liable to fall in love at the drop of a hat, destined to be let loose on the world, who fancied himself in his wildest dreams as an artist, a preternatural self-made, self-priming folk blues prophet, already getting ready for the days ahead when people would be looking back at his life and going through it, even his private affairs, the fools, marvelling at how he appeared, and then disappeared. He knew what was going to happen from the beginning. He knew he would have, and need, a number of different voices. They would all be him; he'd be behind them all.

This first voice on the first album he recorded for Columbia at the end of 1961 for release the following March when he was twenty years old sneaked up from below, from out of the blue and the shadows beyond, with a vague, cocky suggestion of 'let me introduce myself'. This introduction involved him announcing that we are all mortal, nearly shaking himself apart, punching his guitar, singing a dramatically bleak song meditating on the end of a life called 'See That My Grave Is Kept Clean'. He was not setting off in a consoling mood.

The song was made famous by Blind Lemon Jefferson in the late 1920s, the only hymn he ever recorded, containing parts from a Victorian deathbed song, wherein the grave was to be kept green. Lightnin' Hopkins recorded a version in the early 1950s, and Woody Guthrie used its melody as part of his 1940 recording 'Vigilante Man'. It was also part of the repertoire of singers Dylan would be mixing with in early 1960s New York, including uncompromising, irascible local folk-blues institution Dave Van Ronk, member of the Trotskyist Workers League, generous enough to help champion newcomers like Dylan when they turned up looking to compete with him and travel for a while in his slipstream – Van Ronk helped usher Dylan from smaller, more obscure clubs to the bigger Greenwich Village venues like the Gaslight, helping him become talk of the town. Van Ronk welcomed anyone who cared as much about music as Dylan, taken by his gung-ho, take-no-prisoners approach to performing, even let them sleep on his couch.

'See That My Grave Is Kept Clean' is one of a few tunes Van Ronk regularly sang that Dylan recorded for his debut, mostly filled with arranged traditional songs, and in the liner notes Dylan credited Van Ronk with showing him one of his favourite songs, 'House of the Rising Sun'. To get to his first voice, Dylan would admit that he wasn't shy about copying some of Van Ronk's recordings phrase for phrase, taking a lot from how he could spin from a howl to a whisper, the way he inhabited the bodies of the old blues singers that had inspired him. Walking into Van Ronk meant taking on the strange and distant voices and histories that Van Ronk had taken on. Van Ronk had done a lot of studying and curating so that Dylan didn't have to. He could take a few short cuts, learn from the experience of Van Ronk how to channel Lead Belly without sounding crass.

This first voice is of someone who'd been thinking so much about death, and all the accoutrements the song mentions – the coffin, the silver spade that digs the grave, the church bell's tone – that he could sing it as though he was facing death himself, issuing a few last wishes, even if for the purpose of the song. Jefferson really did sing the song shortly before his death; Dylan only pretended, but already his pretending didn't make you doubt he knew what he was talking about.

He'd been listening to the blues so much, he knew what was necessary in the singing to make sure it sounded like the buryin' ground was a real place, that he'd touched those two white horses in a line that were taking him to his final resting place. And the wind that blows through Dylan's entire repertoire, through his entire life, into his voices, was already there in this song.

Roughly speaking – because his voices will slip and blur between records, between the years, come back and fade away again, and with Dylan nothing can ever be specifically broken down into fixed periods, as hard as everyone tries – the first voice, the youngster acting like he was already old enough to know how beautiful things drift away, took him to his second album in 1963, *The Freewheelin' Bob Dylan*. As Hammond sensed he would – there was a brooding look in his eyes – he was starting to write the kind of songs with a curious life of their own that sounded as dramatically original as anything traditional or borrowed that someone as new and young as him would be expected to sing.

Love, of course, as much as anything else, had turned him into a poet; love is what impelled his songs to come from his own intensely felt daily adventures rather than the adventures of others that he absorbed and refashioned. Love is where he found a different kind of collaborator, a different kind of influence, a different kind of audience he wanted to impress. Falling in love, which means falling out of love, became a part of his experimental tendencies, a way of generating the sort of highs and hurts, fascination and indifference that drives his greatest songs. He used and abused love, it used and abused him.

As he dug deeper into an incestuous New York folk scene filled with clever, passionate personalities feeling themselves on a vital social mission, a moral crusade, his craving to belong and make contact with those that could help him make some sort of headway got mixed up with his tendency to feel love quick and hard. He met seventeen-year-old Suze Rotolo within a few months of arriving in New York; he was four years older, but the more immature. He covered his shyness with nonchalance, bravado and secrecy.

As he would say, quick to infatuation, he was dragged overboard by her. An artist and thinker in her own right, she also became one of his teachers, satisfying his ruthless need for new information and new perspectives. Her cultured Italian-American left-wing New York family gave her the kind of targeted informed political awareness he lacked; both her parents had been union activists. She knew the political clubs, meetings, gatherings and marches that he'd feed off, suggested topics for songs, encouraged a more visceral engagement with injustice and struggle than just reading or listening. She imprinted some of her interests onto him because there was something about his creativity that could not be activated unless he was shown some examples.

She helped out her older sister Carla, a Bertolt Brecht fan and early Dylan devotee, who was working as an assistant to the enormously curious ethnomusicologist, folklorist, dedicated folk promoter and inexhaustible worldwide song collector Alan Lomax, just back in New York after a few years in Britain working extensively for the BBC. Carla gave Dylan privileged access to her vast library of old, powerful songs on record and recorded in the field.

Lomax was in determined opposition to insipid commercial music and, committed to celebrating minority artists, had discovered and encouraged Jelly Roll Morton, Lead Belly, Woody Guthrie, Pete Seeger and Muddy Waters; in March 1940, at a 'Grapes of Wrath' evening in New York designed to introduce politicised folk music to a mainstream audience, he introduced Guthrie to Seeger. 'You can date the Renaissance of American folk song from that night,' Lomax said. Through Lomax, Dylan made himself part of another great list, landed another important mentor, with just one step, one dig of the spade, finding a place in history.

Lomax was endlessly fascinated with why people need music, and why people all through history have marked important occasions, moments and events with song – going to war, death, marriage, birth. Dylan found another short cut to immense knowledge, another way of absorbing the lines of enquiry, taste, vision, experience and knowledge of a historically important music specialist.

In the tiny apartment Suze and Dylan were soon sharing, Rotolo became the first person he played new songs to, to see if he was on the right track. He was close enough to the right track that he became increasingly well known locally, and his life got turned into its own non-stop theatre, the small and large controversies he naturally provoked often seeming purposely rigged for his own haywire purposes, putting pressure on their vulnerable young love.

She took a trip to Italy in the summer of 1962, escaping the gossipy social pressure already snaking around Dylan. Her long absence left him bereft and bemused with a lot for a manic loner who likes to be in control to work out. The fraught, exquisitely detailed love songs, obliquely filled with his own life, started to appear. Love as a fuel for expression, rejection teaching him how to reject, and with his roaming eyes he soon found another independent source of energy and information, Joan Baez, a few months older, who could also show him things, give them names, put him in the right places at the right time.

As her fame increased, before his, she took him on tour with her, to draw attention to the writer of many of the new songs she and other folkies were singing with the kind of commercial clarity he didn't have. Somewhere between cruel and callow, he was finding girlfriends for their beauty, their brains and the help they could be to his image and music. He had a way of making things happen, as though he was on a campaign to be someone who arrived somewhere. He'd fill in the details later, perhaps.

He stole his way into Joan's life, as if they were a folk Burton and Taylor, without making this clear to Suze, touring life the perfect location for an intense and clandestine new romance. There was more blissful discovery to turn into song, and more mess and misery, more early warmth turning into frozen feelings. He could act like an adult in his songs if not necessarily in the real life he was turning into song. Carla Rotolo tried to help her sister during a particularly explosive break-up row, fierce Italian-American temper clashing with the fear and fury of a cornered Dylan, which culminated in Dylan and Carla fighting. Her appearance in Dylan's life – after her early generous sponsoring and introducing him to Suze – ends up with an appearance in a Dylan song, 'Ballad in Plain D', where she's tagged as 'parasite sister'. Dylan's often operatic love life could get a little soap opera, leaving a trail of witnesses calling him a jerk, selfish, vicious. Maybe he was simply an awkward aesthete, constantly fumbling through failed courtships.

The pattern would repeat itself, like such patterns do, when he met model Sara Lownds in 1964, and without making it clear to Joan, who felt engaged to him in all sorts of ways, he started living with Sara, and by 1965 they were married. Joan felt the concentrated loving attention, and then a whole world being taken away from her, and suddenly unexpected mean silence falling from his tongue. They became strangers who knew each other's heart, which led to a little, gentle turning of the tables, especially when Joan turned Dylan into her greatest song, 1975's beautifully told 'Diamonds and Rust', pinning him down long enough to reveal a secret or two.

Shameless with his experiences, though all they were good for is exploiting, Bob put it all into song, sometimes making a rejection the shadow of a caress, which was some sort of compensation. And Suze ended up as impressed into Bob's world as Joan, whatever they do and say to distance themselves, by appearing happy together with Dylan on the cover of the *Freewheelin'* album as if their love is forever and she's smiling forever as though she has given her time to someone who deserves her. Even as some of the songs on the record make it clear that their love is both forever and nothing of the kind. Doors open, doors slam shut.

He'd transformed his preoccupations and his inherited mannerisms into a personal style and was sculpting it to his own purpose. The voice didn't significantly change, but the kind of songs absolutely did even as on the surface he was singing the protest songs he would become known for and working out how to write a different kind of love song. They're much more than simply being political songs and lovesick songs, because the universe Dylan set them in is incomprehensible, and needs close attention. The tremendous imaginative power of his ideas stretches them beyond their immediate subject matter.

The interpreter of songs on *Bob Dylan* became on his second album the interpreter of events, of the subconscious and of an America where internal battles are always being fought. Already he had become an interpreter of Bob Dylan songs, and of Bob Dylan himself. He'd become someone who in his own mind could have his own self-titled blues, and he introduced it like he already knew, in the process of unfolding his own myth, trusting himself, that the songs he'd written on the record go way beyond the folk scene where he initially got noticed, way beyond being shrewd, poetic appropriations and manipulations of the blues, way beyond the songs of his early heroes and influences, and are now the songs those heroes and influences will want to sing themselves. The first album set up a certain kind of musical history, and on the next album he walked into it, and rearranged it, creating his very own novel high–low fusion, a world made out of songs, mixing pop culture material with philosophical preoccupations, but still with a sense he could laugh at his own audacity.

In his introduction to 'Bob Dylan's Blues', delivered as though he's chewing tobacco and still acting his age as though he was born before the Depression, a little forecast of his experienced *Theme Time Radio* voice, he makes it plain he wasn't

writing the sort of songs written in the populist-minded indus-
trialised Tin Pan Alley song factory in uptown New York.
His songs didn't come from a factory or a meeting room; they
were written 'somewhere in America', and that was an America
from all across time, an America where he could be swept
along everywhere all at once. His songs weren't designed and
assembled in the recording studio from component parts – he
preferred to record them like jazz, performances as they happened with all their glitches and accidents, allowing for the
unpredictable moments, the surprising turn of events, that
would infuse them with real life so they could breathe, like
they were living things. They were recorded as documents of
a performance, because the unarranged, undecorated songs
themselves contain all the architecture and action.

The songs were also about a number of wild, weird and even
monstrous Americas, as though he had written the soundtrack
to Franz Kafka's first novel, *Amerika*, published posthumously
in 1927 over a decade after it was written. Kafka made an
absurdist dream-world country from his own mind's mythic
elements, set in a time period not particularly identified. Young
immigrant Karl Rossman imagines the country as a land of
opportunity as he searches for redemption. Karl roams across
Kafka's land of the free, overcoming endless obstacles and dizzying reversals until he is admitted to the great Nature-Theatre
of Oklahoma – Kafka's geography is moderately accurate even
though he had never visited America – which is an infinite
stage, as populous as the world. It's a stage where you can
imagine Dylan imagining himself singing the epic songs that
flow throughout his second album, songs fusing the everyday
and the phantasmagoric that would be continually refreshed

by each listener – 'Blowin' in the Wind', 'Girl from the North Country', 'Masters of War', 'Don't Think Twice, It's All Right', 'Oxford Town', 'A Hard Rain's a-Gonna Fall', 'Talkin' World War III Blues', as well as the acidic asides, sort of sardonic foot-notes to the main text, featuring private jokes, sudden rhymes and a sure sense of himself, where he lets us know he's keeping his head or happily losing it – 'Bob Dylan's Blues', 'Bob Dylan's Dream', 'I Shall Be Free'. Believing passionately in something that didn't exist, or was scattered in a hundred different places, he created it, putting his feelings to great use.

Kafka wrote *Amerika* at about the same age as Dylan was writing these songs, both were fond of using parables, and both achieved a sense of internal logic in their writing that is unlike anything else. For Dylan, this meant writing songs that became beloved American classics presenting the most fantastic of scenes in simple terms even as they contained clues about how all creation is re-creation, that songwriters are not only song makers but songs themselves, that every corner of knowledge is a fiction. He was on the limits between cultures, between genres, between languages, becoming a marginal in the centre, a cosmopolitan at the edge.

The first voice is still there on the third album, the more straight-faced, less absurdist *The Times They Are a-Changin'* (1964), because he could still see a use for it, still mostly frame it with the stark unfussiness of his tumbling guitar and trusty sidekick harmonica, as if he was still on the trail he'd been on in the New York folk clubs and still the singer whose only con-cern was protesting the state of the world, even as he protested the state of his life and mind. He had a set of songs, though, that could still use this voice.

It means that when he sings the final track, 'Restless Farewell', at the other end of an album that had begun with 'The Times They Are a-Changin'' and included a handful of more celebrated Dylan monuments – 'Ballad of Hollis Brown', 'With God on Our Side', 'Boots of Spanish Leather', 'Lonesome Death of Hattie Carroll' – it seems he's singing with a mouthful of despair and defiance another piece of aggrieved protest, some more serious news about some injustice or inequality, some terrible state of affairs. It sounds like a plain off-the-cuff adaptation of something plainly traditional about the contemplative wanderer doing his job – reflecting and travelling, occasionally stopping off to spin a few yarns, sing a few songs, open up a little – and the guitar and his voice do nothing to challenge that. He's using his first voice, one we now realise was temporary, and it's perfect for the song he's singing, based on an Irish ballad, where he's making up stories, hiding inside them, but revealing himself a lot more honestly than it first appears.

The last song written for the album was a piece of protest, but he was protesting about one of the first mainstream articles to examine his sound and early fame, with a particular sharp focus on the idea that his whole act was self-conscious shtick. The song is a response to a piece in *Newsweek*, which was taking the whole new phenomenon of Bob Dylan with a plenty large pinch of salt – teasing him for self-conscious, grammatically quirky, obscenity-studded hip talk, trusting none of his stories about his past and his parents, pointing out how this acclaimed new mascot of unconventionality was brought up so conventionally, surprised that such a scratchy, yelping voice was having such success.

The writer didn't seem too impressed that Dylan grumbled

about the commercial side of folk music but was supported by aggressively enterprising management helping him to protect his image and 'fatten his contracts'. There was even a sense that he hadn't written 'Blowin' in the Wind' – which of course he had, it was all his work, and he hadn't, he'd found parts of it lying around – as if the whole point of the piece was to bring his carefully constructed image come crashing down.

He denied that he was once Bobby Zimmerman – and by August 1962 he'd legally changed his name to Bob Dylan; his children would be surnamed Dylan – and denied having any contact with his parents, who it turned out were in town about to see him play the Carnegie Hall having been sent tickets by their son. *Newsweek* had the kind of facts that made Bob uncomfortable, when he was more interested in presenting his past as 'being so complicated you wouldn't believe it'. He was annoyed perhaps that his parents had been brought into it, frustrated a little naively that the article prosaically picked at his nicely building mystique, maybe most annoyed that the writer tried to be language-cute and describe his hair as 'bewildered'. His ego was building nicely too. His paranoia was also taking shape, a paranoia he'd come to rely on when it came to writing songs. Your mind is working at its best when you're being paranoid. You explore every avenue and possibility of your situation at high speed with total clarity. As Thomas Pynchon said, without paranoia there is no art. And paranoia, that bastard child of fear and good sense, can link up with reality every now and then.

*Newsweek* thought he was acting a little entitled and he thought he was being underestimated. They thought he simply wanted to be a pop star and get a load of the attention that comes

NOTHING BUT A VOICE

with being one; he was thinking of winning the Nobel Prize in Literature. Well, not exactly – his dreams weren't stretching that far, and when they did start to really stretch, they weren't aiming in that direction. But he still thought he deserved to be talked about not as an idiosyncratic light entertainer with a stylised eccentric delivery but as some sort of serious writer with a subversive talent for comedy and a great gift for writing ecstatic mysteries. The best response was to write a battling, long-distance travelling song like 'Restless Farewell', full of direct admissions, frank confessions and the rolling, obscuring mists of the mystique the article tries to miserably rub out.

The journalist was just doing their job, challenging the performer, who after all was doing his own challenging, even as he was trying to say such attention was not relevant to who he was and where he'd come from. You would be better off interviewing the music itself. 'I am my words,' he said, which in the sort of no-nonsense article being written about him came across as some kind of confirmation that the journalist was right to be so unconvinced. Who does he think he is?

But then Dylan was right when he said it's more complicated than it seems. The only way he can get right of reply is when he is at his most fluent and flexible; inside a song. Later, per-haps because of the *Newsweek* experience, he mostly dealt with interviews as though he was inside one of his songs, playing himself or any number of other characters that turn up there. Inside the songs, he can be anyone he wants to be, even if in the outside world of mainstream publicity such an approach leaves a trail of confusion and speculation. He dealt with interviews in ways that followed on from the last line of the song, which becomes the last line of the record, and the last line of a verse that seems particularly directed to those questioning what he was up to, those that were trying to disgrace and distract him. He fought the gossip thrown in his face, the rumours covering him in irrelevance, and made his stand.

He'd got a fight on his hands if he was going to be able to keep on writing the sort of songs he wanted to write, which if you think about it are only songs, and there's a lot more dangerous deceit in the world than a singer using a little illusion, a little sleight of hand, in order to make his case and appear on stage. He wouldn't change, whatever happened to him, whatever they said about him – which means he wouldn't stop changing. He'd say farewell – using his thin and vivid folk voice – and the last line is where he looked into his future and admitted whatever did happen, he'd not give a damn. One answer to who the hell he thinks he is. It may not be pretty, but it is more about who he is than a straight-minded civic singing activist.

'Restless Farewell' is a signal, whether he even knew it, about what was to come. It's a signal that he'd just keep moving on, whatever the misinformation, the misunderstanding, the changes in his voice, the changes in the music scene; eventually the line would lead to the Never Ending Tour, where he reacts to an alien music business by setting out on his own come what may. It's a song about what it means when he talks of coming from nowhere as he moves somewhere else, hiding himself even as he seems to say he's got nothing to hide, and using his first voice, the travelling rambler, the 23-year-old acting wiser and wearier, but still a 23-year-old. It didn't immediately have the resonant weight it had when he sang it thirty-two years later.

He performed it on a 1995 *Tribute to Frank Sinatra* TV special honouring Sinatra's eightieth birthday, and there was some confusion about whether it was a song Dylan wanted to sing, or one that for some reason Sinatra wanted to hear, even though it wasn't one of the more obvious established classics. Whatever the reason – maybe it was just chosen by fate – Dylan's complaint from inside a song about how he was being treated when he was outside a song was the perfect choice for the occasion. A song was required and a voice that celebrated the singer and the song in the sort of elusive, mystical way Dylan was protecting when he wrote the song in the first place. Let me play, he was saying, let me find out for myself, and make things up for myself, so that I can write and sing these sort of songs. He never wanted to stop travelling, whatever it took, and this song was about how he couldn't stop even if he wanted to, whatever the rumours, whatever the accusation. It was in songs where he could keep travelling, in songs where he could find the road heading through wide open spaces.

Written at the beginning of a life, 'Restless Farewell' has the same kind of heavyweight reflective end–of–life drama that is packed into one of the great outpouring Sinatra epics, 'My Way', and Dylan's tribute to Sinatra, one American voice to another, one big-time traveller to another, became him delivering with devastating beauty his own 'My Way', a song which summarises his attitude to life and to performance that works just as well as a great goodbye, an ultimate farewell. Being Dylan, writing it at twenty-three, singing it at fifty-five, he was looking forwards and looking backwards at the same time. He was singing it for someone from the generation or two before whose voice had faded without any increase in artistic powers, but he was separated from such a fate by the songs he'd written and the secrets he'd kept, hiding many from himself.

His voice by then had slipped through a few stages, a few shocks to the system; put the two together and it's like a number of lifetimes must have passed, as a swooping, nasal farmhand's lament becomes a deep, embellished and graceful act of blessing.

After the third album, that first voice, the one that places him in a certain history, as though he actually belonged with activists, protestors and singing social critics celebrating the old and distant but intent on changing the world, would be replaced by a second. This is the voice of a quick-witted quick learner reacting to the volatile times, feeding into the roiling speed of post-war cultural movement, turning stolen beat rhythms into a newer sound, transferring existential transience into the pop music of the day.

It was coalescing in 'Restless Farewell' and it fully materialises on 'It Ain't Me Babe', the final track of the fourth album, *Another Side of Bob Dylan* (1964), which can be seen as a love song, an anti-love song, an anti-war song, a song about a woman, about romantic entanglement, about infidelity, about justice, about ethical instincts, about a secret or a series of secrets, about complete indifference, or a song about a generation, about his abdication from being the voice of a generation, about discreetly lowering expectations, about excluding an earlier world view which he never really had in the first place.

It's a song setting up where he was going next, about a change in his voice as he began to shake off the limitations of his folk years and see if a song can in its own way contain the whole world and sketch the universe in a single luminous verse. Or at least he wanted to write and sing songs that cannot be pinned down as one thing or another, and certainly not as mere protest anthems, even if this means losing your mind a little, and losing his initial job title.

The second voice still had the first one inside it, still cutting into and cut up by acoustic settings, as though the folk singer was still travelling between the 1870s and the 1960s, on the road between the beginning of time and the end of days, but it was already on the way to becoming a revelatory third voice. The third voice is electric, as if he'd found a way to wire himself to the mains and shake off all that historical dust he'd used as a convenient camouflage, to connect his first written songs with centuries of tradition and catch up with the Beatles and the Stones. They'd uncovered a whole audience that Dylan craved, being a traveller who didn't mind being on his own but fancied a bit of company. The third voice is the voice of a pop star, or at least the idea of one that Dylan had in his madcap mind, and it became the one most people think of when they think of Dylan's voice, fully charged with eccentric, swooping cadences, elongating and augmenting words and syllables, ending word after word with an emphatic dip or rise, driving right into your skull.

In the Beatle-mad 1965, the sincere, but sly, early-'60s folk singer became the snide, dangerous double-crosser, Dylan going electric as much in how he used his voice as because he was now playing an electric guitar and backed by an amplified rock band with their own singular take on style, harmony, country blues and period clothing. The third voice mostly stayed for *Bringing It All Back Home* (1965), *Highway 61 Revisited*

(1965) and *Blonde on Blonde* (1966), where he was sending out an overwhelming amount of information, writing songs that were like short cuts to spiritual and transcendent experiences, filled with whatever time he wanted it to be. It blasted, quarrelled and spilt out of his body, sometimes like he was about to bury his fangs into your flesh, and it had to, considering what he had started to do with the idea of a song.

The stinging, accusing, unsettling electric Dylan anticipated a few of the punks to come, but he didn't stick there, as some might have wanted him to, the deviously cool, glamorous rock and roll outlaw pushing songs to the edge of the world, letting some tip right over. He used the third voice as a base to shapeshift into country-crooning space cowboy; into intense spirit-raising born-again gospel preacher, the God-fearing Bible basher looking to the heavens; into surreal heart-breaking torch singer, the definitive post-break-up serenader; into bright-eyed, even sweet, pop singer; into self-parodying shaman, trickster-sage, reluctant legacy act, sour, seething rebel rouser, mutant balladeer and grieving, ailing psychic nibbling at the edge of the abyss. And possibly into lost soul fantasising about a nine-to-five life, as exotic to Dylan as life on Mars.

The third voice seemed at the time the end of the road, a convenient place to settle down, a voice to be stuck with 'til death, but it was another act, another reality, useful for communicating the essence of certain dreams, and the dread of certain nightmares, and it was quickly becoming a fourth voice, which came out of a sudden turn to the pre-industrial Biblical rock he made on *John Wesley Harding* (1967) and songs almost thrown away or forgotten like marvellous dreams that were heard on *The Basement Tapes* (1975), where the pop-singing lone raver was suddenly veiled by memory and tinged by dreams, in the mood after all that ferocious scheming and scamming to dissolve into the sky. As always he had a voice in mind, as though he was ready for all eventualities, including near death, and beyond, a voice that spoke in voices, his own and others, a voice that was happy to leave the pop charts behind and head for the hills, making up songs that folded in on themselves that in turn needed a voice that folded in on itself.

The fourth voice has the first three inside it, and hints of others feeding back from some impossible future, but it is something else altogether, the other side of a motorcycle crash, a near-death experience, perhaps death itself, or certainly an enforced change, a radical resetting of style and psyche, a voice meant to set the hubbub his life had become into order. There is something in there that seems so pre-Beatle, pre-Beat, pre-surreal, pre-himself, it is as though he was now so old he just wanted to pass the time of day, casually singing the old songs, the easy-going blues and country tunes, even though his old-sounding songs were as creepy and fantastic with the present and fibres from the future as they were with the past. This quiet, quietly wild, perversely moving part of his fourth voice became a fifth voice, which has the first four inside it, even though it has a calmness, a sense of peace, of slowing down, he'd never revealed before. You can hear these voices on *Nashville Skyline* (1969), *Self Portrait* (1970) and *New Morning* (1970), which is where the voice almost seemed to leave behind the slippery, performing Dylan that we'd got used to, that had gone out of his way to be the image of a protest singer, a folk balladeer, the games-playing pop star. On 'Lay Lady Lay', so calm, deep and smooth, and human warm, the singing version of his speaking voice, there was some thought that this might actually be the real, untreated, unmasked voice of a real unmasked Dylan, where he wasn't acting up or running rings around words. Singing it like it is, like he is. It is just another voice, though, one good for the task at hand, for the way he felt at the time, depending on what he wanted to shine through at the moment he sang it.

The voices exist separately, and sometimes are blended together in different formations, but as the years passed, ultimately one new voice clearly replaced another, as *The Freewheelin' Bob Dylan* became *Bringing It All Back Home* became *Blonde on Blonde* became *Nashville Skyline* became *New Morning* became *Blood on the Tracks* became *Saved* became *Oh Mercy* became *World Gone Wrong* became *Time Out of Mind* became *Tempest* became *Triplicate* and that, it seemed, was that. Unlike most singers, whose singing voices stay the same, as if the whole point is to always replicate the original record, the young tyke, to stay the same age, Dylan allows his voice to move with the times, to change with his age and the breakdown of his body, the errors and shadows in his soul.

Hailed in the 1960s as 'the voice of his generation', naturally impatient, chronically restless, never wanting to sound dated and redundant, he quickly left that idea behind, appreciating how it would fix him if he merely repeated the early voice. His voice changed in the same way a great painter changes how and what, and why, they paint, and it went through various periods, reappraising his roots and his own history.

The sixth voice, around the corner from the fifth, but somehow also from the first, is louder, maybe even his loudest, roaring like a learned rock star leaning into age on *Before the Flood* and the carnival frenzied Rolling Thunder tour, but inside it there is still the dust, the dreamer, the electricity, the anger, the silence, the cool, the flirt, the thief, the hurt, the beat, the pop, the rock, the blues, the human, the money, the country, the joker, the jilted lover, the cubist, the critic, the sage, the lover, the liar, the cheater, the loner, the autistic, the musicologist, the traveller, the painter, the conman, the paranoid, the fuck you, the world, because as he knew all along, he had a lot of voices, and he would need them all to get everything he wanted to say across to all the people he wanted to say it to. He's still the more natural, worthy, post-country Bob on 'Knockin' on Heaven's Door', a near-sentimental song about heaven being under our feet as well as in the sky, which became some kind of deeply possessed novelty hit, and on *Planet Waves* (1974), still exploring all quarters of life, in light and dark, now with a few voices on call featuring various levels of virtues and vitality.

But even this far in, as tumultuous and yet as subtle as the seventh voice is, starting up on *Blood on the Tracks* (1975) and its bitter, broken history of love and all over by the volatile faraway tenderness of *Desire* (1976) and the seemingly lost or about-to-be-lost, self-parodying *Street-Legal* (1978), there was still more to come, because he had only used the voices that he'd needed up to then. For those who get concerned about when some form of deterioration started in Dylan's voice, *Street-Legal* becomes a marker between the Dylan who made his own vocal changes and the Dylan who had the changes forced on him, by his body, stress, substance abuse, carelessness, who to some was already heading into a continual decline.

He wasn't finished, though, and there were still things he could do with his voice, to his voice, and there emerged an eighth voice, containing faded traces of the other seven, but made to praise Christ, when he was either in a spiritual panic, or marching down the clearest path he could find after a divorce from his wife Sara, or losing a sense of his place in the world. Through the albums *Slow Train Coming* (1979), *Saved* (1980) and *Shot of Love* (1981), it was as though he wanted to sing every line as if it was unquestionable, as if the words were being issued from a burning bush.

There were those who saw no difference between sanctimonious self-serving Dylan and sanctimonious Dylan serving and trusting in God, but that might have been a sanctimonious point of view – then again, he sometimes sang as if he thought he could raise the dead, whether a fierce-minded cheerleader for Christ or a fearless poet–jester trafficking in survival afraid for the health and safety of the world.

After focussing on the power of Christ, as if he was storing up some divine strength knowing what was ahead, there was a ninth, sometimes almost disinterested voice that took him through the 1980s, where as compact discs started to replace vinyl he couldn't seem to work out what kind of records to make, or even what kind of records he was expected to make, a time when he would often compose with others, from Sam Shepard to Bono, looking for a way out, or a way into something. Whether he felt it or just the world at large, he no longer occupied the exalted place he once had, his type of performer pretty much out of stock, no longer carried because no longer called for. For a while it seemed all he had going for him was the run-down reputation of a toppled idol, as the source of some indelible phrases, the writer of some classic songs that were starting to detach themselves from their author as he started to slip into academic bibliographies and punctilious dissertations, his authority drifting somewhere strange and distant.

He was preoccupied with working himself out, the other side of Christ, the other side of ferociously failed love, the other side of being Bob Dylan with all that libido and sundry discombobulation, worried as much as at any other time that his past was going to overwhelm him. There was always that dread of being no good, even after his moments of greatness, all that he had done as a songwriter that could hold the imagination like no-one else. Albums kept appearing – *Infidels* (1983), *Empire Burlesque* (1985), *Knocked Out Loaded* (1986) and *Down in the Groove* (1988) – where he just seemed to be going back and forth, using a lot of lines from old films, often writing songs that barely managed to get to their feet, sometimes sunk under weird wafts of '80s synths and drum machines, shoddy reverb and improper slickness, a long way past when he seemed able to create his own reality – plus the inevitable live records and more official greatest hits collections.

Working out how low his '80s could go, he even appeared in a movie that in America went straight to video as a reclusive has-been rock star called Billy Parker, 1987's *Hearts of Fire*. It was as though he might escape – or sum up – the '80s by making his bored equivalent of a flimsy, half-hearted Elvis film, sing a couple of songs for no good reason, kiss his co-star, smash up a hotel room and get in a fight. It's a corny rock and roll movie made by people whose only contact with rock and roll seems to have come from reading Jackie Collins novels. Dylan loved costumes, one man in his time plays many parts, and he could be guilty of fabricating a world in which he could live and invite others to live in, but this was beyond a joke.

Dylan could have been forced to appear in the film in a role he wasn't born to play after losing a bet, or he did it to find out for himself what career suicide might be like, or he played the role just so that he could say the line 'I always knew I was one of those rock'n'roll stars that was never going to win any Nobel Prize'. The film almost totally disappears without trace, taking the fossilised Billy Parker with it, if not Bob Dylan, used to shedding skins, and accepting that whatever happens to him – whatever humiliation, misfortune or embarrassment – can be used as a resource, as raw material that somewhere down the line can be shaped into art. All things have been given to use for a purpose. And at least he never had to do anything like that again.

He tried rapping a few lines for Kurtis Blow and flirted with the tough, aching rhythms of reggae as he vainly searched for a contemporary musical source that could help him out, and in 1988 passively accepted membership of a whimsical, warm-hearted supergroup representing three generations of rock stars, The Traveling Wilburys, more or less keeping a straight face, with George Harrison, Tom Petty, Jeff Lynne and Roy Orbison, as though he'd decided one way to escape the quandary of the decade and break through the tyranny was to have fun with old friends. On the first Wilburys album, 1988's *Volume 1*, each star using a pseudonym, Bob Dylan was known as Lucky Wilbury, and on the second album released in 1990 after the death of Orbison, titled *Volume 3* with superstar perversity, Dylan had become Boo Wilbury.

He was still finding songs – conceptually more successful

than the recording or the performance – that suggested he hadn't lost any of his scrupulous ability to write in a way that probed the universe of spirit, and there was the beginning of a persistent arcane growl that would follow a trail all the way into the '90s, into the Never Ending Tour. It's easy to produce a great playlist of great Bob Dylan songs from the 1980s; 'Brownsville Girl', 'Sweetheart Like You', 'Every Grain of Sand', 'Jokerman' – which in the mid-90s appeared out of the blue and made it into 103 straight shows on the Never Ending Tour – 'Series of Dreams', 'Dark Eyes', 'Most of the Time', 'Silvio' – played 98 times in 1998 alone – 'When The Night Comes Falling From The Sky', 'Dignity', 'Man in the Long Black Coat', 'Tweeter and the Monkey Man' – a Travelling Wilburys song escaped the '80s malaise by ignoring any concerns about sound or legac – 'Tight Connection to My Heart', 'Ring Them Bells', 'Lenny Bruce', Blind Willie McTell', 'The Groom is Still Waiting at the Altar', 'Shooting Star.' There's more; he's gone down as having a bad decade, but he wrote more good songs than most, patiently waiting for the decade to play itself out. Even as he was lost in exile he had a way of making sense of things, or wonderfully making no sense at all, just for the hell of raiding his idiosyncratic mind. He couldn't help himself.

Because of that idiosyncratic mind, the need to issue various sorts of warnings, a voice that couldn't seem to make itself heard like once upon a time, he was so far out from where the 1980s were, a rapid, fickle mess of posing, synthesising and MTV, or even a fickle magnificent mess of Morrissey, or a distracting mess of Madonna, he seemed to have fallen off the planet, so old-fashioned and vaguely unpleasant there was nowhere to go but permanent exile, lost in a bygone age.

The bygone age turned out to be from the future, which he couldn't avoid. He was preparing to be the elder statesman almost as soon as he left Jesus behind in 1983, but he seemed to need to get the '80s out of the way before he worked out how to remake himself as an older performer, seeing no precedent for how someone like him dealt with age – it turned out he needed to actually be old, or at least middle-aged, and his forties didn't quite count, they just put him in a kind of limbo. As the '80s came to an end and he headed towards fifty, he started to get his act together with *Oh Mercy* (1989). One or two things started to click and he suddenly understood something that had been puzzling him. Maybe it was possible to get a handle on this old world after all. Maybe being Lucky Wilbury for a while – and maybe even Billy Parker – reminded him how much he was actually Bob Dylan, without letting that get in the way of being Bob Dylan.

Produced by U2, Peter Gabriel and Brian Eno collaborator Daniel Lanois like some sort of psychic sonic therapist, adventurously encouraging a dithering Dylan to overcome his demons and face up to the glories and terrors of the 1980s recording studio, it was another one of those occasional Dylan albums gratefully received after an apparent loss of verve and a series of disappointed reviews where it was decided he had something to prove. With Dylan, recovery led to rags, but rags kept leading to recovery. In *Chronicles* he devotes almost 80 pages to the recording of *Oh Mercy*, still dwelling over a decade later on exactly how he made it out of the stagnant, paralysing '80s, and how exactly Lanois got so deep inside his head, and got used to how he was a series of moods and sensations, how he changed every day, and played a thousand roles.

*Oh Mercy* became the record that is for many his best since *Desire*, since 1976 – marking thirteen years in some sort of wasteland, where his voice went from young to old, or make-believe old to believe-it-or-not old – and after a little awkward echo from his confused '80s with *Under the Red Sky* (1990) he took this new cracked, scaly tenth voice into the 1990s. He retreated – or advanced, masked – into the all-acoustic *Good as I Been to You* (1992) and *World Gone Wrong* (1993), two albums that rewrote history and reinterpreted American culture through music. Dylan finally shook off the grim '80s by releasing albums without writing any new songs, reviving old policies, refiring himself by beginning again from scratch, as if these folk and blues studies were entirely for his own use, a refresher course in how favourite old songs helped him write his own songs.

After a short run of greatest hits albums and his MTV Live album – the Dylan mini-industry ticking over while the Never Ending Tour rolled on, steadily thickening with its own myth – he was ready for *Time Out of Mind* (1997), the definitive conclusion to some trying times on record, following the longest gap there had been between records of original new material, and an eleventh voice that would make it through *"Love and Theft"* (2001) to *Modern Times* (2006). Having been 'healed' by Daniel Lanois, freed of various phobias about modern technology, he'd now taken over in the studio, producing himself as Jack Frost, creating cubist scaffolds of sound out of his occult feeling for the blues, rock and roll, country, jazz, gospel and soul and any number of outside offshoots, subconscious scenarios and ancient preludes. The modern recording studio with all the plug-ins and EQ's and artificially inspiring effects didn't have to get in the way of generating the wide and wild open undressed spaces he liked to have in his music; the songs could still be as unkempt, disordered, hurt, askew, knuckled, cobwebbed and unfashionably detached as he wanted them to be, sometimes worn to death, beat up, frayed at the edges, waiting for the dust to settle as he headed into his kind of dreamland constantly repurposing his own story.

The eleventh voice became a twelfth, exhausted, outraged, surely scarred beyond help, by *Together Through Life* (2009), a shrunken, internalised blast of a voice he perversely celebrated that year as a form of haywire exhilaration on a weirdist set of traditional Christmas songs and hymns, *Christmas in the Heart*. It was pitched somewhere between zany and ridiculously sane, the sort of songs he could only sing with such a voice, because he took them beyond kitsch, beyond fashion, into a world where, at the age he was, with the mind he had, he could do what he wanted with the time he had left, including being off his head in a way that would have pleased Lewis Carroll.

It was, after all, his right to be odd, at a time when few dared to be as eccentric as him, celebrating life in body and soul as an incalculable, chaotic thing, which is often how he smuggled through his genius, mental vigour and moral courage. Or it was his right to perform a very special other worldly version of 'Have Yourself a Merry Little Christmas', singing 'next year our troubles will be out of sight' like he'd really thought about it, and you could take the thought in any number of ways.

His Christmas album can be for one or two days a year at least, on the back of a good bottle of wine or two, his best album, and it's the roasted, toasty sound of a renowned American singing star full of poetic pretences more alive than most people who reputedly had a 'World's Best Granddad' sticker on the bumper of his car. Writing that makes me realise how it is almost odd to think of Dylan having a private life.

At another extreme, hear the opening song on *Together Through Life*, if you're used to hearing Dylan playing the part from the '60s and '70s and have never seen him on the Never Ending Tour. 'Beyond Here Lies Nothin'' drops from a glum grey sky into a vengeful borderland boogie which does exactly what it says in the title, Dylan surrounded by ash, wrath and memories of something and there's only one way out of things, and his dashed punished voice is the sound of the heart of solitude. Once you get over the shock of him sighing like a furnace, marvel at how as a singer at the end of his tether, at the end of his time, knowing that he knows nothing on the way to being nothing, he pours out his infested soul, and makes every second count.

As he entered his seventies and the 2010s, following through on his Never Ending Tour, where he relentlessly circled the snaking mysteries of his own extraordinary repertoire through a recurring landscape, his voice seemed to be completely dis-integrating, made up of scorched fragments and menacing creature croaks, the sound of a cracked 78, a vortex of crazy brushstrokes, crackling through the air, containing his essence itself, the atoms of his being, sounds abstractly falling together in words and sentences, from sensation to sense. He was singing ghost stories with the soul of a ghost.

When the weathered, artfully dynamic twelfth or thirteenth voice of Dylan appeared on *Tempest* (2012), a few long journeys, dreams, digressions, plots, storms, flames and upsets after the thin, wiry, unrestful very first Dylan voice, you felt it more than ever as a memory of Dylan, part of an aural archive of his existence, his split personalities, ready and waiting for when he no longer walks amongst us. For Dylan, as alarming as his uncompromisingly declining new voice could sound to those who simply wanted an exact repeating of his greatest hits, of his younger selves – or his greatest hits sung by more 'attractive', sweeter voices – this worn, torn born-free late-life voice was the voice he had always wanted, a real, deep, scattered version of the 'authentic' sound he had artfully been pretending to have at the very beginning. Beauty was skin deep; his voice went clean to the bone.

He wasn't using his voice to charm or console, to go one more time through the motions or the greatest hits. He was using it to provoke, to keep searching, and to keep stretching to the bitter end just what a voice can do and be and sound like. He'd repeat a word more and more frequently, and each time with a more caressing emphasis. He'd have his obsessions, and he would explain them over and over again, coming back to them afresh each time. If he's singing something disturbing, something jarring, ecstatic and freakish, as he often is, he uses his voice to deliver the multi-layered, underhand truth. These late-life voices were the voice of someone taking his time, because he'd seen enough and heard enough to know that there was more ahead. After all this time, there was always another voice ahead, which contained every single second the singer had lived, and each second he'd been alive contained a whole life, even if these final voices seemed to be to those who were just passing by to not even be a voice at all.

The raw, scrutinising, lusty 21st-century voices were in some ways his most beautiful, the most miraculous, certainly the most hard-earned, encrusted with past, future and consciousness, twisted around the turn of the century, fractured by time, enriched by thinking too much, straight from a place where the night had dried up.

He was playing at being old as much as the greedy, ambitious, ruthlessly cunning kid had played at being old, but now he really was old, as old as the music he was still rifling through, sorting through the rubble, as old as his ancestors, knowing the same secret things as them. This was a voice with which he could take over from Elvis Presley and Billie Holiday as much as from Paul Verlaine and the weather. It was Billie Holiday that said if she was going to sing like someone else, then she didn't need to sing at all.

This late and later voice was the voice that made it clear however wrong he'd been, he had always been right. However lost he'd got he'd always known where he was, and he always knew he'd got nothing to lose. This was where all his voices had always been heading, to the end of a life, and the very last performance, at the very last minute, finally making it home, a place he'd never been before but which he would immediately recognise.

In his own way always the very first to stand up for himself, and clearly pissed off that he'd been given a hard time about his voice 'since day one', Dylan accepted an award in 2015 with a thirty-minute speech that included a defiant response to the critics:

Critics say I can't sing. I croak. Sound like a frog. Why don't critics say the same thing about Tom Waits? Critics say my voice is shot. That I have no voice. Critics say I mangle my words, render my songs unrecognisable. Oh, really? Let me tell you something. I was at a boxing match a few years ago seeing Floyd Mayweather fight a Puerto Rican guy. And the Puerto Rican national anthem, someone sang it, and it was beautiful. It was heartfelt and it was moving. After that it was time for our national anthem. And a very popular soul singing sister was chosen to sing. She sang every note – some that exist, and some that don't exist. Talk about mangling a melody. You take a one-syllable word and make it last for fifteen minutes. She was doing vocal gymnastics like she was in a trapeze act. But to me it was not funny. I get the blame for mangling a melody, but I don't really think I do that. I just think critics say I do. Sam Cooke said this when he was told he had a beautiful voice. He said, 'Well, that's very kind of you, but voices ought not to be measured by how pretty they are. Instead they matter only if they convince you that they are telling the truth.'

One late-life response to those rattled, even offended by his voice was to turn to music written before rock and roll, before he began writing his own songs, the standards and the Sinatras, the orderly, aristocratic music it seemed he had been over-throwing when he youthfully tore into conventions, bending tradition into riveting new forms: *Shadows in the Night* (2015), *Fallen Angels* (2016) and *Triplicate* (2017). He used his hell-and-fire, heavens-above voice to sing the songs he grew up listening to, and even though the voice superficially sounded ugly and desolate, even tuneless and hostile, his phrasing was impeccable, his musical understanding of the songs exquisite, his love for life undimmed. He still sounded like Bob Dylan, the agitated, nomadic Bob Dylan that always changed the way he sounded, using his voice as much as anything else to camouflage himself, to reflect his enduring belief in the fundamental mutability of song.

Not a pretty singer — although he'd had his moments — but always a profound one, a master of inflection, he was using his voice as he said not to cover songs but to 'uncover' them, to dig into them, open them up and reveal their meaning and their unfashionable, jilted energy. Whatever it was that he'd been looking for as he made his way along from nowhere to somewhere on the way to nowhere, whether that was some kind of God, or answer, or relief, or drama, or peace, or challenge, his voice was strong and true, even when it sometimes sounded like no voice at all, like a sad, weakened monster, eyes full of tears, heart full of rage, a creature from deep in the mind, a undecipherable sign from the cosmos, a desperate wheeze of unease, or an answer to something once asked by Einstein, or Rothko, or Virginia Woolf.

This was the story I would tell once I had heard him sing the first songs at the Hollywood Bowl in June 2020. The story would begin there, with his voice, a voice that had always moved with the times whatever happened next and whatever had happened. A voice that when I first heard it made me decide without really understanding it at the time that the singer was definitely on a special assignment, and he was already the stuff of legends.

# THREE

## OUT THERE

My own Bob Dylan story begins almost as soon as I started listening to pop music in 1970 when I was thirteen, mainly through the BBC's weekly chart show *Top of the Pops*, because it was on television at 7.30 in the evening. It seemed a programme meant for people my age more than my parents, but we'd watch it together, as though it was an entertainment show for all the family. It was soon clear that I was getting something from the programme my parents weren't, seeing something in some of the groups that appeared on the show that they had no clue about, which was a blessing and gave me some space to move into where I could be myself.

By the early 1970s, as television excitingly turned from black and white to colour, which seemed to break all sorts of taboos, the groups I liked the best were the ones who started to look wilder and wilder, not necessarily because of the length of their hair but because of the clothes they wore and sometimes the make-up they wore, especially if they were men. The young mods and hippies of the late 1960s beginning to hit the charts had exaggerated mod and hippie styles and costumes, pushed a few barriers, made use of the colours that could now be seen, and there was the sudden, addictive rush of glam rock. In the middle of grim, broken times, men in make-up and sparkling dress was quite a turn-up for the books.

I began to realise without really understanding it at the time that some of these groups were singing songs to communicate things about sex, pleasure, fantasy and sensation that enhanced, even explained, some of the feelings I was beginning to have that I didn't immediately understand. Fifteen, sixteen years after Little Richard and Elvis Presley had flash-landed into the dreams and homes of 1950s teenagers and seemed to show them the liberating workings of the imagination, a few glam rock performers regenerated for a new generation under completely new circumstances some of the revelations and dramas of these by then historic predecessors. The rock and roll originators seemed back beyond the other side of all that happened in the 1960s, a long way behind everything even as there were clearly overhauled traces and echoes of the dynamic excesses of Little Richard and Chuck Berry in what some of the more inventive glam stars were doing.

Latching on to Marc Bolan and David Bowie in particular with their own singular-angled transformation of sources meant directly receiving their influences, and as well as ravishing spins given to the riffs, poses and costumes of their rock and roll idols, there was the definite presence of Bob Dylan in their spirit and lyrics, packed with symbols and allusions, if not their voices.

The first singles and albums I bought were by Bolan's T. Rex and Bowie's Bowie, and I raided every corner of the songs and sleeves, different types of performance, looking for clues to something, although I wasn't yet clear what. I perhaps started writing about pop music first of all in my bedroom at fourteen, in notebooks read by me alone, one way to figure myself out, to keep looking for clues to something, and also to then work out what that something was. Because, it quickly became clear, there was something going on, and whatever it was quickly became the most important thing in my life.

Bowie wrote a florid, knowing love song to Dylan on his radically theatrical 1971 album *Hunky Dory*, wondering where he was as much as who he was, a variation of the song Dylan had written in his early years for his militant, marching hero, Woody Guthrie. 'Song for Bob Dylan', Bowie's song of respect, confidently putting himself in Dylan's company as Dylan did with Guthrie, immediately opened a route to Dylan, because all of Bowie's references, the collisions he was making with others and otherness, excited instant interest in his sources which surely led to the source of that 'something' I could feel in the air.

Bowie's near competitor Marc Bolan had probably taken his seductive spray of corkscrew hair from wondrous English eccentric Syd Barrett, Pink Floyd originator and eventual exile, but Syd in turn had taken his bird's nest hair from *Don't Look Back/Highway 61 Revisited* Dylan. Barratt had written a song after he'd seen him play in London in 1962, 'Bob Dylan Blues', a sly little parody of his hyper-realistic, too cool for rules, talking blues style that whimsically mocked not so much Dylan but the worshipping fuss that greeted his every jingly-jangly word, as if rhyming alone – as though he alone did such a thing – made him a genius. But anyone looking for some kind of help in writing songs that played around with what a song could be had to keep an eye on Dylan, and Syd never stopped watching what Dylan was doing, and how he put himself together as well

93

as his songs, how he dreamt of characters that seemed to be dreaming of him, from places that are no places and all places, where time dilates and wraps around itself.

Bolan was my favourite pop star. He'd changed his surname from Feld, and some music paper articles suggested that his new name was a compression of Bob Dylan – the first two letters and the last three letters of his own made up surname, B.O.L.A.N. These were the same articles that would mischievously note that the initials of *Blonde on Blonde* were B.O.B., but to me there was the possibility both had been intended.

In T. Rex's 1972 number one 'Telegram Sam', featuring a scattershot parade of the sort of likely and unlikely misfits and spooks that sometimes lurked in a Dylan song looking for action, Bolan drops in ace spook Dylan, using the kind of I'm-a-poet-and-I-know-it rhyme style Syd once parodied – Bobby's alright, sang Bolan, he's a natural born poet, and he's out of sight. It was sung in such a way that its real meaning seemed hidden somewhere else, and it was up to me to go and find out where – it seemed like another vital recommendation from my favourite pop stars transmitting coded messages of intent that I should find Bob Dylan.

To some extent around 1972, 1973, to find Bob Dylan, you had to look backwards, and for a while it seemed you would always have to look backwards. His fast-moving world-making time at the top of a new music scene seemed to have plateaued, and to all intents and purposes it seemed he was never going to be as incandescent, as expert at making resplendent, wounded music set to the tempo of a new era. His album releases had slowed down since *John Wesley Harding*, released in the last week of

1967, the last of eight studio albums since March 1962 which had taken him on a run to brilliance, soaring to transcendence, from freakishly folky, intensely knowing, almost scholarly accurate acoustic bard through to the three increasingly freakish electric albums packed with cryptic games of hide and seek released between March 1965 and June 1966 – *Bring It All Back Home*, *Highway 61 Revisited* and *Blonde on Blonde* – that seemed to produce a one and only example of a pop star achieving Absolute Oneness.

At the time of these albums he was twenty-five, as if he was young enough to know everything, younger than he'd been a few years before, but had done enough years – more than he had been alive – fast enough and great enough to expect a little rest. *John Wesley Harding* as quietly dramatic finale to that extraordinary outburst of form and experience, of fame and dazzle, was a kind of discreetly incandescent, exploratory rewinding, a blood-soaked, semi-acoustic sinking back into the mysterious and fabled American murk and mists where the landscape and the imagination meet. He had been on fire, and then there were the ashes, the dying embers, and he took himself out of himself, out of the world around him. He turned his mind and voice to the divinely commissioned singing of tales of evil and woe, spirit and matter where worldly aggrandisement meant nothing. Meanwhile, there were a few problems that needed solving in his life just in case his dreams dried up.

The accidental overnight stardom and associated high-pressure shenanigans inside limos, hotels, dressing rooms, airports, press conferences, venues and studios had ruptured his mental well-being, with a little through-the-looking-glass help from a dalliance with LSD, the boos after the 1965 British tour from those purists aghast at his new-style electric pop still ringing in his ears. A mysterious motorcycle crash after the release of *Blonde on Blonde* led to rumours of a near-death experience. It was a bad accident, the sun blinding him as he used his beloved 500cc Triumph to try to race ahead of the blur of energies his life had become, spinning off the road and bringing everything to a halt. Everything that had been building up speed since he'd been born as Bob Dylan, delivering himself through a gap in time back in the late 1950s. The accident was a reminder that people – even when they become a Bob Dylan – are unable to order existence because the world has a hidden order of its own. The universe has its own schedule. He was not a master and maker of his own fate – and who wouldn't have believed they were at the time, given all the attention he was getting, whether he liked it or not? – but part of a divine plan that had already been written.

The year before, in his sleeve notes for *Bringing It All Back Home*, bringing up one of his lists that help us work out what's up with his mind, he mentioned that he wouldn't want to be Bach, Mozart, Tolstoy, Joe Hill, Gertrude Stein or James Dean – because they were all dead. For a while, it seemed he'd joined the party. He was dead, or deranged, or had never existed in the first place.

The crash wasn't fatal despite the rumours that at the time seemed to be almost willing a certain kind of instant, legend-making, blaze-of-glory rock and roll death, but it led to the death of a certain image of Dylan the adventurer, arm in arm with the spirit of anarchy, a wild, reckless ride that ended with a terrifying skid, a cloud of smoke and a vanishing act. There was no word from record label or management, no sense of the severity or not of his injuries. Plenty was being read into his words, his actions and deeds, and now plenty could be read into the sudden riddle of his whereabouts, the empty space that started filling the previously well-publicised moving parts of where he had just been.

There was an enforced, abrupt ceasing of the electric campaign leading up to the recording of *Blonde on Blonde*, which had seen him respond to the Beatles and the Rolling Stones with his very own epic, ecstatic theatre, what was seen as the shift between the boyishly buoyant 'yeah yeah yeah' in the Beatles' 'She Loves You' and the exhilarating, limpid rejections of 'no, no, no' in Dylan's 'It Ain't Me Babe'. As soon as he started coming up with his love songs, he didn't hold back with the 'that's enough for me' songs, the kiss-off songs as he left behind a trail of hurt and confusion or was left on his own with hurt and confusion. Even when his songs are nasty they always shed some light.

It was fun while it lasted – he thinks – but he's out of here. He's gone. Or you're gone. 'Don't Think Twice, It's All Right', if you don't think twice about it, can seem a relentlessly lovely song with no bitterness, fear or self-pity, a sweet, simple and blissfully hummable tale of regret, about a split agreed by both parties, if you so desire, but the girl is the reason he's travelling on, she wasted his precious time, and this being Dylan he might just be talking to himself, he just wasted her precious time. It's about a man who was hopelessly, wordlessly in love with a woman who did not love him in return. Or vice versa.

Dylan brought to the love songs of pop music a desire to describe the behaviour of human beings and the world, and that alone for better or worse changed pop music, into something that tried to see and feel things in ways that had never been done before. In the *Freewheelin'* sleeve notes, he admits 'Don't Think Twice' is a hard song to sing, at least the way he wants to – he's not good enough, he says, not yet as good as Big Joe Williams, Woody Guthrie, Lead Belly and Lightnin' Hopkins. He envied their age, at least as a singer. He could act it up, but he didn't yet carry himself the right way to sing the song his mind was somehow the right age to write – ageless in its own way – even if his voice wasn't yet.

In the year the Beatles made *Sgt Pepper* and the Rolling Stones made *Their Satanic Majesties Request*, their response to the 'no, no, no' and Dylan's history-splitting invention of rock as art, Dylan retreated, escaped what had become an unexpectedly messy conflict. One of the first rock critics, helping to make up what that meant, and one of my heroes, Al Aronowitz, said that in the mid-'60s Dylan, like Mao, had won a revolution, and he didn't know what to do with that. Unlike Mao, he was young enough to revolt against his revolution. I met Al once but I've forgotten everything he told me about his friend Bob Dylan. Maybe he mentioned this to me.

Dylan had been through his own apocalypse and found somewhere to heal, where, according to Al, one of the things he spent his time doing, in revolt against his revolution, was building a dirigible. In Woodstock, a former artist's colony a hundred miles north of New York, he withdrew into family, his own, a growing brood of children, and the family of musicians with The Band at the centre.

The Band had been the Hawks, a Canadian group of supreme, individually distinctive musicians, Rick Danko,

Richard Manuel, Robbie Robertson, Garth Hudson and Levon Helm, who'd backed rockabilly king and fellow countryman Ronnie Hawkins and then set out on their own, coming to the attention of Bob Dylan via his A&R man John Hammond in 1964. They backed Dylan on his 1965 tours including the notorious British tour, which became D. A. Pennebaker's famous documentary *Don't Look Back*, the band fusing in the myth and mayhem of it all with Dylan, inspiring each other, so that they became not just a band but The Band. They became comrades-in-arms, a ragged troupe of soulmates, from a place where court jesters, bohemian writers and warriors shared similar personality traits.

Working with such an extraordinary collective, each one with their own quickfire style, critical spirit and taut, languid way of playing inside the moment and around the outside edges, accelerated a change from what could be more or less defined as folk to something that enclosed a wilderness of ideas within a few bars of music, a rooted, rootless music, freeing itself of time, easy-going and in suspense, that could never be safely defined. The Band were perhaps the only musicians at the time that were capable of surprising Dylan, and keeping him on his toes in the privacy of his own home was the perfect way to relax him; they looked like charming gardeners or maybe amiable assassins and they made his soul blossom.

In their modest Woodstock homes, they stayed up all night and ignored the pressures of the world, wasting hours making music for the sake of it, the time they enjoyed wasting not being wasted time. They improvised and experimented around their own home-made scenic reckoning of the sound of America with a kind of chilled frenzy, a sinister charm, getting ideas from each other's expressions, or lack of expression, taking turns at being genius, heading lightly into the dark, darkly into the light, for their ears only, as if no-one would ever hear what they did and it didn't matter. A lot of those songs, on fire with wisdom, whimsy and the burnt-out ends of smoky days, Dylan was happy to chuck into the waste bin, as though the only point was that he had experienced them, shrugged them off, but they were saved from oblivion by being taped by a more practical-minded Garth Hudson.

It was a form of slow healing, sleeping, eating and playing according to their own herky-jerky rhythms, an escape into their own time, their own worlds, as if musically they might be all on their own. While the Beatles and the Stones, and Frank Zappa and Jefferson Airplane tried to find out what part of the city Dylan had made his own, he disappeared into the country, but a secret part of the country that led to the gothic threat, ramshackle glee and strung-out wariness of 'This Wheel's on Fire', tossed off in one session as though songs were just creeping up on them from behind the wall, and what atmosphere and threat there was on the land settling through still centuries before there even was a wall. When dream folk band Fairport Convention heard some tapes of the then unreleased songs The Band and Dylan were teasing out of their isolated togetherness, bassist Ashley Hutchings reported hearing a strange mishmash of styles and drawled lyrics coming out of the speakers. 'It sounded subterranean; there was this strange cloak of weirdness covering them. We loved it all.'

Dylan hadn't quit, he hadn't gone entirely quiet, to some extent he was as active and artistically analytical as he had ever been, still with a potent work ethic, trying on new voices, but he had come to some understanding that in order to understand the world, one had to turn away from it on occasion. He'd checked himself inscrutably heading for the stars – or heading towards danger – in Pennebaker's watchful myth-building documentary as he recovered from the crash, and was a little disturbed at what he saw, someone based on him beginning to believe too much in his own self-creation, crackling with energy but also a narcissistic neurosis. At merry, messy press conferences, wary of traps being laid, of hounds snapping at his heels, facing unnecessary interrogators confused by his intensity, and the improbable ways he explained himself, he was saying things like 'I expect to be hung like a thief.' There was a look in his eyes like he had suddenly realised that everything around him was alive. He could feel the heat closing in.

He sometimes came across a little testy, a mite snidey, with a hell of a temper, especially when he was feeling righteous, which was getting to be about all the time, and after being thrown from his motorbike he wasn't dying to find out what would happen to him if he kept being so careless with his temper. He thought he was just having a quick reaction to bullshit, lashing out at the insanity and hypocrisy of the world, but caught on camera it wasn't necessarily a good look. When your temper becomes frayed, your sensibility is in shreds. Watching the rushes of *Don't Look Back* became part of his post-crash therapy, which perhaps involved learning – or relearning – how to put his madness to good use and keep thinking clearly.

Fame looked like a lot of nothing, too, just a lot of social frivolity, and it seemed a sure way of stamping and stereotyping you, stopping your own self find its natural dimensions. Fame seemed a form of incomprehension. Now he was a rich man, he was still wanting to live as a poor man, with a preference to be nobody, just in case it was the money and fame that was going to get in the way of his music. He preferred to be out of step with his time, because over time it turned out that was the best way to go on doing what he wanted to do. He adopted the pace of nature.

In early 1968, there had been a brief return from exile, Dylan looking smart and healthy in a fine blue suit, if with evidence of an enigmatic smile that hinted he knew some would think he'd come back from the dead. He appeared with The Band, temporarily called the Crackers, to play a tribute show for Woody Guthrie, who had died on 3 October 1967, honouring the departure of one of his heroes, and using the opportunity to stage a new arrival without going out of his way to take over. Others performing included Richie Havens, Odetta, Tom Paxton, Ramblin' Jack Elliot and Ry Cooder, but Dylan swooped in from another world, cloaked in an otherness that he'd never shake off.

Dylan and the not-yet Band were as loosely sublime as heaven, finding other sorts of deviant folk music deep inside traditional folk, playing Guthrie's 'Ain't Got No Home' as a dreamt anthem, with the power Dylan brought with him from his own songs, which lifted Guthrie's music into a different dimension. A few purists thought it was a little blasphemous to interfere so casually with Guthrie's spirit; Dylan thought it was wrong to sing him on the straight and narrow, that his songs were there, like all songs, to be changed, to be taken somewhere else, to keep them alive.

If anyone was going to bring Dylan back from the dead, it was Woody Guthrie, and Dylan would bring some echoes and memories of Guthrie into the records he made over the next few years, some sort of abstract, idealised imagining, a surreal inhabiting, of the kind of songs Guthrie might have been writing if he'd lived through the 1960s. The first recording session for *John Wesley Harding* took place two weeks after Woody's death, and one of the songs in that session was 'I Dreamed I Saw St Augustine', where the narrator/dreamer is on an uncertain hunt for the ultimate, feeling intense faith in something he doesn't yet understand.

The albums now came less rhythmically, and some of the music he was making didn't get released at the time he was making it – *The Basement Tapes*, capturing some of those informally powerful home recordings with The Band, was released eight years later, after the music it had structurally and tonally influenced – or else, in the form of the mostly reviled *Self Portrait*, steeped in cracked, hidden history, it seemed part of some calculated self-sabotaging attempt in this quasi-afterlife to purposely distance himself from the haywire fame and misfortune, from being held up as some kind of electromagnetic world-changing guru. It appeared to some as though he was deliberately undermining his own achievements. 'What is this shit?' *Rolling Stone* asked in their first review of Dylan in a new decade, turning on their hero and his trite, ugly-seeming *Self Portrait* with the kind of spite they'd picked up from their now apparently fallen hero.

Even the exquisitely rendered peace and consciousness of *Nashville Skyline* was greeted with some alarm, as though he had handed in his revolt, freedom and passion, traded in his transcendent civic conscience, abdicated from certain iconoclastic movement-building responsibilities to become some kind of bland, derivative cowboy singer, a more or less straightforward and suffocatingly ultra-respectable country act. The vicious swing of his pre-crash music had shrivelled up; the pop star surrealist gloriously illustrating the chaos of the mind and escaping the laws of gravity had become a strangely reassuring down-to-earth realist. Of course, all was not what it seemed. The first post-crash album, *John Wesley Harding*, his retreat into resurrection in 1967, had effectively invented country rock and the later alt-country, and one or two genres not specified, quietly energising American popular music. And where some thought the pedal steel guitars and crooning about a mockingbird meant Dylan was kidding around, *Nashville Skyline* confirmed the resolute love he had for Nashville and country standards as not merely a repository of pickin' good-time music but another nourishing route to the sublime, to seeing deep into things. He wasn't becoming country; country was becoming him.

Pop and rock and roll singers, from outside, didn't make country music at the time – at least not those who were bringing with them all their other knowledge, from music, literature, theatre, history, and adding a different set of self-conscious energies to basic, well-worn country templates. Once Dylan had put his mind and methods to country style, country music was never the same again, not necessarily as the crossover music it would have become anyway but as another enriched, enlightened sound.

Change is rarely straightforward. This still wasn't the Dylan that seemed to have invented a new kind of rock in the '60s; even inventing a new kind of country music seemed more an act of subdued conservation than convulsive disruption, but his renovation of country music was part of how he was renovating himself after the scars he received playing the role, whether he fully knew it or not, of triumphant, trickster disruptor. The world had fallen in on him; he restored himself. If the world itself fell, there would be hope, because there was love. Country music turned out to be the most useful music to move into to enact a response.

In 1970, there was the unbold but carefully golden *New Morning*, happy with the kind of happiness that comes when you stop searching for it, imbued with the calm his wife Sara and kids brought to his life, a deep breath after laughing, and mocking and rolling, too hard. It was a little too early for me to be aware of it at the time, and the new releases that came after were made up of greatest hits albums; a single released in response to the murder of Black Panther member George Jackson; a soundtrack to the Sam Peckinpah film *Pat Garrett & Billy the Kid* (1973), featuring a twisted Dylan cameo as Billy the Kid's dubious, cryptic sidekick Alias, and a moodily literal, steady-as-a-rock hit single, 'Knockin' on Heaven's Door', which made more sense by Alias than Dylan but then they may be one and the same; and an album of random record label-compiled outtakes that some received at the time as his most offensive, and has got pressed into online history as perhaps his only one-star album. The spasmodic early 1970s release schedule and lack of live shows seemed to be saying that Dylan was destined to exist in the distance, in a world he could control, out of harm's way, concentrating on being safe in his own skin, occasionally appearing to confirm he could still write a song, and still read the history of music with astute insight, but the days of revolution and the constant disorientating shuffling of identities and voices and ravishing dislocations of perspective were long gone.

The offensive single-star album, compiled without the direct input of Dylan and indifferently called *Dylan* (1974), was released seven years after his apparent disappearance, but some of the anger directed at it seemed part of a general annoyance that the missing Dylan was letting his fans and sundry supporters down. He'd given them so much promise, and then slipped into the woods to become a husband and a father, a part-time painter, a country crooner, a revivalist serenader and even happy. How dare he!

At fifteen and sixteen, treading along dizzying trails, I caught up with the revolutions, stories, protests, photos, writings, make-believe, characters and gossip and the unprecedented, magnificently unruly song dramas of Dylan, all that 1960s Dylan that still sent shock waves through anyone coming to it new, hearing songs that had a kind of voodoo Biblical heaviness as well as a scintillating lightness of touch coated with mystery that meant that nothing made since had made them seem smaller or slighter. The loves of my life were mostly the records being released around me, from the charts of the moment, or from an underground that few visited, but Dylan was somehow like my first love, even though it was difficult to see how and where that love had begun. The groundbreaking literary critic and scholar Christopher Ricks, a superlative writer on T. S. Eliot, Milton and Keats, argues that Dylan was an equivalent literary figure. He once said that you don't find

Dylan; he finds you. How did Dylan find me, ultimately possess me as only he can? How was I bitten by the bug?

Maybe it didn't actually begin with a record, but a book, *Tarantula*, which consists of words presented not as poetry or prose or autobiography or lyrics or hoax or comedy or speech scraps but a wired-wiring, jumbled tumbling barrage of everything. As Dylan picked up mind-splintering velocity between 1963 and '65 there was lots of his seemingly non-stop writing that didn't make it into his songs, but spilt and spasmed over into fragmented, fiery sleeve notes, including the beat-up Beat autobiography of 'Eleven Outlined Epitaphs' on *The Times They Are a-Changin'*, containing traces of songs, drifts of memory and whispers of poems, and a self-baptising survey of influences and inspirations where he rummaged through sources and excitements as a kind of self-appointed critic savouring the special. On the quiet he was already, accurately, if only in his dreams, feeling their equal, on the way to surpassing them; in one-line reviews he talks of the mystery of Marlene Dietrich, the love songs of Allen Ginsberg, the narrow tunes of Modigliani, the cries of Charles Aznavour, the quiet fire of Miles Davis, the bells of William Blake, the saintliness of Pete Seeger. Some of these other writings, containing words and thoughts – 'strokin' my senses' – that kept themselves to themselves, became a book started in 1964 and eventually published in 1971, five years after his crash postponed its appearance.

Post-crash Dylan lost interest in it, because it reminded him too much of the Dylan that prowled, powered and artfully dodged through *Don't Look Back*, when he thought if everything was under control he wasn't going fast enough, the Dylan wrenched from the continuity of time who was of a mind to write as much as he knew as quickly as possible. The Dylan that couldn't find a way to stop his racing mind, whose brain was a receiver of consciousness, who'd started to get trapped in the idea that the world was made up of an infinite succession of dreamers. For a while, he was under the absurd illusion that he had gained understanding of a chaotic, meaningless world, or he had read that he thought he understood, or that he thought he was under the absurd illusion he did. He was, he protested for his own benefit, just a song and dance man.

When he wrote what became *Tarantula*, as a 23-year-old who adored the pulse and power of words and had literary heroes, their minds managing to occasionally touch, when he was speeding up commercially as much as anything else, the thought of writing a book appealed to Dylan's vanity, and also to a mainstream publisher looking to cash in on his increasing pop notoriety. Fame if just for a moment had one or two advantages.

On the cover he looks like the one and holy surly, renegade pop star with penetrating gaze, transparent skin and transcendent cheekbones, the one who hadn't yet crash-landed, who perhaps hadn't slept for a while, very at home in the shadows, in his own vibrant space. His hair has the 1965 medusa tousle, as though ideas are exploding out of his skull, that was spreading like wildfire through British pop stars. The title is perfectly just so, with that odd kind of glorious inevitability about a Dylan project even when it's completely unprecedented, the word just hanging there over his head like a spider, and he might have found it dipping into Nietzsche, or because he was imagining what would have happened if a spider had bitten the white rabbit that Alice chased down the hole. Maybe he felt that he had spiders, some with a mean streak, making themselves at home in his mind alongside the worries that he had stored away.

As part of some kind of spell, the titular tarantula might have been handed through the gloom of time to Dylan by virtuosic nineteenth-century gothic master Edgar Allan Poe, who was a consistent, naturally shadowy spirit in the songs, winking self-consciousness, dark dreamworlds and unworldliness of Dylan, his occasional detours through the heart of darkness, even perhaps helping a little with the title for *Time Out of Mind*. Poetry for Poe was the rhythmical creation of beauty in words, and that was high up on Dylan's own list of motivations.

He identified with Poe's 'love that is more than a love', his 'giving the future to the winds' and his 'all works of art should begin at the end'. Poe also lied compulsively about his own life, laying traps for future biographers, and when he arrived in New York for the second time in 1837, he settled in Greenwich Village, encouraging its bohemian reputation, and the city became home to some of his greatest triumphs. Not long after Dylan arrived in New York in 1961, he would visit one of the homes where Poe once lived to pay a fan's homage.

Dylan would say that sometimes, not feeling he was who people imagined he was or wanted him to be, it was like he was an imposter trapped inside a Poe story, in the deepest corner of a catacomb, and he was too much inside his head, feeling he was losing his mind. Becoming insane with long intervals of horrible sanity. And there Edgar Allan Poe was, drifting through the masquerade of *Tarantula*, breathing an atmosphere of sorrow.

A tarantula pops up in the epigraph to Poe's tangled, fanciful 1843 story of piracy and slavery 'The Gold-Bug', a kind of Victorian Indiana Jones story, where puzzle-loving Poe introduces the idea of making and deciphering codes, coining the word cryptograph on his way to inventing the idea of the detective story. It's more Sherlock Holmes than *Pit and Pendulum*, filled with clues that can lead all the way to Dylan's capricious puzzle of a novel that is filled with puzzles, many destined to remain unsolved. Why should things be easy to understand? Mysteries force a person to think. We need to have mystery in our lives otherwise we grow up thinking everything in life is easily solved. Sometimes the truth is right under your nose, but you still need to find it. It's a story about madness, and along the way exposes the madness of reading meanings into a text, and of reading things into the idea that Poe's tarantula was also Dylan's, inspiring a fever of ideas.

'What ho! What ho! this fellow is dancing mad! He hath been bitten by the Tarantula,' the epigraph ran. In the Italian middle ages, the bite of a tarantula allegedly inspired disturbing symptoms, including a blazing fury in the eyes and a 'wild emotion in the countenance'. The dance of the tarantula was the disease the spider is said to have caused, the violent spasms bought on by the bite. A frenetic tarantella traditional folk dance emerged in southern Italy, where the dancers would be accompanied by accordions, mandolins and tambourines. The dance imitating the frenzied movements of the bite victim was said to be based on an emergency cure for the hysteria, as though dance could defeat the poison, wild self-expression could suck out the venom and conquer sickness.

Another place Dylan might have found the tarantula was the epic, implacable American tragedy *A Streetcar Named Desire* by Tennessee Williams – where Edgar Allan Poe makes a brief appearance – written while Williams was listening to blues music, to Ella Fitzgerald, to his favourite song, 'If I Didn't Care' by the Inkspots. In memory, he once wrote, everything seems to happen to music. (Williams loved Dylan's 'Lay Lady Lay', calling it one of those songs that helped him when there was too much distracting noise in his head. He decided that Dylan was on a similar path to him, of reinvention, of discovery, or telling a story, and he loved how Dylan was loving a woman in the song so fully and beautifully. He even toyed with turning her into a character in one of his plays. He heard great yearning in Dylan's songs, in his voice and his lyrics, and this yearning was forever moving towards some kind of understanding. He would lose himself in the journey Dylan was creating, and he would feel saved.)

An influential 1947 play, *A Streetcar Named Desire* was powerfully recreated as a 1951 film with a script by Williams featuring Marlon Brando as rough, brutalising, animalistic Stanley Kowalski and Vivien Leigh as voracious, tortured, wilting Blanche DuBois. She was one of theatre's greatest creations, a decayed Southern belle out of Poe by way of Baudelaire. The play and the film is a battle between realism and fantasy, between one set of deceptions and another. 'I don't want realism,' cries Blanche at one point, 'I want magic! Yes, Yes, magic!'

Blanche conducted a seedy past at a hotel called The

Flamingo, but when she's asked if she ever stayed there she replies that the Tarantula was the real name of the hotel. The Tarantula Arms. 'Tarantula!' her shocked boyfriend exclaims. A flamingo doesn't convey what she got up to inside one of the hotels rooms. A tarantula makes it clearer. The hotel was like a big spider, where she took her 'victims' and had 'many intimacies with strangers'. Like a tarantula hunting prey at night-time to survive, Blanche hunted men — including other forms of snakes — for a different kind of survival.

(Cate Blanchett would appear as the mighty, alert and worn-out Blanche DuBois in a 2009 production of the play; other real-life characters she has spectacularly shifted herself into being include Katherine Hepburn, Queen Elizabeth and Maid Marion and, in Todd Haynes' *I'm Not Here*, Bob Dylan — as tricky as any character she has played including Williams' Blanche DuBois, Ibsen's Hedda Gabler, Chekhov's Yelena Andreyevna, vampy supervillain, psychic supersmart Soviet agent, a telepathic elf, evil stepmother, TV news producer, mournful ex-wife, femme fatale, the spirit of Armani's Si fragrance, vigilante teacher, Irish investigative journalist, pregnant American journalist, glamorous Russian dancer, snooty punk rocker, Second World War British spy, French art historian, American socialite, CIA officer, notorious 1960s anti-feminist, unknowable woman cursed to be born at the wrong time. It took one — a master shape shifter — to know one.)

There is a poem by Federico García Lorca — Lorca briefly turns up inside *Tarantula* — 'Las Seis Cuerdas' ('The Six Strings'), combining the playful and the harrowing, whimsy and dread. In a few brief, stark words the Spanish poet and one-time musician compares a guitar to a tarantula, with its 'round mouth' through which the sobbing of lost souls escapes. The guitar makes dreams weep, and like the spider it weaves a huge star to catch sighs floating in a black wooden water tank. You can imagine Dylan's hands on the guitar, one plucking, one finding the chords, weaving webs, songs built with the strength and lightness of the spiders spinning, his hands moving in such a way it might freak you out if you thought about it too much.

(Another of Lorca's guitar poems talks as Dylan often did of wind and water, of whispers made of thunder; it is impossible to silence the guitar as it weeps as the wind weeps over snowfields. Whatever Dylan's manifesto of the mind and poetic methods consists of, it definitely includes much that he found reading and/or sharing with the volatile Lorca, a fan of *cante jondo*, 'deep or profound song', the original outsider version of the more commercialised flamenco music, a Spanish blues: poetry as a game, life as a game, but not the self as a game; in everything there is an insinuation of death; he didn't worry to be born so he will not worry to die; there is no straight road in the whole world, only a massive labyrinth of intersecting crossroads; you cannot fail to see the beautiful, aged Walt Whitman and his beard full of butterflies; only mystery allows us to live; everyone being curious about what might hurt us; the poem, the song, the picture is water drawn from the well of people, and it should be given back to them as a cup of beauty, so that they can drink and understand themselves; letting the years carry us along is the most important thing in life; he wanted to be a poet from head to toe, living and dying by poetry.)

Some saw *Tarantula* as contract-fulfilling pretentious drivel packed into useless pages, the kind of Kid Kerouac speed-of-America stuff he could get away with at the time because no-one could keep up with him, and no-one dared ask if he meant any of it. If he hadn't been Bob Dylan, no-one would have bothered publishing it. It was all about the money; monkeys might as well have typed it out.

I didn't care for the naysayers, buying it as the kind of fifteen-year-old experimenting with J. G. Ballard, William Burroughs and Philip K. Dick, staring at the crowded pages in books by James Joyce impatiently waiting for the moment I knew would come when it all started to make sense, swooning over the chains of gold Arthur Rimbaud was hanging from star to star. *Tarantula* seemed to come from those places, and this was a time when I flattered myself that I was weird enough to appreciate it. Better to be weird, I decided for myself, than worry about whether the book made any sense. Sense? The sense he was making in his songs, about the way things turn out, about the way things change from day to day, about what to do if you don't know what to do, meant that there was going to be a lot of sense pressed into this weirdness, even if it was a study in nonsense. I think the point is that he'd done enough even by then to have his nonsense respected. And the songs he'd written were the directions you needed to read to be directed in the right direction when you read his book. It was like Bruce Springsteen said about the first time he heard Bob Dylan, as a fifteen-year-old kid, how it 'thrilled and scared' him, touched what little worldliness he had at the time, and amplified it – it was the same for me reading as well as listening to him.

The way I saw it, he was advising you in whatever way came to his mind not to be dumb. He was showing us the workings of his bright, dogged mind, and as this was the mind that had written 'Like a Rolling Stone' and 'Subterranean Homesick Blues', relishing word play as the best kind of mindfuck, the best way of driving out devils, it seemed like a very good offer. I didn't want to resist these sentences where language was taking immense pleasure in itself.

He'd already surprised the largely conservative entertainment world by being a singer who wrote his own hits, a rock and roll star who aligned himself – however abstractly, ultimately – with radical causes, and now it seemed he was a pop singer who shared an affinity with the stream of consciousness of Joyce, with the Burroughsian attitude that language and image were methods of social and political control, used by those in power to dictate the terms of reality. The creative and interpretive composer who had investigated how and why songs were written the way they were and decided there were many other ways they could be written was here investigating how sentences are constructed and wondering if there might be other ways of locating and dislocating sense. He was deadly suspicious of the prearranged patterns which had been superimposed on reality, and sometimes this led to a song as perfectly poised and recognisable as 'Don't Think Twice, It's All Right' and sometimes to the slithy, gimbling rhythms of *Tarantula*, which, unless I'm clutching at straws, were just as much influenced as his songwriting was by the fal-de-riddle-eye-do of old English folk songs written by Anon and the rapid, rooted, flowing, fired-up hip fast scat syllables of bebop.

Dylan was Dylan because unlike just about anyone else he could make some kind of equation out of a sailor's tune as old as time plus hyper het-up jazz speeding through his veins multiplied by the tears of the blues divided by moving shadows and the contaminating of reality by dream plus myself being myself at speed. With *Tarantula* Dylan was running away with himself, but he was still thinking things through. It was writing by someone more devoted to music than grammatical rules. As Gertrude Stein said, 'The great question is can you think a sentence.' As Charles Bukowski said, 'There's no clarity. There was never meant to be clarity.' For Nietzsche, nonsense was a necessary condition of happiness. Vladimir Nabokov wrote 'Ink, a drug'. I'd even believed that Dylan, building huge libraries in his mind, had come across 'Notes on the Art of Poetry' by Dylan Thomas.

Singer Dylan would repeatedly deny over the years that his name had anything to do with the poet Dylan but he obviously knew about him and surely couldn't resist a peek or two – see later for my own take on this. In 'Notes on the Art of Poetry' Thomas begins by marvelling how there are such goings-on in the world between the covers of books, 'such sandstorms and icy blasts of words, such staggering peace, such enormous laughter, splashing all over the pages in a million bits and pieces'. The words, words, words he wrote were alive forever 'in their own delight and glory and oddity and light'. Directly or not such a sense of rhythm, such gleeful, intoxicated ways with words, would make it into Bob Dylan songs, and into the writing that never made it into songs.

Inside the book, even if it is just a million scenes spread out over a billion scraps of paper as Dylan once said, wondering himself what the hell it all meant, what you can see and feel and cut your mind on is that shredded, untrustworthy, almost hysterical speed he was moving at up to and including *Blonde on Blonde*. It was as though he felt compelled to record every thought he had ever had. The impertinent, vatic thrill of his music, the howling maelstrom of voices is there for the taking as the words riot amongst themselves on the page, jumping in and out of whatever he'd been thinking, or taking, at the time he wrote them, finding a little space in an unnerving manic rock star day to sit at a typewriter and gleefully, or grimly, smash the logic out of some sentences, which meant smashing the logic out of some memories.

This was during the time whenever he was writing that he couldn't be dragged from his desk by wild horses. Perhaps he was hoping in the middle of one of these sentences he would forget himself – writing as a deeper sleep than death. Perhaps he was having a tantrum. Or writing had become his prayer, the only way of achieving peace of mind, the only way of keeping going. Words and sentences were his paint. He liked the way they smelt.

The words, collected like they were, laid out as lines on a page because what else were you going to do with them, joined together like a mob, are Dylan's wild free-associating mind caught up in time, reflecting his experience of the '60s as he unfolded his own myth, of the '60s themselves, when he was right at the royal, irrational centre. Risking senselessness, in a fight that sometimes got pretty violent, he was trying to find out the reason he wrote, and deciding it was because he must, and the book was a piece of his life, a voice from it, a sign of his spirit. It was effectively a collection of his energies when energy was all he was, the energy of the mind as the essence of life – hence there were those who genuinely felt he was in the process of discovering the secrets of the universe. It was his job.

You didn't have to read it all – you didn't have to read it at all – but as an object, a possession, a thing that exists because Dylan did, it was and remains one of my favourite Dylan artefacts, one of my favourites of all his voices, ripples of pure movement, deeply symbolic of how he loved everything that flows, from rivers to words and in the end life itself. It said to me, for better or worse, that there is enough cutting and tightening of sentences in the world; why not try the other extreme? Dylan had pounced on his prey.

In a wider sense, as a side product, published five years too late, *Tarantula* in the early 1970s seemed to underline how the myth of Dylan was in free fall, out of control. It was part of a few remnants of his '60s falling to the ground in slow motion as though they were all scattered consequences of the motorcycle crash.

As I experienced Dylan in my own time, working it out for myself, a kind of after-the-fact approach which suited the enterprise, the greater question being asked about Dylan in those early 1970s was whether he could ever so visibly and audibly equal those mid-1960s albums that already had been sealed in time as masterpieces set in stone: *Blonde on Blonde* or maybe *Highway 61 Revisited* as his *Citizen Kane*, *Freewheelin'* as his *Chimes of Midnight*, *John Wesley Harding* as his *Touch of Evil*, *The Basement Tapes* as his *Immortal Story*, *Self Portrait* as his *F for Fake*. Would he ever live as loud again?

There were those deciding it was never going to happen when he released *Planet Waves* in 1974, a first album of new songs by Bob Dylan since the modestly mysterious *New Morning* of 1970, and the first album of new songs by Bob Dylan that I bought. It and he didn't seem to fit anywhere near where music was at the time, except that by being a Bob Dylan album, it slipped into view, hard to ignore, even reached the top of the album charts, and became a part of the puzzle that was still being built.

I had some of his other, earlier records, but *Planet Waves* was where I joined in with an ongoing Bob Dylan, when his voice was now set in the '70s as though his '60s were finally quietening down a bit, learning to let go, letting him out. It's one of those Dylan albums that sometimes sneaks up on you to become for a time your favourite of his; it can slip by nice and friendly, even a little simple-sounding, and then you realise the songs hit some sort of truth about the ebb and flow of life, and we have to live, no matter how many skies have fallen. I've always been pleased it was the first album I bought by Dylan that wasn't from the past; it's one of those that floats a little free of some of his more tabulated phases and eras, as though it's been granted some kind of independence, Dylan coming onto the world and catching a few falling stars for the delightful heck of it.

It features, as a man of letters with a distinctive mind, some liner notes wondering fast about how to track down his spiritual homeland, if it even existed. The notes, blurring essay and poetry, seem connected to the electrically fantasist self-examination of *Tarantula*, because in one game he was playing he was still using this kind of writing to look for a surprising new hand.

He was back in a relationship with The Band, who after their own towering, impalpable records were now much more than his band. They prepared for a joint tour which would be

Dylan's first tour for eight years, and *Planet Waves* grew out of rehearsals. Despite how close they seem in the imagination, it was their only real studio collaboration, and in that sense it was by Bob Dylan and The Band even if it wasn't credited as such, a one-off strategic integration of the tenebrous scrutinising of Dylan's mind and the grounding high resolution of The Band's playing. Dylan could get a little *Tarantula*, revealing a little disdain for reality, a resigned nihilism, a relish for paradox, and the uncanny musicality of The Band warmed up or calmed down the haywire mood. Together for the first and last time on studio record, marvelling that they happened to find themselves on the same planet at the same time.

The record didn't satisfy those craving for a return to some over-idealised, impossible '60s past, the one more in the mind of fans and critics than Dylan himself. In the long run it got overshadowed by what we were about to receive, but the combination of Dylan's intensely reflective doubts and fears, sometimes seeming to sink into the cold abyss of himself, and The Band's five soloists, certainty bursting out of them, was as emphatic, even as ecstatic, if sometimes in reverse, as anything he'd done since *Blonde on Blonde*. It was a hint of where he might have been without the crash, a different sort of recovery from the psychic dislocation of 1965 and '66, one without the eight years in between.

If it was another one of those Dylan albums that wasn't going to set the wider world on fire, but didn't spoil the history, he still sang songs of love and fate, death and phantoms, deftly, softly, intensely, often figuring out what to do with his time even as he felt like an enigma wrapped in a dilemma surrounded by a conundrum; was he still in unforced, comfortable solitude, still happy at home, sending out the occasional jaunty, occasionally irresistible result of making music with The Band, or was he trying to work out how he could escape being one kind of Bob Dylan, where his better work seemed behind him, a definite purgatory for someone who thought liked him, and become another kind of Bob Dylan, one who after all that could still produce records, write songs and make gestures that seemed as thirsty for the marvellous as the classic songs that now seem fixed in the all-time? Was there new Dylan music that could compete with and connect with his enormous, overwhelming past?

The *Planet Waves* alliance with The Band led to a shared 1974 tour that then became a full-blooded live album, *Before the Flood*, putting Dylan in the kind of swift, decisive, driven-again touch with his classic songs that suggested he wasn't over-whelmed by them, he had found a way to pull them forward and make them as much a part of his present as his past. The two records in different ways revealed Dylan coming back from the country, in from the outside, or maybe pulling people over to where he was. Dylan was becoming more than yesterday, more than a possibly concluded series of big moves, off-centre appearances and well monitored off-stage antics.

I was more and more a Dylan fan, even if I wasn't one of those who were getting so wrapped up in him they annotated his every move, hunted every rare bootleg, tracked down his every whereabouts, comparing his breath on one version of a song to his breath on another. Dylan had done enough to ensure, I figured, thinking about music in the way someone who wanted to be a rock critic would, that even if he never again did anything revelatory or artistically significant, he was as important in the story of rock as anyone had been or would be. He had nothing to prove; count the songs he had written that you could play forever without using up their power, without getting bored with them, the life inside them always seeming to lead to new life, and count those he had influenced.

And then in the first month of 1975, the calm of his marriage allegedly breaking up in real time around him, Bob Dylan released *Blood on the Tracks*, and ultimately I was happier I was eighteen when that appeared than I would have been if I had been eighteen when *Blonde on Blonde* appeared. This was a Bob Dylan that seemed to belong to me, to my then and now, and it was a Bob Dylan breaking free of all those past associations.

There had been the long-drawn-out pause in the 1970s, filled with a combination of miscellany, retrospectives and hints of a comeback, or some intermittent version of his cataclysmic energy. And then out of more or less nowhere a set of songs, a devious, cathartic saga, that seemed to be the result of years of consideration, calculation and speculation, and a couple of months of art school, learning the basics of cubism, as though the previous few years had been an actual prelude, a build-up of tension, a clearing of space and clutter so that when the results of his deliberations were concluded, they landed free of any expectation that here was going to be the return to form, the predictable extension of his '60s intensity.

After all that excitement that had got in his way in the 1960s, he'd spent time, one way or another, not just living a life and having a family, but bringing things back to where him making an album was nothing more or less than just him making an album. And, of course, without great solitude, no serious work is possible, and even if that idea didn't seem part of the rock

122

cycle that had bloomed around him in the '60s, escaping the crowd in all sorts of ways was definitely part of his system.

*Planet Waves* and *Before the Flood* were like his own support acts to his own reveal, and they gave no clue about what was to come; the former was an example of the easy, unassuming but actually intellectually rigorous way Dylan could play with form and drift or zip through a song that met all the requirements of being as teasing and tantalising as a basic Dylan song would be, and *Before the Flood* was a sign of how Dylan had recovered an appetite to make different forms of unsettling theatre out of presenting versions of his old songs in new times and new contexts.

Another part of the prelude came a few months into 1975 with *The Basement Tapes*, an official release of some of the songs he had casually, sometimes a little hazily recorded with The Band in 1967, off duty, off screen, off kilter, which added to the sense that Dylan was picking up speed again, even as the timelines were all mixed up. The relative silence and erraticism, the lack of presence, all those gaps in time and space were suddenly wiped out ... the smoke which lingered after the motorcycle skid finally cleared ...

... because then there was *Blood on the Tracks*, which for all he had done – as a presence and an absence, as a series of voices and then all but voiceless, a cosmically cool cultural icon and then a puzzling disappearing act – dropped into view as though this was where Bob Dylan was beginning. Everything since the crash existed to precipitate a dramatic shift in course and a way of writing songs that now weren't necessarily made up of other songs he had found or remembered but of influences that came more from his own experience and his own continuing accruing of technique and style. And then, though he had just proved with The Band how much as singer and musicians they were in perfect nimble sync, he wasn't working with The Band. He had returned to 'a band'.

Dylan's nameless and amazing band in this case included on some overdubbed organ the magnificently elegant studio keyboardist Paul Griffin, who had played on *Bringing It All Back Home*, *Highway 61 Revisited* and *Blonde on Blonde*; as soon as Dylan has a band behind him it includes the very best musicians in town, and that town is New York, so the best anywhere. Griffin brought a stand-alone resplendent gospel swagger and the necessary improvisational swing to match the mental earthquakes of 'Like a Rolling Stone' – moving over to the piano, allowing Al Kooper to sneak into the organ seat and smuggle his surprised, almost desperate presence into the song, flamboyantly asserting his existence – and some positively deep and generous piano at the beginning of 'Just Like Tom Thumb Blues'. On 'One of Us Must Know', Griffin worked with and around Dylan every word of the way, bringing a whole history of twentieth-century piano playing from Gershwin and Rachmaninov to Ray Charles right into this unprecedented sonic cosmos, being invented off the cuff, rehearsed in the act of doing.

Dylan made alien and illuminating with language, not limiting himself to reality, and Griffin supplied instant musical translation, from someone who learnt to play in church, hitting the moment, not for a moment considering the importance of what he may or may not be involved with. Just doing his job, helping someone else do his, but in his own way as a musician jumping rapidly from session to session during the heyday of the great session musicians he was moving as fast as Dylan was, up to speed with the prima donna speed of Dylan's mind and intentions as he jumped out of his skin, Griffin's playing as beautifully balanced and co-ordinated as a bird's wings.

Griffin once said music saved him from something horrible, and the relaxed but taut, soulful gratitude he felt spilt all over Dylan's first band sound – which of course was a band that didn't last for long – simultaneously elevating and grounding Dylan, and however nasty, possessed, outraged, self-absorbed and obsessive Dylan was being for the sake of a song, and the sake of a thought, Griffin brought some pure love into the sound which it needed even as Dylan's mind was somewhere else, battling for different kinds of rights, at times experiencing only himself. Griffin represents the kind of musician with their own levels of greatness who Dylan could always trust to take care of a certain strange sort of business very few understand, but which meant he could sing the language he creates the way he wanted to.

Griffin also linked Dylan not only with his own personally defined history of popular music, idiosyncratic and mind-expanding, but also with a more general sense of popular music, so that Dylan's contracting and expanding mid-1960s studio ensemble, with Griffin, included the keyboardist who helped create pop music's essential sound – the first choice of producers like Jerry Wexler for Aretha Franklin, Bert Berns for Van Morrison and Burt Bacharach for Dionne Warwick. There is a world where the greatest pop songs of all time include 'Like a Rolling Stone', Dionne Warwick's 'Walk on By', Van Morrison's 'Brown Eyed Girl', the Isley Brothers' 'Twist and Shout', the Shirelles' 'Will You Love Me Tomorrow?' and

Don McLean's 'American Pie', and Griffin played on them all, as well as records by Nina Simone, Quincy Jones and John Lennon, an often anonymous traveller leaving plenty of sense and spirit behind him. And there he is travelling through and tracing the right kind of truth and time on *Blood on the Tracks*, giving his undivided stargazing attention to 'Simple Twist of Fate', 'You're Gonna Make Me Lonesome When You Go' and 'Buckets of Rain'.

I remember hearing *Blood on the Tracks* for the first time in splendid isolation, treating the playing of the record as a kind of ritual, the way playing a record could be in 1975, as pure object, commercial product, conceptual project, fashionable item, mysterious expression and, if you were really lucky, actual work of art. A record you had been looking forward to, saving up for, a special occasion, and you gave it some time, you got yourself in the mood, you stared at the sleeve as though that was the first sound of the record, the invitation to come inside, into another new world. The sleeve to *Blood on the Tracks*, as usual with his records up to then featuring a carefully chosen image of Dylan, side-on in sunglasses, is a deep, intoxicating ox-blood red, and Dylan is presented as someone somewhere between young and old, famous and obscure, permanent and ephemeral, here and now, lost and found, known and unknown, what-he-is and what-he-is-not.

It's now accepted as one of Dylan's most revered albums, maybe his greatest, but at the time it was simply another Bob Dylan album, coming quicker after the one before it, so it was almost back to the giddying '60s pace, but it came with no great sense of anticipation, no sense of where it was going to

126

fit stylistically, lyrically, emotionally into his musical history. There was a story about the making of the album, which was a mystery at the time, though later books would be written about where the hell *Blood on the Tracks* came from. Dylan had made a couple of attempts to record it, first of all in New York in September 1974, and at the end of the year in Minneapolis. The more austere New York sessions could have formed the official released record, but five richer-sounding Minneapolis tracks were added to five bonier New York songs on the finished record, which wasn't noticed at the time, apart from by a few determined stalkers, and certainly didn't seem to matter. Eventually, on the six-CD *More Blood, More Tracks* collection of first stirrings, other versions, sketches and outtakes, including a dozen tries at 'You're Going to Make Me Lonesome When You Go', you could hear both sessions, even plan your own perfect version of the perfect record, even though you already seemed to have your own perfect version of the perfect record. It turns out there was an infinite set of possibilities for an album that maintained how only through the eyes of love can you find infinity, and nothing lasts forever.

The first time I heard it in all innocence, as soon as it began, something stirring from within, a determined guitar jangle that pushed all fixed points out of the way, Dylan wandering into town as though for the first time, drifting from New England to New Orleans, stung by a haunting presence, telling a compelling story where the story itself seemed to be missing, there was an immediate sense that he was seeing, hearing, feeling, knowing, needing life in a different, more complex way, noticing the smallest shifts in feeling, the doubts and fears at the heart of trauma. As each song began, using the

127

usual instruments, and arrangements in some relationship to the usual musical styles, it became apparent even to a teenager that this Dylan more than even the other Dylans was somehow using song and voice and a subtly splintered series of perspectives to perceive the infinite complexity of life.

The songs sounded like songs that could be labelled 'folk-rock', but it was as though Dylan was seeing undulations in the world that no-one else was seeing and giving us a chance to see things through his eyes and hear things he was hearing. Through what were love songs, or breakdown songs, or crumbling-marriage songs, certainly songs motivated by the falling in and out of love, songs of light and dark, rows and romance, blame and counter-blame, symptom and cause, self-estrangement and powerlessness, voices answering voices, he was allowing us into the most private regions of his mind, even if just for the briefest moment as we passed through the song as though at the same moment as him, the listener and singer aware of each other's presence but not sure which one was the ghost in this particular arrangement. There was also the sense sometimes that Dylan was listening to himself from within the song, amused, alarmed, enthralled by his own performance, the story he was telling, the story he was part of, jumping in and out of the action at will, as though he was hearing it for the first time. He's got insider knowledge, but he's hearing what happened – or what might have happened – for the very first time.

For each second of each song you felt the world a little more intensely, as intensely as Dylan felt it. With his earlier, ingenious, relentless songs at the intersection of smart and crazy, you could sense him experience this intensity, witness it from about as close as seemed possible, but never quite feel inside his mind and its apprehension of the world and his memories of it like you did with *Blood on the Tracks*. He'd found a new dimension with its own series of micro-climates and found a way to put us in there as well.

Did I feel this immediately? Yes and no. There was something going on, but I knew enough to know that I would need time to work it all out, and after forty-five years I still haven't had enough time, even as I know the settings, surroundings, disclosures like I've lived inside it since I first heard it. What I did feel immediately was how Dylan sang certain words like it was the only way possible that these words – and moods – could ever be sung, whether he was being deliriously vehement, inside the very menacing heat of events, in 'Idiot Wind', which would claw at my memory if I only ever heard it once, or as delicate and resilient as he was in the intimate time twisting dream space and shifting shapes of 'You're Gonna Make Me Lonesome When You Go'. This song would create after-effects that are still in play, both because it was obsessed with words filled with fantasy and reality like dragon, target, purple clover, Queen Anne lace, Crimson hair, flowers on the hillside, blooming crazy, easy, slow and lazy, right and wrong, sad and bad, back and forth, situations and relationship, Verlaine and Rimbaud – which jumped out a mile and took Dylan with them into their sordid affair – compare, crickets, Honolulu, Ashtabula and tall grass, but also because it seemed as though he sang the song like he'd been considering it for years and at the same time it had just come into his mind, as he's swept along through life like a river.

He sings every word, each line, the whole song, which is as light as a feather but springs deep out of life, as though the ultimate influences on his songwriting are actually time and space. It contains a series of calm, extraordinary vocal leaps, surprising news, and emotional feints that remain amongst my favourite Dylan moments, for the way they make the world, for no good reason, or because he has so spectacularly offered us a kernel of himself that he has saved, a more wonderful place. He sings like he understands how in the mind everything is possible, like he might have found a way to outsmart his passions, knowing how his passions often outsmart him.

There had clearly been some kind of leap from *Planet Waves*, as emotionally and enjoyably bracing as that had been, and whereas previously wherever he was in his songwriting, you could sense the various sources he was working and playing with, this sound was less obviously connected to a disruption or abstraction or elaboration of tradition. All his previous findings had somehow been discarded, as if he had been inspired by source material no-one had ever heard before, increasingly by source material that wasn't musical. It was as though where Picasso said that to draw you must close your eyes and sing, he was saying to sing you must close your eyes and draw.

It was set in its own sound world; he'd broken through genre into a territory all his own that took reality as its starting point on the way to drifting somewhere beyond reality. As soon as I had played it once I played it again immediately, because he had taken control, and Dylan was again wandering into town for the first time and the songs seemed to be the same but shifted elsewhere, as though even in their recorded form they were changing shape. I would keep playing it at the time, all the time, and the songs kept shifting, the places they were set revealed more of themselves, the real and made–up characters

130

featured in the songs seemed to be living inside the songs, and growing old – or younger – where they were. While you went on living it went on living too. The record was so alive that while you weren't listening it had shifted like a river, moving on and moving away. When you returned, it was the same river, but somewhere else. If anyone has ever done anything like this record, using songs to make something so fantastically real out of memories of reality that isn't called *Time out of Mind* or *Modern Times*, then please let me know.

During 1975, still writing for myself in my bedroom, I started to put together a fanzine called *Out There* that I had decided was going to be my qualification papers when in all innocence I applied to become a writer for the *New Musical Express*, my favourite music paper. Bob Dylan in the year of *Blood on the Tracks* was obviously going to be heavily featured, even as punk music started to move into the centre of my attention, including punk music made around Manchester, near where I lived.

There were long features I had written on Brian Eno and Patti Smith – punk poet offspring of Bob Dylan and Virginia Woolf – and I marvelled at the transfixed, invigorating ways Bettina Jonic, a Croatian artist, actress, singer, dancer and friend of Samuel Beckett, sang songs by Bertolt Brecht and Dylan on a 1975 album, *The Bitter Mirror*, as though Brecht was from Vietnam-era America and Dylan from Nazi-era Germany, in the hothouse of 1930s Berlin. Jonic embraced both Brecht and Dylan with a voice that would be just at home singing Schubert or Gershwin. She sang songs like 'It's Alright, Ma (I'm Only Bleeding)', the vivaciously vicious plea for some kind of help that Dylan would admit he would never have thought of writing without Brecht, and Jonic backed by a kind of European wonky-tonk, a spastic formality, relentlessly built up the strangeness, pushing to breaking point a song written about reality being pushed to breaking point.

A friend of mine from Stockport who I only knew as Barry who lived, breathed and sometimes wept Bob Dylan supplied some comprehensive inside knowledge of the best, most prohibited-seeming Dylan bootlegs. I got the feeling apart from me Dylan was his only friend. He was a couple of years older than me and was a customer in the town centre bookshop where I worked after leaving school, selling a lot of Middle-earth fantasist J. R. R. Tolkien and the romantic middle-east spiritualism of Lebanese-American Kahlil Gibran, whose 1923 *The Prophet* had become a '60s counterculture sensation, but also a lot of books about and by Dylan.

I'd stay up all night with Barry in his cold, lonely-seeming council flat listening to Dylan, marvelling for hours how the B-side to 'Like a Rolling Stone' was 'Gates of Eden', which on the *Bringing It All Back Home* album was tasked with somehow taking you from 'Mr Tambourine Man' to 'It's Alright, Ma (I'm Only Bleeding)'. One way of moving from one more or less world of rhymes and reasons to another via some kind of nightmare, which we decided was one of Dylan's most exciting tours through time and space. Then there would be hours seeing how you went via 'She Belongs to Me' to get from 'Subterranean Homesick Blues' to 'Maggie's Farm', and then we'd fall half-asleep to the album's last track, 'It's All Over Now, Baby Blue', a little embarrassed to be in the same room together as we drifted into our own very personal emotions, lost in Dylan as he sang on the verge of waking up, everything interesting him, nothing holding him back, his masquerades disclosing the reality of souls, his sadness somehow comforting.

We'd drink the oddest grassy tea, a little scared he might at any moment have an epileptic fit – which he was prone to – feeling once and for all like grown-ups as we heard Dylan describing the grown-up world as a dangerous, lonely place to be seen, on illicit records some of which made him sound like he was a million years away. They sometimes seemed taped by someone who was sat millions of miles away from the stage.

When I hear a song like 'Visions of Johanna' now I can still taste that tea, and remember a long, wavering version from an Australian bootleg with a picture on the front of a kangaroo with the head of Bob Dylan, on which he sounded like he had drunk some of that Mad Hatter's tea party tea as well, or just had a fit.

I never saw Barry again after our occasional, almost too raw, Dylan listening sessions, but I imagined, if he made it to hear the puzzle of the *More Blood, More Tracks* outtakes and digressions laid out over a few hours, that he would spend days playing with the tracks. He would drive himself happily mad getting trapped in indecision – and trapped in Dylan's mind, a pile of broken mirrors – wondering which version of which song was best, and why, and why did Dylan change his mind between one and another, and occasionally substitute one word for another as though he was replacing one world with another. If you so desired, *Blood on the Tracks* could cease to be an intimately immense story of the fictionalised break-up of one particular fictionalised marriage – now you see it, now you don't – and become some sort of mammoth quasi-scholarly investigation into the unexplainable. Which is maybe what a lot of Dylan studies were often about.

I put Barry's detailed bootleg survey in *Out There* alongside an interview I'd found that Paul Krassner may or may not have done with his friend Dylan. It might well have been made up. Krassner, meta-prankster, artistic hoaxer and San Franciscan surrealist, was the founder of one of the first radical underground magazines, *The Realist*, and co-founder of the Yuppies. He was known to make things up and his obituary of Lenny Bruce was published, with the comedian's permission, two years before he actually died. He once asked Dylan how come he was learning Hebrew. Dylan replied, 'Because I can't speak it.' He asked him how he felt about the Holocaust. 'I resented it,' he said. Dylan once laughed with Krassner about how his young son wanted to call him Son and wanted Dylan in turn to call him Daddy – then suddenly made sure the interview he was doing hadn't begun yet, because he was out of character, and opening the door to the forbidden. Krassner might have made all this up too, like the time he took an acid trip with Groucho Marx, who apparently had a pleasant, sometimes moving experience.

I liked Dylan filtered through Krassner's careering, whimsical mind, which helped seed the counterculture and which had a completely different, less pious way of detecting what about Dylan was significant, and what was insignificant. Through Krassner you could glimpse a real tarantula Dylan, which actually seemed more preternatural than the swirling but increasingly controlled myth. And it was this Dylan, especially now he had reset himself after a few years of drift, reconnecting with earlier currents via the momentous discoveries of *Blood on*

134

*the Tracks*, that made me want to put him on the cover of my fanzine, even as punk was happening, as Eno was developing ambient music, and to put Dylan on the cover seemed eccentrically, even extremely set apart from modern music movers and shakers.

The fanzine got me a job at the *NME*. I passed the audition, and had plenty of music to follow, review and love or dismiss. In a way, because of my background and alliance with punk, post-punk and Manchester, Dylan wasn't part of that job. Within a few years, into the 1980s, as music changed very quickly, Bob Dylan slipped even further away from the centre of a progressing music scene, stumbling, sometimes it seemed a little blindly, through an irregular release schedule of original albums, indifferent to the normal standards of pop and rock, at his most caustic and unforgiving, more punk than anyone. I would have years when I wished I hadn't put him on the cover, especially during those 1980s, when new recording techniques and electronic methods proved difficult for Dylan the song recorder to navigate, when MTV-driven visual styles were too disappointingly literal and basic for him.

One of the great video directors of the MTV age was Kevin Godley, as part of Godley and Creme making definitive miniature dramas for Visage, the Police, Peter Gabriel and Kate Bush, and Herbie Hancock. I never met Bob Dylan – outside of my dreams, or were they his – but Godley became one of a few first degrees of separation I had from Dylan. He told me a story of how he had been summoned to meet Dylan when he was in London to discuss the idea of making a video. He was told to turn up at the Hammersmith Odeon to see Dylan play a show, and when he got there was given a place at the side of the stage to watch. He was there at the end of the show, and was surprised that Dylan, as the audience stood and cheered, walked straight up to him, put his arm around him and started talking about ideas for the video. The audience were calling for more, Dylan was already somewhere else in his mind.

He was due the next morning to meet Dylan for breakfast at his hotel. When he walked into the breakfast room Dylan was already seated, but to his alarm there was someone he knew sat at the next table – Brian Eno, the conceptual musician who at the time was producing the records of the biggest rock group in the world, U2. Eno spotted him at the same time as Dylan, and both would be expecting him to come and sit down next to them. Godley had to make a quick choice, almost, he said, like choosing the favourite of your two children. He sat next to Dylan, sensing Eno's annoyance behind his back. He sat with Dylan, and couldn't remember a thing they talked about. Maybe Dylan told him about a dirigible he had once made.

In the video '80s, Dylan seemed to be drifting into the wilderness, but then he'd been there before, seemed to have started out there, and it seemed the inevitable end to his particular legend, riding further and further out towards the horizon, still doing things unlike anything else, but taking his genius with him, playing songs only for a few lizards, ending up for the sake of legend in a place called Devil's Point, a sacred place but also a place of danger, death and organic uncertainty where the fog is isolating and unsettling. Better that ending than more greatest hits sets and more albums of songs he hadn't written.

It was during this period that he set out on the Never Ending Tour, heading out into his own logic, part of the history he dreamt, his own journey into space, when the 1960s seemed as far away from the 1980s as they did from the 1930s. But then Dylan wasn't really of the '60s; in some ways he was more of the '30s, but a '30s all in his mind, which really set him so far to the side of everyone else he was actually further ahead than anyone would have thought.

I often thought he had been the wrong choice for my *Out There* cover; it should have been Patti Smith, it should have been the Sex Pistols, or maybe even it should have been Marc Bolan. I should have chosen Eno. I loved Dylan, but he was often at the back of my mind, needing to be caught up with again, because there was always so much to catch up with. He was at the back of my mind, but never far away from being right at the front.

I never worried if time passed without Dylan releasing an album, which would now have the 1960s and *Blood on the Tracks* to contend with – along with the spontaneous, migrant magic realism of the Rolling Thunder tour and the exotic itinerant south-of-the-border epics of *Desire* that kept his 'comeback' spinning in the late 1970s. It never concerned me if he drifted off so far from where the pop world was, as if he had got trapped in his own mind, locked inside his own history, or had forgotten how to write new songs. Sometimes a pattern of absence might be repeated, where Dylan seemed to have crested, and new albums were replaced by another greatest hits collection, or another flatly titled live album containing some greatest hits, as though they were end-of-career tributes.

I'd learnt from those few years between 1967 and 1975, when family man Dylan was idly prospecting for gold, that eventually when he found a new horse or caught the right train he would arrive back in town, one he'd never been in before, with some compelling new discovery, nothing like what was happening around him, but another album that caused pop culture traffic to stop, to let him back in. It was never clear how much he'd struggled to find a new audience, or whether it was even about finding another 'Like a Rolling Stone', or if it was just about finding a place to call his own again, but even if he never had hits again, not like he did in the '60s, he produced something that didn't necessarily make people permanently forget his hits but proved he was still in the process of discovering himself. When he seemed to be lost, he always found a way to return to himself.

Even after another of those 'comebacks' in the late 1990s and early 2000s, when for a while Dylan was once more clearly the right choice for the *Out There* cover, I would still often think I had got it wrong. It wasn't important to anyone but me, but in terms of my own arrangement with Dylan, one of the millions that help make up the overall sense of Bob Dylan in the stunning, prodigious time our lives overlapped, I would feel a little guilty that I felt this way. *Blood on the Tracks* remained my favourite album, sounding fully and thrillingly the same as it did when I first heard it, but different in hundreds of ways as well, and yet my mind still wasn't made up about whether I should have put him on the cover or not.

After *Modern Times* in 2006, which has spent a few weeks on and off as my favourite of his albums – but then most of them have – and increasingly a few more Never Ending Tour shows, whether in Paris or Cardiff, Bournemouth or Oslo, I decided that of course I had been right, and I haven't changed my mind since. It was obviously the right thing to do. It was as obvious as it is that a photograph of Bob Dylan should go on the cover of this book, which in some ways becomes the sequel to my Bob Dylan *Out There*, my solo debut as a writer. My first voice, which has become my late-life voice.

As I got closer to seeing him live in 2020, I worked out how this book was going to continue my relationship with Bob Dylan, which was getting close to celebrating its fiftieth anniversary, because it was now going to become a book where I put together versions of Dylan with my own, if only to celebrate my own correct judgement in putting him on the cover of *Out There*. Maybe I would take the fanzine with me to the Hollywood Bowl, and in my expensive seat right at the front I would wave it at him when we made eye contact, as we surely would. Because he knows everything, he would pick up in a flash that what I was saying was, in my very own way, I wouldn't be here if not for you – and I am about to write a book because of you, a book which will begin at this exact moment, and then I would go on to put his perfectly ever-changing imperfect voice at the centre of the story, which I hoped would please him. The look in his eye would probably freeze me to my seat.

He wouldn't care that this was what I was thinking, and because I had grown up surrounded by the rousing sardonica of Dylan, hearing him almost every day for almost all of my life, reading about him and reading him as though it might help me start to make sense of his life and therefore life itself, even when I had many other things on my mind, I wouldn't care that he didn't care. Something had brought us together, in our own special way, a way that was unlike anyone else's togetherness with Dylan, and when it comes to life, we spin our own yarn, and where we end up in life is in fact always where we intended to be. And then sometimes everything is going along as usual when all hell breaks out. It's like when you hear a song by Bob Dylan for the first time, and you seem to be in one place, in one story, following one set of circumstances, and then half way through the next line, after a couple of words, you're somewhere else, and the sure if unmanageable world you thought you were in has completely disappeared, the stone under your feet has turned to sand, a cold wind blows from the banks of the river, and suddenly the stakes are raised.

# FOUR

## TAKING HOLD OF HISTORY

In 2020, a pandemic crash-landed, and everything changed. One moment, things made sense, even if sometimes they didn't, in a controlled, pushy sort of way according to Sky News and CNN, and then very little made any sense at all. A threatening shape-shifting adversary radically remade our daily routines and ruptured our habitual rhythms. It was enough to make you wonder if you were on the right planet. It was as though we could all now see the dead end of the imagination. The clock that ticked yesterday so well stopped ticking.

Everyone, however old or young, suddenly had to adapt to a new reality and deal with uncertainty on an intense scale. The year plunged into the night; there were new forms of an almost avant-garde social interaction to get used to. Cities started to drift into their own emptiness. Skies were cleared of jet planes. Oil was cheaper than water. Polluted cities seemed to clear up in days. We could breathe more easily, but that didn't seem right. Birds sang louder and wild animals turned up in town centres out of the blue as if the streets and store fronts had become part of their domain.

A host of restrictions were placed on us; at times there were only a handful of ways to leave your home that were legal. We started to wave to each other through windows, avoid crowded places as best we could, make hopeful but forlorn contact with six, seven, eight people at a time through Zoom on our computer screens, which didn't necessarily bring us closer and actually further fractured any sense of belonging. Shops closed probably for good, comforting TV soap operas stopped production, exams were cancelled, students sent home, death became part of the everyday, much of it passed to us through lifeless numbers that kept on rising. We even collectively started to speak a different language filled with new terms, to do with distance, furlough, faces, handwashing, disinfectant, surfaces, temperature, a loss of taste and smell, the science of this, the science of that, essential, non-essential and the new normal. Everything was so unprecedented the word 'unprecedented' became the word of the year.

Masks were no longer only worn by self-consciously kooky pop stars attending the Grammys, or provocative archly branded fashion accessories made by designers like Off-White. At first, the scientific community didn't consider masks any use as protection. Then they did. Or better than nothing. Or better than that. They didn't necessarily save you, but they might save others. Whether you wore one or not said a lot about where you were politically, emotionally, psychologically, practically in dealing with this abruptly everyday life-or-death situation. And never in all my life had I heard the word 'mental health' said so many times by so many people. In fact, until 2020, despite coming into close contact over the years with suicides in the family, and relatives suffering anguished mental breakdowns, I don't recall hearing the phrase mentioned once. In 2020, there was no stopping the public displays of stress. Experts appeared daily on television to warn us we were tipping over the edge of a mental health crisis. Not that we hadn't been tipping for years. It was just never so emblazoned into the everyday. The world needed a chapter break, just to catch its breath, but it didn't know how to get one.

I will of course be suggesting that the songs of Bob Dylan, containing precious and illuminating material, exist for many reasons, but a significant one is how they can be used to help you make sense of times changing so rapidly and radically you almost have to change your own appearance every day to keep up. If Bob Dylan's songs could keep Bob Dylan from losing his mind – and that's definitely one way of looking at things – then perhaps they can do the same for others.

Once the damned impact of this vicious new coronavirus brutally unfolded, leading to lockdowns, curfews, quarantines, sieges, social distancing, loss of freedom, loss of nerve, loss of the normal, loss of basic if flawed societal coherence and for many a general sense that they had experienced their last encounter with the outside world, a whole lot of people joined me working from home. Many of them seemed a little shell-shocked, but for me it was a case of 'welcome to my world'. It is actually a lot weirder than you might think considering it's based in the place where you live. Solitary and largely detached from social life, inhabiting your own island, it can lead to a dis-orientating form of detachment and dislocation, which actually makes you extra qualified to be a Bob Dylan listener, even a Bob Dylan explainer.

For many years in a world of offices and office hours I was one of the very few working from home, which had its perks, but also a whole pile of insecurities and one or two definite dangers. For the privilege of not having a boss, of making up your own hours, of regularly raiding your own fridge, of being able to watch TV and listen to music whenever you wanted there was a continuing sense of unease, of worry that there would be no more work, or if there was work, that it wasn't paying enough to keep you going. And of course for many working-from-home room dwellers, there were the constant deadlines, the ever-present pressure that you must complete in time and satisfy requirements or else you wouldn't be paid. Not to mention the lack of holiday pay, of bonuses, of a pension, all of those things some seemed to consider part of the fabric of the universe, not simply a post-industrial lucky break.

Before 2020 only around 5 per cent of people worked from home, and for many, especially those working in offices, following the usual hours, it was something viewed with suspicion. It was an idiosyncratic, possibly even self-indulgent choice. Surely it was not possible to do any work at home, with all the temptations and distractions surrounding you? And what about a lack of discipline, of personal hygiene, of a communal spirit, a lack of an employer organising your routine, co-ordinating the daily demands on your time? What about the idea of a weekend, which very quickly melted away as days led into days that more and more resembled each other – days with no clear regular structure, which was familiar to those used to working from home but alien to those who couldn't get to the office? Each day could be the same and totally different from the day before.

And if working from home was always going to be the future, a new post-internet, post-office world of freedom and the trust of your employers, where you were paid by the idea, paid for completing pleasant, even pleasing tasks in your own time, it was meant to be a future where actually you worked from anywhere, not just from home. You worked wherever you fancied, continually moving your workplace into different zones around the world, which was so easy to move through. The pandemic put paid to that. Locational flexibility was one of the first things to go. Not only were you destined to work from home for the rest of your life, you might end up doing everything from home, imprisoned, even as you were serviced by Amazon, Facebook, Just Eat, Uber and eBay – or was it us serving them?

An increasing number of people were also losing their jobs, because all manner of conventions and structures that once seemed fixed and forever were shaken from their moorings. I was lucky enough as the lockdowns began to have some work. It could easily have been that I had no work – as a freelance writer at a time when journalism was becoming an even less secure profession than it ever had been – but in the weeks at the beginning of the year when the virus was lurking around the edge of news bulletins, at the edge of people's awareness, I had signed a deal to write a book about Bob Dylan, to be published around the time of his eightieth birthday.

There is a world of course where a 'Happy Birthday, Bob' is too obvious for words, but then Dylan has been known to have his obvious moments, and at the beginning of 2020, it seemed some sort of hook was required to remind people – most following the usual fashions and trends at a time when the latest and the loudest and most 'liked' keeps winning attention, lost in their own worlds, stuck in their own cultural niches – how important and insightful Dylan was, when the idea that Dylan was oracle, prophet, maker of worlds, sharer of knowledge had faded back in time. And of course Dylan himself had said, no doubt meaning the opposite, hoping to stem the tide, responding to 'the gazillion' of books written about him with more to come, that he 'encouraged anybody who'd ever met me, heard me or even seen me to get in on the action and scribble their own books. You never know, somebody might have a great book in them.' You never know.

He may not have been setting things in motion like he used to, he may not have been challenging the culture around him like he had been known to, but there seemed little point, just because fashions change – hell, he'd set a lot of them in motion – in ignoring how he was completing himself, completing various patterns of behaviour, and reaching eighty with his ambition intact, his myth still ready for action. Why not celebrate him as some kind of emotional and spiritual futurist at a time when such a figure seemed a good thing to have around? He didn't burn out, and he didn't sell out – whatever some might say about the *Self Portrait* album in 1969, the religious years, one or two of the live albums, one or two albums in the 1980s, or some of the television commercials for beer, cars and underwear he got involved with.

Some might complain that there was a sell-out when he sold his complete song catalogue – if not any songs to come – in the winter of 2020, planning for some sort of future, exploiting a certain freedom of choice. This only represented one Dylan, the businessman coming from a family of businessmen who saw absolutely nothing wrong in 'doing well', and why did this Dylan exist any more or less than all the other Dylans that had appeared one after the other? According to the rule applied by others he seemed to sell out, trash the sublimity of his music, as though the songs now only existed in a corporate deadzone, but not according to another set of rules, one decided upon at a certain time by one particular 'Dylan'. It didn't mean he'd given up on life, that he was running from his calling. There are all sorts of ways of co-partnering with the universe and creating meaning.

The songs themselves had taken on a life of their own, and maybe they were responsible for the decision, settled for the realities of life, submitted to its necessities, for the sake of their own survival, and oddly for the sake of their immortal soul. Dylan was never so sure about his. It never seemed a reason to doubt his word, to questions his motives. And whatever money was received in return for owning the publishing rights of his songs, it still seemed an underpayment for all those memories and benefits and that fantastic fascination with his own mortality.

He was someone who was good to get to know whatever your musical and artistic taste, because he always kept an eye on the disorientation of a transitional era that reached a crescendo in 2020. And when you pay attention to Dylan, the intricate metamorphosis of his thoughts, his way with words and his care for the voice, you learn something new every day. Not just about him, and his songs, and the voices he's been using along the way, but about how the mind creates, resisting the crushing pressure of reality and its impact on the inspiring power of contemplation, about how to make sense of the tangible and intangible world, how to have a presence in the world, how to appreciate the importance of the imagination. About how to make sure your life isn't a waste of time. Maybe just about how the vivacity of language can help us deal with a world turned upside down, as reality takes a tumble, and how a certain kind of grand scepticism can help you work from home. Don't ask me how. But I have my own proof that it works.

After the Dylan concert I was going to make the beginning of my book had been postponed, I needed a new way to start, to get to all those voices he'd passed through and left where they were. March quickly got darker and stricter once it was clear this was a serious, unpredictable pandemic spinning a mad, clingy web around the world, surging into our consciousness, a meta-infection apparently with a mind of its own that seemed to be reaching inside our collective soul.

Cancellations, withdrawals, closures increased, hours that could be spent outside decreased, became an equivalent of wartime rationing, and the very idea of social life came crashing down to earth. Musicians and performers, losing venues and festivals to play, were immediately challenged to consider new ways of singing, of hosting online dance parties, of reaching an audience, forced to switch to uncomfortable new abstractions, to using flat screens to communicate, members of a group separated from each other as they tried to look engaged and close to the vibe in their own sad-seeming separated digital window. Almost overnight there were performers using YouTube and the new-fangled Zoom to play songs, livestreaming from home and their backyards as if from somewhere in space, to let everyone know they were still around. They started to play live in the way they made records themselves, apart from each other, their parts compiled and pieced together, musicians who played on songs often never even meeting each other.

If I hadn't been writing a book about Dylan I wouldn't have

thought much about what he was doing, assuming he had just disappeared into the shadows, into whatever his domestic life was, keeping himself to himself, like he liked to, orchestrating his own absence, finding out in his own private way what a difference a day makes. Waiting somewhere for the rest of us to catch up.

His latest voice certainly wasn't going to be his Zoom voice; we wouldn't get to see him in front of a bookshelf or lining the shelves behind him with his favourite album sleeves. This would be one of his silent periods, which have their own attractions – at times you felt that he was a singular example of a classic guarded modernist who lived a monastic life, even a zealous post-modernist who spent his days in a small cork-lined cell. Who knew what he got up to out of sight, apparently living on the quiet in the City of Dreams, a city one way or another teetering on the brink. He wouldn't be obediently occupying a blank square on a screen, guitar in hand, maybe dog at his feet, faithfully singing a favourite old hit however suddenly appropriate the lyric as the idiot winds howled, the riot squads seemed restless and the times changed by the hour.

In the woke present, alive to difference, hyper-aware of process, dangerously quick to make its mind up who were the heroes and who were the villains, who were in the wrong and who in the right, Dylan tends to be too slippery, too remote, too mysterious, too much a fugitive detached from emotional frankness to be made welcome. Too ill at ease and too happy to feed off himself. There are just too many of him. And famously he has a difficult relationship with protests, with marches, tending towards the Ginsberg view that collective action is likely to lead to further authoritarianism.

This old white man is also too much of an absurdist to become any kind of hallowed modern icon in the woke world; absurdism doesn't sit alongside the speed of social media and its synthetic activism, tokenistic cancellations and pretend progressiveness. He's opted for the kind of privacy and solitude that doesn't fit well with the age of social media. It doesn't make him anti-social or cause him to reject the rest of the world. You need to breathe. You need to be.

There was a lot of cancelling and sloganeering, a lot of advice and concern, escalating anxiety about how the lack of live performance started to make the world feel less exciting, but few as far as I could tell seemed to respond to the moment and the world's new situation to come up with innovative ways of making sound, challenging orthodoxy and truly reaching people. There was plenty of retracing of steps from behind a screen, a torrent of quick bursts of cheery if desperate dancing as if that counteracted the evolving estrangement. There was a sense of panic about loss of income, a real fear that once venues closed they would never reopen, but no radical sign of discovering some new way to develop a scene, to make responsive new music, to react spontaneously to the pressures pouring in from every direction. Maybe it was impossible, and all that could happen was an attempt under the circumstances to create new comfort zones, hold onto the familiar shape of the past as it was being wrenched away from us, and find ways to keep in touch and support one another when everyone felt lost and increasingly lonely.

At the end of March, at the start of the unsettling first official lockdown, rumours emerged in the usual online places that Dylan was stirring. Dylan, or whatever the Dylan organisation is these days, maybe him on his own in his kitchen with a laptop, dutifully broadcast bulletins through his neutral if busy official website. The news was unexpected enough to sneak its way through the boundless thickets of information perpetually spreading across the world. At first any news about Bob Dylan cutting through the interference was a little disconcerting, at a time when the daily death count was increasing, and those over seventy-five were definitely at higher risk.

There was a song on its way, with a title no-one recognised, and perhaps this was a final message from wherever, a requiem of sorts. For some, for me, fingers hovering over keys working out the beginning of a book about Dylan, it was quite a moment. For the faithful, and especially those who had their tickets for the latest leg of the Never Ending Tour, now lost, it was an event, a wonderful curfew compensation. Seeing what the title was going to be, 'Murder Most Foul', added to the excitement. It sounded like quite a show, and this from the artist who once completely rearranged the very idea of show business.

To those less concerned with the current whereabouts and mentality of Bob Dylan, with an unhelpful fear of the uncanny, it was merely another communication amidst the millions seeping, tweeting and headlining into the world every second of the day, an amount of information, a heady mix of nationalism, reality TV and remorseless tabloid scandal that had contributed to a general cultural complacency and a collapse of common ground. Their loss, the faithful would think; they should pay more attention.

Dylan, it turned out, as though anyone would have doubted it, was using the strangeness of the times with all its noise and indifference better than anyone and using the ability of the internet to distribute a song without notice. The lack of build-up and the sudden reveal was the build-up. Even just the act of appearance was a suggestion, whether it mattered or not, that Dylan was never as contemporary as now, turning up as the world turned dramatically new; he always had something to say to those a long way outside the faithful whether they knew it or not.

It wasn't as though, as with 'Like a Rolling Stone' in 1965 and its rabble-rousing attention-demanding snare drum start, he leapt into readiness as a wide-awake world hung on his every word, on his every unexpected juxtaposition, but then these were very different times, fractured into pieces that were increasingly impossible to keep glued together. No; Dylan and his new song, which might have been an old song saved up for such an occasion, gently settled into the world a few seconds after midnight on 27 March, at the early edges of what was now officially a quarantine. Because many of us now had a lot of time on our hands, Dylan generously provided us with his longest song yet, a seventeen-minute equivalent of a Shakespeare history play with a title taken from *Hamlet*, Shakespeare's longest drama – 'Murder most foul, as in the best it is / But this most foul, strange and unnatural' taking us straight into our very own 'strange and unnatural' times while sifting through time and the contents of his mind as both music fan and dreamer of history. A little message on the website thanked fans 'for their support and loyalty across the years' and then gave a wink, a nudge: 'This is an unreleased song that we recorded a while back that you might find interesting.' Dylan had never seemed so topical since the early years of the 1960s when he made his name as a direct-seeming topical troubadour, commenting on the times as they happened, as they were changing.

A few reviewers guessed it was from the *Tempest* sessions, another title shaken out of Shakespeare, possibly with some additions and remixing. *Tempest*'s title song is another extended myth-making meditation, another vast trance-like collage, on a great twentieth-century event, a significant hinge in history, the sinking of the *Titanic* – forever topical as far as Dylan is concerned – tangled up with time and reality, shuffling references to James Cameron's film for some oblique cinematic emphasis, and strewn with Biblical phrases and spillages from the Book of Revelation, which the captain of the *Titanic* reads, knowing he's lost the race. It inevitably becomes many other things as well, including an appreciation and an appropriation of folk songs reacting to the tragedy with a mix of journalism and wonder – he sings it as though we already know the melody – and a transcendence of folk tradition – he sings it as though it doesn't matter if no-one even considers it has a melody, or even ever hears it. Dylan dreams a song, and sings his dream, and there's a watchman on board dreaming the sinking, as though that's actually what it was, a bad dream, something you could wake up from, even if the next time you fell asleep the dream came back again.

You could see 'Tempest' as a way for Dylan to write about the 9/11 attack on the Twin Towers, on the financial crash of 2008 – the difference between first and third class, between poverty and wealth, although the rich and the poor end up in the same watery grave. The song becomes a voyage through life itself, which must come to an end, the ship representing the world, whose end is near, the veil torn asunder. The passengers are on their own, without a home. The sea is history. It's where we came from, it swallows us up. Peaceful sleep is ever there beneath the dark blue water.

The story of the *Titanic* becomes a story about life's fragility and the fate of humanity. It's a shanty written for a long journey, written for the saddest of sailors as they head out to sea. The sad Celtic air, the ancient, maudlin ballad structure, the deathless piling up of verses with no relief in sight as Dylan slowly counts down the turbid ebb and flow of human misery led some to think it was dull and meandering. Their loss.

And the voice Dylan is using is perfect for the reading of this news in limbo: cracked, creaking, retreating into another world, beaten up by time and concentration, by smoking and sneaking around in forbidden zones, but impeccably timed, gracefully subtle, bitingly solemn. The voice of someone who seemed to know Jonah and hung out with Noah – back when History was beginning, a rumour without an echo – and who's had a few adventures of his own on the dangerous seas, getting close to Captain Ahab and his damned white whale, if only in his songs, which are as free as waves, laughing and buoyant, liquid, uneven, yearnfully flowing in the wake of a ship.

(Those that concluded Dylan was indeed announcing that *Tempest* was to be his final album, with a reference to the fact that *The Tempest* was Shakespeare's final play, were corrected by Dylan himself, who reasonably pointed out that *Tempest* and *The Tempest* were two different titles.)

You can break down the hundreds of Dylan songs into more manageable shapes by imagining them as his equivalent of Shakespeare's histories, comedies, tragedies and romances, filled with their own enigmas, disputes and dilemmas, and

Dylan was a historian in the way Shakespeare was, passing stories from one generation to the next, freely mixing legend and myth with historical fact, juggling, borrowing, pickpocketing, adopting, recasting material from a variety of sources, caring more about what could have happened, what should have happened rather than any attempt at 'the truth'. Holding up a mirror to the past in order to learn how to amend your own life, and especially anticipate events.

Dylan had a lot of records and singers to play around with, which gave him some kind of advantage over Shakespeare, the advantage of being alive four centuries later. He had a vivid constant bustle of references from twentieth-century popular culture to toss into the mix: his legends, daredevils and myths, the poets, actors and singers, those unlikely builders of an age, who recorded songs, had them played on the radio, who acted other characters outside themselves, sometimes based on themselves. Dylan kept adding to a catalogue of records and idols that inhabited his mind and now it included this song, all these musical moments, lifeboats made out of art, symbolic song lyrics and artistic achievements that despite it all made life worth living, which sure gave him something to think about, that helped invent so much of his mind. Times are tense, and songs are still part of those tense times, part of how you weather the storm, which can often be a data storm. Many of his songs contain other songs, grew from other songs, melodies lifted vigilantly and constructively in the time-honoured folk tradition, featuring slanted, salted-away references, discreet, glancing mentions and adapted quoting – as well as other phrases, lines, fragments, translations, sound bites taken from poems, novels and other sources – and here he seems to be owning up, blatantly filling this song with other songs, a series of hyperlinks you can follow in your mind, or on Spotify for real.

'Murder Most Foul' begins with the outrageous assassination of President John F. Kennedy in 1963, theories, memories and experience floated from various points of view and fancy, and then extends infinitely here, there and everywhere into the history of rock and pop, as if it is where the music begins and ends. If you played everything that's mentioned and recommended, all eighty songs, they would last for hours, an intercultural song cycle sneaking out of Dylan's mind and threading into others just as the death of Kennedy leaked into the American cultural bloodstream. (*The Realist*'s Paul Krassner more exuberantly stated that all that happened in the '60s, from Vietnam to the assassinations of Robert Kennedy and Martin Luther King Jr, exploded out of the bullet hole in Kennedy's skull.) The reverberations from Kennedy's death led to the hippy dream of Woodstock and then the Hell's Angel nightmare of Altamont, Dylan somewhere else at the time but around to be the one who puts it all in song, the one who writes and sings the history.

Each song inside 'Murder Most Foul', each group, each singer, each title, each stolen line, each new kind of love song for a new kind of century is a fresh beginning as the world crashes down around him. Or it's the souring of idealism as the world seems to be breaking through into a new age of hope. As the soul of a nation is torn away, as the tension accumulates, the dawning realisation of the consequences of the assassination, and a certain unstoppable energy grows, he turns his playlist, his co-creators, his rapt name dropping, his encounters with film stars, comedians and jazz heroes, his memories of hearing them for the first time, his radio request show within a song into a series of mantras, as if they can build up enough magical and spiritual power – just by being spoken – to save the president, and save our souls. A song can ward off evil for real . . . He knows there's no chance, but he just can't help believing. Music is his religion.

In 'Murder Most Foul', as well as the music and the special guest stars, there were also, of course, deviants and ne'er-do-wells, killers and the killed, and a lot of characters named Jack – a disc jockey tasked with the playing of each song (Wolfman Jack), a president of the United States of America (Jack Kennedy), the assassinator of the assassinator of the president of the United States of America (Jack Ruby). There was a Jack in 'Tempest' as well, Jack Dawson, the Leonardo DiCaprio character in James Cameron's *Titanic*, who appeared in 1912 to be giving the Bob Dylan of the future some lines to appropriate; he's just a tumbleweed blowin' in the wind, he says at one point, and paraphrases a line from 'Like a Rolling Stone' about having nothing to lose. The Jack of Hearts, the enigmatic bank robber, charming rogue, wandering, mysterious stranger – possibly Dylan himself hiding in his own clothing – a figment of the imagination from Dylan's murderously cheerful, urgently unfathomable cabaret frenzy 'Lily, Rosemary and the Jack of Hearts', might be lurking in the shadows in both songs as well.

One song starting with a dark day in Dallas, the other with a pale moon rising, 'Murder Most Foul' is in a similar spare, sorrowful, intermittently ecstatic trance zone to 'Tempest', not so much a song as another example of a new unnamed kind of strangely radiating sung performance where a number of ideas, time zones, meanings and emotions could all happen at once. Somehow, a holy grail playlist of favourite music could co-exist with a swift, comprehensive history of western civilisation, an evocation of true hero Kennedy with a condemnation of post-truth shyster Trump. Saints and sinners rub shoulders with each other, the mythic and the modern flow in and out of each other, a sense of dread exists as he puts a positive spin on loneliness.

Dylan's unwavering, seventeen-minute voice, on its own, disembodied, on the other side of the troubadour, the preacher, the prophet, the crooner, the war correspondent, the Beat reader, the stand-up comedian, the eulogist, the blues singer, drifted towards the silence he could always see coming. The barely-there instruments of his discreet co-conspirators loitered on the edge of their own withdrawal, but the words, the connections being made between Dylan's list of irresistible, born performers and their methods of expression, made it all sound as weirdly solid, while in many ways not being there, as the mind.

In 2020, as events amassed around us, threats coming from all directions, with almost too much happening to make us think it would ever become, safely, history, written by the survivors, Dylan's 'king' in the 'Murder Most Foul' history was Kennedy with his own sense, as Hamlet pronounces before his death, of 'had I but time'. Let him not die in vain. Perhaps there's hope that those traumatic events can now be simply part of a song, taking its place amongst other songs. A song where a mesmeric history of show business can be on Dylan's mind as much as a distressed contemplation of just how unsafe the world can be, when a powerful, rich, successful young man can be so suddenly wiped off the face of the earth. Life goes on, for real and in song, even after everything seemed lost, the reliability of the world completely undone. History might haunt us, but we're around to be haunted. As a kind of pilgrimaging figure emerging from the shadows, he sets off from Kennedy and the assassination as he set off from the *Titanic* in 'Tempest', going deeper and deeper into a wider, oceanic sense of history, and into a treatise on how meaning gets into things and lives.

The *Tempest* album wasn't big enough for both visions of history. He put it in his back pocket, and when a pandemic struck like an iceberg, and there was somehow a feeling language was becoming exhausted, too many words had already been put together into too many combinations, what could possibly be left, he pulled it out.

Dylan was close to Kennedy and not just because he happened to be there in America in the last year of Kennedy's life – he's close to Kennedy in some of his songs, even a friend, and in 'I Shall Be Free', from *Freewheelin'* (1963), his second album, a song which is somewhere between playful and profound, nuanced and nonsense, and not as po-faced as the title sounds, even gives him some advice. In the song – where else? – Kennedy rings Dylan to ask his pal for help about how to make the country grow. You can inevitably read a lot or nothing at all into his answer about growth: Brigitte Bardot, Anita Ekberg and Sophia Loren. Dylan's sly enough to know how interested Kennedy would be in such a threesome, or so. By the end of the song, where he's somewhere between Jack the lad and jack-in-the-box, larking around and perfecting his lopsided allegorical energies, he's catching dinosaurs, making love to Elizabeth Taylor and catching hell from Richard Burton – Burton and Taylor had met on the set of *Cleopatra*, released in the year of *Freewheelin'*, a film so expensive it nearly sank Twentieth Century-Fox, and had an affair that was a worldwide scandal, even condemned by the Vatican. Dylan had a lot to keep up with in 1963 and was happy to do so, until it all blew up in his face.

Back in 1963 Dylan was in the process of becoming well known for the first time and already plotting a kind of escape from becoming that particular Dylan. It was the year he shifted between being off the radar and being a kind of new star, and the year when the life of America's first television president was shot short, just as young people with their heroes and idealistic ambitions were beginning to push past an older generation.

For Dylan, the shock of the assassination, a sense of personal loss, has never stopped. For all the changes, in voice and character, in age and image, this is one moment where part of him stayed where he was and who he was. History fell apart all around him. Dylan felt the world shift under his feet, feeling his insides shake, things fall apart. He even got the jitters being seen as 'the voice of his generation', because it's not what he asked for, not what he intended, and if the president of the United States could be murdered just because he had a way of standing up for things that seemed a little provocative, then the voice of a generation was something of a target as well. He'd rather have been seen as someone who was striving towards reason, as a shadow, or a dream, something that wouldn't make an easy target.

In 1971, he admitted how rotten he felt about Kennedy's death, as much as anyone, but pointed out that if he was actually more sensitive about it than anyone else, he would have written a song about it, which until then he hadn't, unless you consider that all of his songs had Kennedy in there somewhere, if only because all his songs were his entire imagination, every experience he'd ever had, compressed into different forms, rhythms and structures, all part of a greater whole that we never get to know.

The night after the assassination, stunned like he was stoned, he wondered about how in his shows he'd play a song he'd recorded a month or so before which was going to be the title song of his next album, *The Times They Are a-Changin'*. It seemed to him right that he did sing it; some took it as a call to action, the way the words grandly rang in the ears of an audience, making them feel at the centre of things, but it was more a plea for some kind of alliance, written about the bitterness towards authority he could feel in the air in the months before Kennedy was shot when the chill of McCarthyism was still lingering.

He'd written it a few weeks or so after he'd heard a song called 'Das Lied von der Moldau' ('The Song of the Vltava') at a musical revue he'd seen in Greenwich Village, *Brecht on Brecht*, celebrating a politically literate, vital, cynical and amoral singing poet ancestor. Brecht's own peculiar, mesmerising voice had been described in one magnetic 1920s cabaret-style proto-pop star performance as 'raw and abrasive, often crude like a street-singer or a music hall minstrel, and it was pervaded with an unmistakeable provincial intonation. Sometimes he sang with something approaching beauty, and he enunciated his syllables very carefully.' Witnesses noted the particular way Brecht clutched his acoustic guitar to his crotch, how he had a devil-may-care self-consciousness about his hips that Elvis would have thirty years later.

The song's lyrics were written by Bertolt Brecht and included a line where 'the times are changing, no violence will help that'. That line didn't escape the notice of Dylan, endowed with panoramic attention, whose job had become as much as anything to notice things, and the gaps that separate and connect them, and pass them on. Notice, and be aware. Pay attention, and sort out the rules already in place. The world is changing and there is nothing anyone can do. Things can happen one way, but they can also happen a completely different way.

The Vltava is the longest river in the Czech Republic, and Hanns Eisler's music to 'The Song of the Vltava' was based on the second part of *Má vlast*, a six-part symphonic tone poem evoking his fatherland, written by the Czech composer Bedřich Smetana between 1874 and 1879. Smetana's 'Vltava', also known as 'The Moldau', was a musical description of the course the river takes through Bohemia, beginning with two small springs flowing in Smetana's words 'through woods and meadows, through landscapes where a farmer's wedding is celebrated, the round dance of the mermaids in the night's moonshine'. Smetana in turn had adapted the sixteenth-century melody 'La Mantovana', which was also the basis of the Israeli national anthem, 'Hatikvah', and lapped up via a Swedish folk song, 'Oh Beautiful Farmland', into Stan Getz's 'Dear Old Stockholm' of 1951, made famous by the first Miles Davis quintet in 1956.

Davis hunted for folk sources to transform and re-evaluate as diligently as Dylan, both of them testing material they felt they could do what they wanted with, to see how far they could take it. They'd give themselves permission on behalf of their imaginations, which was theirs and theirs alone to play with.

'The Times They Are a-Changin'' came out of how Dylan remembered some Irish and Scottish folk tunes and their 'come gather round, people', how he adapted a Carter Family song, first as 'Paths of Victory', then with a devious shift in the timing to 'The Times They Are a-Changin'', but it also came out of the Brecht song with its neutral view of change – some things stay the same, some things become something else, some things are for the best, some things not so much – and its adaptation of the accumulating dynamics of the Smetana piece, and how words can roll, rise and fall, dip, turn and swerve, implore and deplore over the top.

When Dylan sang it live for the first time after Kennedy's death, admitting he had no understanding of anything, in a country where everything had just gone haywire, he didn't know how the audience would take it. He thought it might come across a little blasphemous, maybe as some smug manipulative pontification suddenly struck irrelevant, and he might be stoned by the audience, looking for someone to take it out on. In the end, the song seemed right to the audience, sensing it's really a song about renewal, and they applauded, because that was all they could do under the circumstances, but he thought it was a little weird. What were they applauding? Eventually, very used to the weirdness of it all, and the way the song now had a life of its own, long past his control, he sang it underneath crystal chandeliers at the White House for President Barack Obama in 2010, part of 'A Celebration of Music from the Civil Rights Movement', marking a time when musicians were answering Martin Luther King's question 'What are you doing for others?' Using just a pianist and bassist, he scrupulously whittled it down into a regretful quasi-waltz, just to say he did have some control over it, that he hadn't been completely captured by it.

Obama was more thrilled to meet Dylan than Dylan was to meet Obama, or at least Dylan kept his feelings to himself. He didn't turn up for the chance to get photographed with Barack and Michelle – unlike all the other performers including Joan Baez, Natalie Cole, Smokey Robinson, the Blind Boys of Alabama and John Mellencamp – and briefly shook hands with the president after he'd not so much celebrated protest music as sighed all over it, bowed his head a tiny bit, smiled an even tinier bit, folded his magic carpet, then wandered off to wherever the next stop was, the next person he was due to meet. For Obama, the way he definitely wasn't clamouring for love or anything, Dylan was everything he wanted him to be: 'You don't want him to be all cheesin' and grinnin' with you. You want him to be a little skeptical about the whole thing. So that was a real treat.'

Dylan had mastered the protest song in 1963, as an exercise, as a rite of passage, an inevitability considering where he'd come from and the music he first fell for, but look where it had got him, and America, and President Kennedy. He felt the need to go looking for other, less solemn, less dead-on ways to seek psychic security and take on forces of injustice, negligence and corruption. He was taken with the dramatic, elegantly malformed way that Brecht, sometimes with Kurt Weill whipping up delirious, stormy melodies, sometimes with others, adapted, reinterpreted and recreated his sources, remaking their very soul, adding modern social and emotional significance, even as that came with accusations of plagiarism, piracy and shameless appropriation.

This is why when he skulked in and out of the White House forty-seven years later he sang 'The Times' not as any kind of affirmative, sing-along uplifting anthem, the light at the end of the tunnel, making the universe seem just a bit kinder, or even as anything that really had anything to do with him, but from deep inside some dream he was having about how the past continues to change according to the way the winds of consciousness are blowing. He'd entered wider popular culture because of these kind of songs, but he never wanted to be captured by them. He didn't want those early songs to be a prison. Why did he play at the White House? Well, he still had a job to do, of some description. And he almost fell for believing that the election of Obama meant it 'looked like things are gonna change now'. He was still prone sometimes to believe what he read.

Dylan shared with Brecht a scavenging, magpie temperament, an excess of feeling that could tip over into caddishness, an icy persona, a love of roaming and a way of building up his sense of history from wayward bits and pieces. They both read quickly, fighting for ideas, determined to master all manner of genres and grand themes, ready to make use of their dramatic potential. The wider they read the freer they became. They both identified with those who stood alone.

Like Brecht, Dylan was at ease with the riveting fragmentary energies of modern art and literature. After experiencing and studying Brecht, after his confounding protest peak with 'The Times They Are a-Changin'', Dylan became more interested in a montage approach to constructing songs, capturing the infinite, sudden or subterranean interaction of different feelings, connecting disparate elements inside a song that might provoke people into new recognitions and understandings. He moved on from literal, intensely logical and flawlessly common sensical protest where he was so obviously being of service, sometimes nearly sinking into dangerous solemnity, before most of the world had even cottoned on to how perfectly he conceived the protest song, entwining vigilant observation of current events with melodic and talking-song methods used down the ages to transmit opposition and hope.

He quickly ducked out of the way because he didn't fancy doing that forever, didn't fancy being appropriated himself by the greedy, careless mainstream, and took on Brecht's more mobile, transgressive and in themselves adaptive methods of layering reflection and self-reflection, reference and self-reference, sweet and acid, flow and flux, his approach to showing people how to perform the act of thinking and search for their own answers. Dylan started to exchange roles and identities, making himself a kind of montage, and he started to experiment with how songs could exist inside other songs, and you never necessarily knew whose thoughts he was singing, or who he was singing to. He got ideas about how to deal with the writer's dual existence, as fallible human and immortal creator.

As the Kennedy song he finally got to write or had been writing for fifty years – alighting on all manner of symbolic comparisons between now and then – slid into the recently changed world of 2020, becoming, oddly, after nearly sixty years, Dylan's first ever American number one, the violence and division and American turbulence that Kennedy's death symbolised was still boiling. Number ones weren't what they once had been, a special event, a distinct way of punctuating history itself, but America's arguments with itself hadn't changed.

A climate of violence, hate and extremism seemed increasingly set in stone, the polarised American Way. The civil rights activists and demonstrators of the early 1960s were now the civil rights activists and demonstrators of the twenty-first century, still being beaten and harassed as national anguish was intensified by a messier, radically partisan non-stop media and inflamed by America's first social-media president. A president who made his expert subject – his religion, his way of filling a maimed, empty mind – the haywire logic of the sort of conspiracy theories that blossomed following the shooting of Kennedy. The hard selling of conspiracy theories was how he crept into your mind and got things to stick as if they had the hold of truth whether you wanted them to or not.

'Murder Most Foul', a song about songs about life and death from the writer who won a Literature Nobel Prize for songs as much as words, could easily have been a farewell. Given the dismal, dizzying nature of the period, he might have been seriously ill at a time when serious illness was on the news every hour. Little Richard, one of Dylan's great arousing, pioneering inspirations, died in May, and as an accidental farewell one of his songs, 'Lucille', is on the totemic 'Murder Most Foul' playlist, the soundtrack to a kind of paradise, a party for the ages, in between Jelly Roll Morton and Chet Baker. The song's a roll call of death as much as a litany of sacred hearts and high spirits.

At the end of the song, the last song on the playlist is the song we've just heard, and which should now be played again – we have just experienced history, and now we should examine it more carefully now we know what's happening. The song seems more of a farewell because we are asked to play it again, so that everything can start again, and everyone in the song, listening to the song, singing the song, constituting part of the song is still alive. It was a way of pausing the history that had developed inside Dylan's life, or his life as a performer, a history which was now at its most alarming and, dreadfully, most amazing. There were still songs, and stories, and they can contain infinity, following Nietzsche's doctrine of eternal recurrence. To avoid the mental terror of an eternal universe, he proposed that the universe would eventually return to its original state, and the same things play out again and again. Play murder most foul. Dylan had managed to compress forever into a song, like he'd always hinted he could.

A month later, at the end of April, losing ourselves in lockdown, our ruptured new reality, filled with a strange combination of apartness and togetherness, came news of another unreleased song by Bob Dylan.

Somehow this seemed even more thrilling than the first reveal, which would no longer be a mere one-off: a tweet of all things that contained nothing but the hashtag #icontainmultitudes. Yet another great piece of show business, Dylan riding on the back of Twitter to add some ravishing glitter to his well-tended mythical status by using a one-line manifesto as a kind of ad slogan, pointing out that inside Dylan, the worlds of his songs, there are multitudes of people, real and imagined, restless and settled, taken from fables, literature, film, folklore, other songs, or made up by him, each with their own stories, which represent something, or which may have something to do with Dylan, maybe how he sees himself, or are just from places and times which interest him. Or it's just his way of referencing the whole world as it's taken shape inside his mind.

This time, showing his hand once more, making it clear that his playful, sly, sincere method of invention always did involve the inspiration, assistance and guidance of others, known and obscure, he used the title to kidnap something of Walt Whitman, the great proto-modernist American poet of democracy. His first collection, *Leaves of Grass*, published in 1855 as the Civil War was looming, in the years before America achieved a kind of literary independence, contained a radical new form of open, honest free verse soaked in settings and celebration of a self 'afoot with my vision'.

The artistic prophecies and poetic propulsion of Whitman, William Blake and Arthur Rimbaud, struggling with the same conflicts as people in the modern world, preparing us for a world we would eventually find ourselves in, encouraging others to create their own systems rather than being enslaved by others, snapped together inside the poetry of Allen Ginsberg on the way to Bob Dylan and thence to Patti Smith and Kurt Cobain. Dylan, now with his Nobel Prize, stepped forward to inherit the mantle of Whitman, who might have been warmer as a character but didn't have Dylan's connections.

'Song of Myself', from *Leaves of Grass*, includes arguably Whitman's most famous lines:

> *Do I contradict myself?*
> *Very well then I contradict myself,*
> *(I am large, I contain multitudes.)*

Whitman himself was riffing off Ralph Waldo Emerson, who in his 1841 essay 'Self-Reliance' said that 'a foolish consistency is the hobgoblin of little minds ... Speak what you think now in hard words, and tomorrow speak what tomorrow thinks in hard words again, even though it contradict everything you said today. To be great is to be misunderstood.' On the other hand, Herman Melville considered self-reliance 'the masquerade in kingly weeds of a wild egoism, anarchic, irresponsible and destructive'. You pays your money, you takes your choice. Whatever gets you through the night.

Dylan had his Melville moments – in his Nobel Prize lecture, grudgingly delivered just days before he would have missed a deadline making him eligible for the £800,000 prize, he made much mention of *Moby-Dick*, and the author's tremendous ability to synthesise a carefully selected wide variety of cultural sources. It turns out most of his information, possibly including the line about cultural sources, was lifted from the SparkNotes summary of the novel. For this new song, though, he was in a Walt Whitman state of mind.

The self is always evolving into new selves, changing as it is exposed to new experiences and events. The self is a hoax, a passing phase, a form of obedience, an absurd idea. People are not the static, consistent entities they are presumed to be. The self that existed yesterday is not the self that exists today, and Dylan with a self always becoming began 'I Contain Multitudes' with today, tomorrow and yesterday, which was something he had learnt ages before from poetry, from painting, how all time can exist in one place, one thing happening after another in the same place and time, leaving the reader, or the listener, to sort out the rest, including what order things come in, and where we go from there.

In a song full of 'I' he offers clues about who he is or isn't, or at least who he is or isn't in this song, which for now contains his self, and a few other selves, some of them his own, which gives you a sense, in a swift, delighted summary, of Bob Dylan being vain, combative, unstable, a drinker, a creep, unapologetic, a painter, ready for all kinds of action, an outlaw, a dandy, resourceful, in possession of some slender knowledge of William Blake, operating in a world that contains the Rolling Stones, the David Bowie and Mott the Hoople of 'All the Young Dudes', Anne Frank, Indiana Jones, Beethoven and Chopin and of course life and death. Turns out he's in bed with both of them, the existential saucepot.

He becomes the song in the way Walt Whitman would become one of his poems and the song again is about what a song can be about, and about how you build it up from nothing using bits and pieces you find and in Dylan's case the channelling wonder of your mind. Like 'Murder Most Foul' – and 'I Shall Be Free', 'Desolation Row', 'A Hard Rain's a-Gonna Fall' and 'Gotta Serve Somebody' – it is one of Dylan's list songs, rooted in Homer's lists of war heroes in *The Iliad*, in the family lineage of many of the books of the Bible, there in Whitman's 'Song of Myself' and 'I Hear America Singing' and Allen Ginsberg's 'Howl', a carefully compiled inventory of things, names, places, thoughts, images, feelings and beings.

This catalogue listing of everything on your mind and for the moment everything in the universe was most elaborately displayed in one sentence by the blind, beautifully speculative Argentinian writer Jorge Luis Borges in the form of an essay containing entire libraries, 1949's 'The Aleph', a taking and shaping of infinity, a warping of infinity, its meaning becoming something different on different days. You could see how as a young man Borges wrote poetry in the style of Whitman, believing for a while that Whitman was poetry itself, even when he left behind his bardic voice and tone admiring how everyone could find themselves in Whitman. In 'The Aleph' the first letter of the Hebrew alphabet is a point in space that contains all other points, where all the places of the world co-exist, the simultaneous co-existence of all things, everything in the universe. Hamlet imagined himself being king of such an infinite space.

The one majestic sentence where Borges relays the things he's seen that lifts life into the special includes, amongst much more, a silvery spider's web at the centre of a black pyramid, a woman in Inverness he would never forget, simultaneous day and night, his bedroom with no-one in it, the delicate bones of a hand, the survivors of a battle sending postcards, a Tarot card in a shop window, his own face and his own bowels, the circulation of his own dark blood, the coils and springs of love and the modification of death. You can hear it being sung in much the same way as 'A Hard Rain's a-Gonna Fall', and even if Dylan had never seen the sentence before he wrote the song, and those of his songs containing lists leading up to this par-ticular list, then he was definitely on the same wavelength of knowing. He was definitely on the road looking for the Aleph, that point from which you can view all other points in space and time – and in Dylan's case, the Aleph is that point where in one song you can hear all other songs.

(Whether he knew it or not, whether he shared a spirit or simply researched the thinking of Borges, a Dylan manifesto, by someone who once said it was like a ghost was writing his songs, it visited him and then went away, can be rooted in the apprehensions, imaginings and expectations of Borges; he said he was all the writers he had read, all the people he had met, all the women he had loved, all the cities he had visited; being with someone and not with someone was the only way to measure time; whatever happened to you as a writer was a resource, including your humiliations, misfortunes and embarrassments; to fall in love was a religion that had a fallible god; Borges was trying to bribe you with uncertainty, danger and defeat; writing was a guided dream; the original was unfaithful to the translation; a reader should misunderstand the text, they should turn it into something else; his name was someone and anyone; he'd come from so far away he didn't expect to arrive; the task of art was to transform what was continually happening to us; all men who repeated a line from William Shakespeare were William Shakespeare; life itself was a quotation.)

In the old days, that part of the twentieth century when Dylan ran riot as fabled rock star, songs were singles, objects that took up space, they had a place, they came in sequence, but now in an era of content delivery systems they were unfixed announcements, they were random messages preparing the way for some other performance, some other production or P.R. campaign.

After 'I Contain Multitudes' there was a third reveal, not as such a single, with another title, 'False Prophet' – one of the comedies, black like he was hammering on Edgar Allen Poe's door, black like a shadow placing flowers on his grave – that seemed to show Dylan was using them so as to refine his biography, his mighty brand. These new songs were part of an album, one that few saw coming. 'False Prophet' made its soundless appearance with an opening verse about an unending day of anger, bitterness and doubt that seemed plague perfect, as though it was all part of Dylan's great pattern, part of some greater timing.

After being lulled by the first two previews and all their slow-burning turning over, here he was going out of his way to prove there was rattling, raging life in the old dog yet, he could still make a racket, and he was boasting like he meant it about his worth and his augmented ways. He was old enough to not remember when he was born, or the day that he died. He was having a good time in the face of a cataclysm, just in case you were one of those who hadn't paid attention to him for a while.

It turned out Dylan, wherever he was, was preparing the way for his first album of original songs since *Tempest*, one that seemed primed to exist in a time of intense awfulness, of the worst doom and gloom a generation or two or three had ever experienced, and along the way, rolling it all into one, play more excessively with who he was, and what you could do with a song and a voice. A time when the end of the world headed our way every day was his time to shine, when working out how to live was an hourly mystery. Nobody knew what the hell was going on, and that suited him down to the ground. He'd taken the opportunity of losing his Never Ending Tour dates to keep working and collect some songs and show the world what being awake really meant.

If you thought he'd lost his voice, he was now – or then, it wasn't quite clear when these songs were from, they could have come from any time in the past ten years, give or take the odd reference to the past thirty years – singing with the kind of low, authoritative precision not of a waning, croaking, fatally wounded champion but of a quick-thinking, clear-sighted vocal dramatist with a cosmic sense of rhythm and an enchanting human touch who after all followed tenacious, high-rolling Frank Sinatra as much as muscular, low-moaning Howlin' Wolf. He had been using those Sinatra albums as research to get some clues about what to do with a voice that could sound as old as time, and twice as damaged, that had bloomed and then faded with amazing punctuality. There was a lot of waste weighing his voice down after decades of hard living, moody struggles and long touring, and another twist of genius was how he was finding ways to be gentle and luscious as well as damned, even ghastly.

As Allen Ginsberg had noticed relatively early on, Dylan found a way through his singing to focus all his intelligence and consciousness on his breath. He talked of how Dylan had become a column of air, where his total physical and mental focus was this single breath coming out of his body. He was not a singer as such, but he used his voice like a singer, and like no-one else ever had, experiencing and reflecting time like no-one else, and along the way, his voice changed as much as his mind and self did. His voice contained multitudes, a colony with certain delusions of unity.

And Dylan was still breathing in 2020, when the very idea of the absolute miracle of breathing was concerning people more than ever.

*Rough and Rowdy Ways* had a title nicked from a 1929 Jimmie Rogers song that gave away little about the contents, except that the song's opening line was 'For years and years I've rambled' and it ended with 'but I can't give up my good old rough and rowdy ways'. The album had a cover that didn't directly help either, as if Dylan couldn't be bothered pretending it was any sort of album like they once were when there were records or even compact discs. Now these sort of things were just songs linked by proximity, and whatever conceptual intent might be present, and there was no sign yet of anyone working out what the sequel might be to the seven-inch single, the record album, the miraculous vessels of his more official prime time years. Dylan had done his bit for the album, but he didn't have the time or inclination to work out what was next. It was released – or whatever the word now was – on June 19 in the year of Covid-19, like it was a sign, like there was no such thing as a coincidence.

I took the album as a definite sign. A first new album since *Tempest*, proposing a new way of thinking about what his final album of original songs was going to be. Here, perhaps, was the end of a reign, his last words and testament. No more phantoms to follow. Until the next time, or not.

The overall work of Bob Dylan had been updated, changing everything that came before. This was the right time to write a book about Dylan and his voices; here was another voice, even if it was difficult to pin down exactly where and when it came from. The voice was a mystery, and it would take me through to all those other voices, with their mysteries, and reasons. I had lost my original Never Ending beginning, but I now had a new, better beginning, a significant shift in the story, a place to start from one voice in order to catalogue all the others.

I know, I know. We're nearly two hundred pages in, and the book hasn't actually as such begun yet – depending in which order you are reading it. But this is a book about Bob Dylan and so things happen when they happen. Some things happen when they should, some things when they shouldn't, sometimes it all goes on at the same time. What did you expect? Think about the twelve lines or so of *John Wesley Harding*'s 'All Along The Watchtower', one of those Dylan songs that seem to offer a swift resume of a marvellous, mysterious imaginary 500-page book that touched on every topic under the sun. An entire unwritten novel is reduced into a condensed kernel; a rich, complex interpretation of some epic Bible stories compressed into a two-and-a-half-minute song.

The song relentlessly pushes you back and forth through destiny and time's sheer change towards an inevitable fate, and in Jimi Hendrix's supreme, incandescent reading his swooning, saturated backwards solo turns into perfect sound Dylan's capturing of a world made of time, a tireless labyrinth, a maze built of mazes. Dylan's Biblical rock imagined an existential country ballad form as the music of revelation; Hendrix veered away from the original, taking nothing as gospel, and envisaged a more brutally beautiful Biblical rock, jumping from Dylan into the soul of existence. Hendrix added a couple of minutes to the song's length, but also somehow centuries of emotion.

Hendrix's acknowledgement of Dylan and his agile integrity and the astonishing elasticity of time would become, when he now played it, Dylan's acknowledgement of Hendrix's ability to turn his swirling imagination into sound. So, the song said, there are many ways to begin and end, to address what has happened and what happens next and in what order.

Dylan released his thirty-ninth studio album and it was like a gift in the middle of dark, disturbing times. It reminded me of how the bated-breath-wait for a new album release by Dylan, T. Rex, Neil Young or David Bowie lit up the early-'70s version of dark days and troubled times, and the release itself seemed powerful enough to get rid of the darkness for ever, and in some ways it did. A new Bob Dylan album! Just as I had been thinking more deeply than ever about him, his origin story, the turnover of his voices, the make-up of his faces, paying even closer attention to his songs, and the songs within the songs, and within that the flickering spaces between one thought and another where Dylan is perhaps at his most present, in permanent transition. If I were the praying sort, rather than just the sort who wrote 'If I were the praying sort', this would be the answer to my prayers.

I could begin my book.

# FIVE

## LOVE MADE VISIBLE

Here he is, with a look in his eye that says, *Here I am, what are you going to do about it?*

You've been here before.

Relax. Concentrate. Dispel every other thought. Let the world around you fade.

'What's happened to me?' he thought.

One day, they'll say he never existed, and that it was someone else who wrote all his songs.

When Bob Dylan was a little boy, he was not Bob Dylan.

Bear with me. I was just thinking how best to begin a book about Bob Dylan. What would be under the circumstances the correct, the most suitable first line? How to begin a book about someone who made sure he was better than anyone at coming up with the beginnings of songs, of albums, of books, of genres, of escapades, of stories, of answers in interviews, of his own individual story, which never stops changing shape, which becomes a whole series of overlapping moments, emotional permutations, self-portraits in disguise, developing behaviours and competing fortunes? Dylan once said that every line in 'A Hard Rain's a-Gonna Fall' was the beginning to a different song.

In his opening lines, the snap, crackle and pop of how his songs begin, straight into the fleshy, flashing being of things, no messing, you will find sharkskin suits, wounded flowers, God speaking to Abraham, ambassadors to England and France, hot chilli peppers, Noah's dove, dead streets, the hour of his deepest need, boats and ships being built, a woman passing herself off as a man, benches stained with tears, the colour of the sun cut flat, pistol shots ringing out, a rumbling in the sky, postcards of the hanging, the Lone Ranger and Tonto, the ghost of Lenny Bruce, Gregory Peck, the night playing tricks when you're trying to be quiet, you've got a lot of nerve. The air is getting hotter. You have to find out what's happening next. Don't follow leaders, but follow him into temptation, into a whole new life.

He is better than anyone, sometimes despite appearances, and emphatic disappearances, at finding a clean slate, turning over a new leaf and being spurred into action, passing by everything in a rush of air. Finding the right words at just the right time with an opening line to die for because what's on his mind should be exactly what's on everyone's mind, no matter who you are.

Better than anyone at creeping out of the bushes like a fastidious detective investigating his own crime, probing his own flaws, because old men ought to be explorers, not settled in their ways. He's got some intimate messages, some good rocking tonight and a lullaby or two, he's taking stock and judging a life. He appears out of gloomy nowhere, where the way up and the way down are the same, trying as always to make some progress, on his quest to continually be remade, in order to arrive at what he is not. He looks familiar, wearing a hat as some kind of hint of his honesty, perhaps even his humility, but he is also so 'other', as if he is almost casually getting ready to meet the otherness of the divine spirit. Which makes that guitar he's got in his hands and that harmonica slung around his neck very odd indeed. But then for him Beat was short for Beatitude and he could see a way where Johnny Cash and Jean-Paul Sartre were drinking pals.

If you ever think his story has finally settled down, ready to be definitively sorted and sifted, neatly tied up and concluded, something turns up to make it something else again, another rumour, another theory, a radio series, maybe another book, another song from the unknown, another performance, another piece of business, another birthday — especially one of this more celebrated big ones, with a zero at the end — even something that actually hints at what the end of the world will be like, the end of all human things.

There he is, with the perfect song, with the perfect opening line, with every following line perfectly poised, or roughly speaking where it should be, with a voice — selected from the many that are available — that seems to contain all human knowledge as the world teeters on the brink of catastrophic collapse. A song that fundamentally concludes how to accept the hand you're dealt, where he exercises his freedom in a revolt for or against absurdity, and somehow in the middle of a dark world getting darker by the day he can see a distant point of light and a dim hope.

It might be a love song, this perfect song, because however hopeless things get, however furious his deal, love is one of the most persistent ideals in his writing. Love, as renewal, must always be there in the middle of despair, as a way of getting through. Of all the meanings that can be assigned to Bob Dylan, and let's say, for the sake of a list, a list of one hundred meanings topped off with a leopard-skin pill-box hat, up there in the top ten would be the fact that 'love was his meaning'. As you contemplate this, wondering how love is so constant for someone who can sometimes seem a bit of a cold fish, even a cruel, high-handed reprobate – he could never be called loveable, but maybe that's part of the act, the performance art, the self-conscious stunt of someone acting as though he's gripped by martyrdom – why not compile a list of his greatest love songs, where pure love gets caught red handed, chased, arrested, interrogated, tried, condemned, locked away, released, executed and resurrected, to be played in support of this particular meaning?

Making up this playlist is one of at least a hundred impossible tasks that come up when you consider the wider contribution and wider worth, the self-invented mania, of Bob Dylan, a man reborn as an idea, but think about how much you'll find out about love from courtship to catastrophe, from fulfilment to disappointment, from just tonight to everlasting love if you give it a go: 'Tangled Up in Blue', 'Brownsville Girl', 'Most of the Time', 'Sara', 'One Too Many Mornings', 'Ballad in Plain D', 'Dark Eyes', 'Every Grain of Sand', 'Isis', 'All I Really Want to Do', 'To Ramona', 'She Belongs to Me', 'Nettie Moore', 'Visions of Johanna', 'Absolute Sweet Marie', 'Spanish is the Loving Tongue', 'Dirge', 'Boots of Spanish Leather', 'I'll Be Your Baby Tonight', 'Hazel', 'Is Your Love in Vain', 'Simple Twist of Fate', 'Precious Angel', 'Wedding Song (Who Loves You More)', 'You Changed My Life', 'One More Night', 'When the Deal Goes Down', 'Mississippi', 'Saving Grace', 'We Better

Talk This Over', 'To Be Alone with You', ''Til I Fell in Love with You', 'I Threw It All Away', 'Make You Feel My Love', 'Shooting Star', 'If You See Her Say Hello', 'Most of the Time', and have I forgotten 'If Not for You'? No.

It was one of the first, if not, consciously, the very first, songs I ever heard that had been written by Bob Dylan. I heard it at fourteen in 1971, at the beginning of my time with Dylan, actually sung by fragile Australian nightingale Olivia Newton-John, who didn't really like the idea of it that much, and had only heard the darling George Harrison version from his third post-Beatles record, the gently monumental triple album *All Things Must Pass*, which featured Dylan lurking like a ghost, holding George's nervous hand, replacing John and Paul, who'd been a little rude and thoughtless to George. Here he was part of a dream where Dylan had been a Beatle, treating George with a little respect, like a brother, because he definitely had something.

At the time I couldn't work out why I liked the Olivia Newton-John song so much, because she herself seemed so lightweight, and smiled emptily an awful lot, and was presented as the girlfriend of chaste, unsullied Cliff Richard, a troubling thought. But even as a teenager just discovering pop music I could tell there was something in the song, as light as it actually was for Dylan, that wasn't lightweight. Turns out, I think, that it was untypically light for Dylan because it was so full of light, shining on a whole lot of loveliness, which Dylan has a thing for, even as he spends so much time in the dark considering thorny topics like disease, deception and suffering, and getting acquainted with dirty visions and the nightmares of history. There was a hygienic radiant innocence about it, as if it were a way of possibly discharging sin and error, of putting something sweet and natural in the way of material injustice. Or it was how Dylan felt about love on the day that he wrote it, when for once he felt, or forced himself to feel, that the world wasn't such an unpleasant place after all, a place of trial for individual souls.

I soon heard the writer of the song himself singing it with one of his straighter, less shrouded voices, emptied a little of the disruptive characters filling his mind, on *New Morning*, which suggested he was emerging from some form of darkness I knew nothing about at the time. I very quickly fell in love with him, or at least with his voice at the time, with the voices he had a few years before, with what he could do with a song, whether it was a dainty love song, or a chiming, rhyming drama beyond reason compressed into a few condemned, condemning highly strung minutes.

At the time, there was no clear sign that Bob Dylan wasn't just fading away like a '60s legend, someone from the past, his star power and greatest songs behind him. Pop moved fast then, hits, sounds, new faces and latest trends dropping in and out by the week, the young swiftly replacing the old even if the old at the time were not yet thirty. Once you were thirty, you hit your revival years, the on-the-road years, where the road was mostly out of town, going nowhere, maybe into the woods with no way out. There seemed no chance that actually for some the road would go somewhere relevant, often back into the centre of town, where you'd find your name in lights a few more times and win a few more awards.

There was no significant proof that, eventually, to begin to comprehend Bob Dylan – and all the songs that were yet to come, let alone those he'd already written which would grow in power, and become something else again and again – you would need to complete at least a hundred impossible tasks. What about a playlist of songs to listen to while you get your mind around those hundred impossible tasks, which I have been doing as I get myself together on the way to thinking about how to come up with the best opening line to a book about Dylan: 'Won't You Please Crawl Out Your Window', 'Jet Pilot', 'If Dogs Run Free', 'Clothesline Saga', 'Yea Heavy and a Bottle of Bread', 'Highlands', 'The Ballad of Frankie Lee and Judas Priest', 'All the Tired Horses', 'Wiggle Wiggle', 'I Shall be Free', 'Desolation Row', 'Murder Most Foul' . . . and a song that could make both lists, and many others, 'Sad Eyed Lady of the Lowlands', with a title blown up out of the name of his wife at the time, Sara Lownds, who he was calling his astrologer, his oracle, his seer, his psychic guide, even if it ended up, once Dylan had got carried away even more than usual with the pure sound of the words, as being about others, and other states, temptations, relationships, ideals.

He got so carried away with the song, he said, once he'd finished it – band ready and waiting in the studio to play it, not expecting it to be so long – that it was his best song ever. Once he'd rolled out yet another song brimming with the moment and a more raucous invention of cool, after he'd seized the opportunity to come up with another classic, he was often thrilled at his own furious, mobile audacity, by what he could do at the time with inside jokes, random asides, supernatural attitudes, an argumentative temperament and an imagination always leading him in surprising directions.

He couldn't wait to tell someone in the outside world, especially a passing friendly journalist, diligently hyping up his own work as part of how he was taking control of his own biography. As far he was concerned, and he wasn't shy in saying it – back when one of his many voices was the voice he used to elaborate on his music and exaggerate his presence through regular interviews, taking an almost malevolent pride in his intelligence – he was the best person around to write his history and explain himself and his role as a fully self-conscious theatrical character as much as rock star. Neither of them entirely real.

Some say 'Sad Eyed Lady of the Lowlands' is the best love song ever written, a gauntlet tossed in the faces of those who favour the summer's day, the 'couldn't hear a robin sing'. He surrounded his love with an intoxicating atmosphere of imaginary brightness. Some seem concerned it might be a pretentious, knowing, smarter-than-thou parody of the ultimate love song. Maybe – it's the mid-'60s, he's turned on the electricity, turned up the volume, raised his voice, a sane man had just entered into rivalry with a madman and didn't stand a chance – he's at the imperial peak of his powers, cutting to the chase, cutting to the quick, pulling the rug out from underneath all the sceptics. He himself feels so attractive he now knows everything there is to know about the power of attraction.

There are all these ways he's found to dare disturb the universe, of transforming an observation into a state of mind, and he's showing off, playing games with his listeners, developing a historical sense of what it was he was doing that would take him as an artist way beyond his twenty-fifth year, luxuriating in the idea, valid or not, of being a poetic genius. When meaning goes missing language is abundant. He's trusting every move he makes, and every new turn he takes, and there's few around at the time to challenge him. Ask him anything. He has an answer. Or a better question. 'Judge a man by his questions rather than his answers,' said Voltaire. Questions open a space in your mind; answers often imprison you.

His songs are filled with questions, as if he put a barrier up against all the things he was always asked, about a song's meaning, about who the hell he is, about the smallest and biggest questions. Who's he talking to in his songs? Who's asking? Maybe he or whoever it might be is asking you, me, an enemy, God, the crowd, a passer-by, a gambler, a girl, a go-getter he once met, someone he's about to meet, the judges, jokers and Jacks, maybe he's only asking himself, questions with no answers that describe the boundaries of human existence. He asks how can you ask me again, who killed Davy Moore, who's the friend, why is he by the door, which side are you on, should I wait by the gate, what are you going to do when the shadow comes under the door, why do you have to be so frantic, can you please crawl out your window, where have you been, my blue-eyed son, how many black cats crossed the trail, are you ready, all the 'how many's' in 'Blowin' in the Wind', is there anyone that knows, is there anyone that cares, can't you hear me crying, won't you descend from your throne, has anybody seen my love, is your love in vain, how can the life of such a man be in the palm of some fool's hand? Sometimes there might be answers to the questions he's asking, and the answers would break his heart.

Maybe in 'Sad Eyed Lady' under pain of deadline he's taking himself far too seriously, because that's how he gets things done. Maybe he just couldn't stop the spontaneous overflow of powerful feelings – a restless demon had got inside him – even if all he set out to do was write a simple love song, just to see if he had it in him, and along the way found a way to put feeling together with thought. Out of his skull one way or another, he was listening to the voice in the wind telling him to write everything down, so he did. He's agreeing with Saul Bellow, who said that you never have to change anything you got up in the middle of the night to write. That's why I'm not changing any of this.

Maybe it was the only true way he could reach Sara; for a time there everything about her was how he wanted to be. He'd found a soul that resembled his; a miracle. Of course, really, he was just being selfish, to be so inspired by her. Mesmerised, whether for a moment or a lifetime, by the character of a woman that made her beautiful to him, by the idea of love as an immortal force that defeats all obstacles.

Tom Waits said the song was a dream, a riddle and a prayer. Or was that 'I Dreamed of St Augustine'? Some say for all its length and billowing layered meaning that Dylan was on the hoof as he was writing it, covering up as he went along for what might appear its flaky corniness, its sloppy-seeming fetishising of female melancholy, its vague, incoherent overdosing on metaphors, its indecent stash of religious triggers, or disguising what it gives away about his solemn, boyish imagining of an ideal woman, a holy mystery, a radiant jewel, heavy with grief, and his quest to win the lady's heart with his loneliness, his darkness and the hunger of his soul. Some hated it then loved it, often for the same reasons. Some loved it the older they got and as, funnily enough, the song turned out to be less adolescent-seeming and more a devastating study of what remains beyond reach – like the lady, like the strange ways of being in love, and like the song itself, standing in on this occasion for all his songs.

It is a song with an opening line that, erotically, cryptically, mesmerisingly features the words 'mercury', 'mouth' and 'missionary', which set him up to do a lot of explaining, which sent his head spinning. Once his head stopped spinning, and he got to sing it, with a voice that sounded like an undiscovered country, and a sound that could be called ghostly soul, it took up one side of *Blonde on Blonde* from 1966, when Bob Dylan looked like many people always wanted him to look, the spiritual mock-heroic rock hero, and sounded that way too – murdering and creating rock and roll all at the same time, aiming definitively damning digs at empty squareness, America's closed minds and phony attitudes.

'Sad Eyed Lady's' eleven steady, graceful – some said plodding, some said funereal – minutes trailing across one side of a record like he'd been listening to some symphonies helped *Blonde on Blonde* become the first conceptually minded double album of original songs ever released. For all its eleven minutes, a near-static instrumental suspension, time passes quickly, or at dream speed, which is no time at all, as though human time has ceased to be.

Dylan was making things happen as others followed and mimicked and took on what he had taken on and turned into something new. If the amped-up Beatles, Who and Rolling Stones had made him say 'play it fucking loud', the records he made in quick time right after told them, and everyone else suddenly in the game, to 'play with appearance and reality'. Songs didn't have to be about one thing. The world was changing too fast for that. People were losing their grip on reality. Stability was giving way to confusion, but then doesn't it always? Strap on an electric guitar and amplify not just sound but the conflict between order and disorder, youth and age, light and dark, language and reality, the plain and the exotic, love and hate. Play it louder than life. Make those fantasies sing.

The loyal, exhausted, freewheeling music men who played 'Sad Eyed Lady in the Lowlands' in a few takes, in the early hours of the morning, initially caught out by the fact there was more to come long after they thought they'd peaked, found themselves disorientated by Dylan's Lady, just as Dylan had been, following her into a labyrinth, worshipping her in order to create her, getting himself wrapped around her little finger, never understanding the extent of her power, only knowing it existed, and knowing how she echoed all the complicated, enigmatic, abstracted women who featured on *Blonde on Blonde* and in Dylan's wider reading and dreaming.

Maybe what he's saying is that his imagination is female, and he's exploring his own imagination, cataloguing some of what it contains, indexing its visions. It's a song about what's on, what's in, his mind, which will include new wife Sara, her ethereal gaze, her gentleness, her geranium kiss and saint-like face, but also all those things he finds in his imagination, the crosses, ghosts, songs, messengers, fingertips, glass, dead angels, convicts, John Steinbeck, cowboy mouths, Spanish manners, Arabian drums, decks of cards, with the jack and the ace missing, which says a whole lot about what Dylan won't let inside this part of his fantasy. The narrator in the song, who may or may not be Dylan, is listening to the song just as Don Quixote is reading *Don Quixote*, and Hamlet is watching *Hamlet*. Which makes the rest of us the fictitious ones; in one relationship to the song we are the imaginary ones.

In the song he never gets to meet the Lady, and he doesn't appear to have ever sung it live – it's not clear if it's shame that's stopped him, or too much real feeling in the song, or a desire to leave this set of desires where he left them at the time – but if he did, I would love to hear it before 'Tangled Up in Blue' from *Blood on the Tracks* in 1975, which seems to be a song written and sung by someone else altogether, but also the same person, who could do so much with a love song. He could make it reflect the glorious, awed beginning of love and the shattered, shattering memories of love that move around and beyond space and time. The space and time that has become something so different because you found, and lost, love, and all the connections and sensations that come with it and then end up nowhere. From holy hope to desperately no more. In one slow, swooning song, he comes across love as though for the first time; in the other, possibly the other side of the same relationship, written just eight or nine years later, love is caught up inside an urgent interaction of the unexplained and the unexpected, the ordinary and the sublime, emotions and experience constantly shifting between different realms of existence.

To reorder the love song, to sink deeper through air and sense into the vertiginous experience of love, he had to go through the heady, high-flown Lowlands to get to the magnetic, time-bending comprehension, the stirring inklings and recognitions, of 'Tangled Up in Blue' with its clearer if distorted autobiographical elements. In between, somehow, came the fragrant admissions of 'If Not for You' and its soft, sweet depiction of true, full-moon love, a song helping to temporarily avoid the temporality of all things, the undefeatable passage of time. How better to appreciate love's bitter mystery than by moving through these three songs: we see three completely different contexts in which love operates.

Dylan wasn't necessarily writing many love songs at the time he wrote 'Sad Eyed Lady', and he never wrote another as long as this one; in the months before, packing in a complete joke of eureka moments, driven by an anarchic joy, with a hell of a glint in his eye, he had written 'Farewell Angelina', 'It's All Over Now, Baby Blue', 'Like a Rolling Stone', 'Can You Please Crawl Out Your Window', 'Positively 4th Street', 'Highway 61 Revisited', 'Queen Jane Approximately', 'Ballad of a Thin Man', 'Just Like Tom Thumb's Blues', 'Stuck Inside of Mobile with the Memphis Blues Again' and 'Visions of Johanna'. For whatever reason, he was averting his eyes in matters of romance, but not losing sight of how love proves to be creatively invigorating. Even if you have never heard these songs, I think just by looking at their titles, at the places and mentalities they seem to suggest, you can tell that Dylan was making up the counter-romantic Dylan by the hour, by the song, title by title, line by line.

The mournful 'Sad Eyed Lady' didn't necessarily fit with all of that spectacular invention, all the glamorised, galvanised emotion, where he was, let's say sensationally, in a frenzy of writing, sarcastically blasting language open in a period of agitating socio-political flux, switching effortlessly between ivory tower and saloon bar, even though in the end all Dylan songs fit with each other, in whatever order you end up making for yourself. But apart from whatever else it was, it proved how Dylan was trying to make a song something more than a song in the way that Beethoven was trying to make a string quartet more than a string quartet and T. S. Eliot was trying to make a poem more than a poem.

He might have failed, he might have succeeded, it might just be a song about a song that must be finished because the band are waiting drinking, sleeping, smoking, playing cards, and it's been a long day and it's the middle of the night. (All Dylan songs are as such songs about songs – songs written about songs that are about how people construct an intelligibility from the randomness they encounter; how people choose what they love, and sometimes lose it; how people integrate loss and gain; how they undergo and consolidate experience by wish and dream.)

'Sad Eyed Lady of the Lowlands' might be a song about how faith comes slowly and painfully. For better or worse, it encouraged a lot of rock musicians – look at Pink Floyd, at the Grateful Dead – to write longer songs, to forget the three minutes if just for a while, along with the cosmic woe of 'Desolation Row' from the year before, a restless anthem from some extreme campaign in favour of lost souls. Dylan nonchalantly crossed the threshold of the three minutes, and as time, place and people converged never once thought of turning back.

Ostracising himself from the fast-forming clichés of the counterculture, he'd just completed a quick, livid turn from the topical to the apocalyptic, from the conscientious rambler to the transporting ascetic, from wanting to change the world to wanting to change himself. He'd turned from critically observing America's darkest elements to contemplating the visions in his head, moved from the news and the marches shared with others to his own memories and perceptions, belonging to him alone, which he seemed to share even as he kept them private. Thinking had become his way of marching, of fighting, of attending to the issues of the day, and of avoiding them.

As a kind of deliriously static, ecstatically realistic song sequel to Eliot's *The Waste Land*, Ginsberg's 'Howl', Steinbeck's *Cannery Row*, Kafka's *The Trial*, Freud's *The Interpretation of Dreams* – Dylan fully fancying himself as a guardian of the world's knowledge – 'Desolation Row' needed all of its eleven bleakly beaten consciousness–flooding minutes, which in performance could sometimes turn into forty-five, just to give some of the characters in their elaborate disguises some space. Allow them a chance to roam a little in the landscape he had created for them and enjoy the life he'd given them even if all was not rosy and the world was falling.

The characters find themselves repeating their lives in a different order in a place they may end up in longer than any other place. They included Ezra Pound, Eliot, Casanova, Nero, Robin Hood, the Phantom of the Opera, Einstein, Noah, the Hunchback of Notre Dame, the Good Samaritan, Bette Davis, Romeo, Ophelia, Cain and Abel – Dylan liking to take real-life people and fictional characters and make them seem like his own creations, filled with possible motives and intentions. You might think Dylan – out of Borges, or maybe again just thinking the same things, in some way being the same person – has the idea that all people are but one person, but you don't so much analyse the song as join in and mingle a little.

A Google search to find the meaning of either song will get you over 75,000 hits (and that's just those in English), and one way or another the song can make you leave home, and take it from there, it can make you wonder yet again when you write a book about Dylan how on earth you will alight on the correct first line. Something happened, and goes on happening, featuring people piercing or just drifting through other lives, as with most Dylan songs, which are never about anything in particular, or never just the one thing, but ultimately mean what they say, and/or will get round to saying.

All put together, as a continuous work in progress, his songs and albums record a journey made by one individual making contact with many minds that goes from the beginning of everything to the very end of time, and the energy, the vital signs of Dylan, will keep evolving even as reality, the normal we had got used to for better or worse, breaks down once and for all. He's always been ready for such a time. He's been ready for anything, whether he saw it coming or not. And, he realised, glancing over his shoulder, everything is always something else. God gives you one face, and you make yourself another, and a mask can tell us more than a face. God gave you a voice, and you make yourself some more, to go with the new faces and the masks you wear.

His death will not stop him changing shape. Death will be a fresh start in disguise. He will continue to occupy our thoughts in the same way as when he was alive. Death will add more shape, more shapes, and the living shape he is can be traced a long way back before he was born, into the distant centuries, ancient artefacts and long-lost legends he found the time to connect with, and filter through his seething mind into his songs.

It can seem as though he once made acquaintance with those who planned the universe and gossiped with them about some of their schemes. They had gone to a lot of trouble. He figured it was rude not to see as much of it as possible, and let others know what he'd found out. Hearing what he did find out, and the way he told us the news, as if he understood the big picture, it's possible to surmise he might have been related to one of those cosmic planners, someone wearing black clothes who taught him a whole lot of tricks including how best to be amazed at his own existence and pass on some details.

Because his mind goes a long way in many directions, the precise beginning of human existence can literally be found, not necessarily at the beginning, in many Dylan songs – now there's a playlist to compile: top ten Dylan songs that reveal the secret about how human life and consciousness began – and that's just one of the things that make successfully beginning a book about Bob Dylan a complicated thing to pull off. Perhaps the opening to this book – I know, I know, but being a Dylan fan means the beginning is always today – needs to be a line that is somewhere between 'In the beginning God created the heavens and the earth' and 'Somewhere in La Mancha, in a place whose name I do not care to remember, a gentleman lived not long ago, one of those who has a lance and ancient shield on a shelf and keeps a skinny nag and a greyhound for racing.' With a little reference to 'I begin with the first sentence – and trusting to Almighty God for the second', 'If I'm out of my mind, it's alright by me' and 'I am an invisible man'.

In the end, you begin. You quit talking about it, getting a little prematurely worried about death and all that, about the one hundred impossible tasks ahead of you. You just start, for heaven's sake, whatever it is you are starting, wherever you start, because the beginning is always today, and you really do have to decide. Before you know it, you find that you have begun and everything after that will just unfold how it was always meant to, one step, one word, one fact, one lie, one drama, one secret, one task, one voice at a time.

The invisible man with elsewhere eyes might even appear. Landing on his feet with a smile on his face: he's got a smile like a dagger that can cut the sun in half. There's a face there for sure, a face perhaps only Picasso could see correctly, lending itself to windy and rainy weather. Sometimes it's a face he's torn from someone else, an angel or a stranger, with some strangeness in the proportion. There can be many faces within his face, he's very good at making a face, under the cover of skin, but sometimes he can seem to be faceless. He doesn't want the responsibility. He writes – or you could say he entertains, the surrealist showman, putting the shock of the new into show business – in order to have no face. In his ideal world, do not ask who he is and do not ask him to remain the same.

He'll be playing the artist who is always beginning, always busy being born, always pursuing beginnings, always watching, watching, watching. He knows exactly when things begin – when it all starts to go weird. Then you go on until you come to the end, and then stop. Once being born, defying the odds, sparks flying upwards, there is no turning back.

Others have found a way to begin a book about Bob Dylan, because there are many to write, because there are many Bob Dylans, each with their very own voice, some taking more time to deteriorate than others, each with their own shadow to escape or just plain deal with. There are many ways to be a Dylan fanatic: a devotee, a believer, an academic, a chronicler, a groupie, a critic, a colleague, a disciple, a dogmatist, an amateur studies geek, a kind of ally, a trainspotter spending so much time trying to work him out or simply a paying member of the audience. As one or more of those, I need to write a book about Dylan and the many Dylans that plough the fields and scatter the good seed on the land. It has become my job to do this. Dylan and me, the kind of book that must happen when Dylan hits a particular birthday, and once more there is a torrent of rediscovery.

I clock in and I clock out. I work from home but try to establish for the sake of being well ordered in my working life some equivalent of office hours. And in this particular job, there is plenty that needs to be done, which means spending more time alone. Which might actually be a help in getting closer to understanding Bob Dylan, and how he works, and why and how dreams work, and that dreams – for a better, kinder, even wonderfully stranger world, a utopian future, the promised land – mean work.

Work is love made visible, said some prophet or other for some reason or other – as you work you weave the cloth with threads drawn from your heart, even as if your beloved was to wear that cloth. And here I am at work, weaving, as if that might make it clearer how Bob Dylan does his weaving, and sowing, and the general managing of his affairs. Make it clearer how Bob Dylan chose his habits as though his life depended on it.

As part of my work now that I have this job, sitting in the front row of the Hollywood Bowl, or locked down at my writing desk, imagining where he came from, before he was anyone, before there is a voice, I begin a book about Bob Dylan by writing:

Step out the door and see what you can find.

Bob Dylan's 1940s Duluth family home photographed on 14 October 2016, the day after he won the Nobel Prize in Literature.

High School. Hibbing, Minn. NH 78

The 'castle in the sky'; Bob Dylan's High School in Hibbing, Minnesota.

James Arness as *Gunsmoke*'s righteous Marshall Matt Dillon.

Lead Belly: 'The hard name of a harder man', said Woody Guthrie.

Bardic rogue Dylan Thomas at the BBC in 1948.

Woody Guthrie: 'If you want to learn something, just steal it.'

Odetta, 1961, playing the small bodied guitar she nicknamed 'Baby'.

Bob Dylan reading a copy of the *US News & World Report* in 1962.

Dylan with a Gibson guitar and harmonica at a recording session for the *Bob Dylan* album, November 1961.

With producer John Hammond during the *Bob Dylan* sessions.

With Joan Baez during the Civil Rights March in Washington D.C., 28 August 1963.

With Suze Rotolo, September 1961.

With wife Sara at
Heathrow Airport, London,
September 1969.

With poets Allen Ginsberg and Michael McClure and guitarist Robbie Robertson, San Francisco, 1965.

Another day in Woodstock, January 1968.

In the writing room above the Espresso Café on Tinker Street, Woodstock, 1967.

With Richard Manuel of The Band, Denmark, May 1966.

With George Harrison at the Concert for Bangladesh, Madison Square Garden,
1 August 1971.

The Rolling Thunder Revue with Joan Baez, New York,
December 1975.

In the hat he wore
through the entire
Rolling Thunder
Revue tour in 1975.

With Sheryl Crow celebrating his Album of the Year Grammy for *Time Out of Mind* in 1998.

Moustache, hat, tie and microphone; Bob Dylan in Austin, Texas, on 4 August 2010.

Patti Smith sings for and on behalf of Bob Dylan at the Nobel Prize Awards Ceremony in Stockholm, December 2016.

# SIX

## BORN TO LEAVE PLACES

For those that think the artist, the creative practitioner should have no other biography than their works, you can skip the next part. Then again – beware – this life, before there were any published, recorded works, might actually be a part of those later songs, the voices to come, as the features of character start to materialise and the artist unfolds in a different dimension as a result of the shadows, ghosts, whispers, energy, crises, memories and dreams existing before he was born, and in the years between being born as Robert Zimmerman and being born as Bob Dylan. They were separate, different lives. But there are always separate, different lives as Dylan moves on, past himself, and each one replaces the next but owes something to the one before, or the one before that, or the one yet to come. And somewhere, somehow, he started to get interested in words, images, his connection to other people and the part of the world he found himself in, and some sort of motivation, some intention, started to emerge.

He developed a fierce curious streak, or simply found himself with one – curiosity has its own reason for existence – and there might not be any psychological insight into imagining it began as he decided as a five-year-old to follow the muddy footprints of a deer along a trail in the hills around his home just to see where they went, and it might not even have happened, but it's worth following those deer tracks just in case they take you somewhere. The muddy deer tracks that might not have even existed are as good a way as any of imagining a way of understanding someone who interested his heart in everything. He grasped at everything, even if sometimes all he caught was the wind.

Before he was heard outside his narrow, limited, provincial world, there is the silence of his early years, as he began living a life that will become the plainest, if still enthralling, part of his biography, and possibly for all the gaps and assumptions the most simply real and helpful, and the most unreal and unhelpful. He was born somewhere or other, his ancestors were of this type with this set of beliefs, he did this and then he did that, he read, listened and watched stuff, these are the rooms he dwelt in and passed through, people he met, people he forgot, and none of that tells us very much unless you read between the lines and read things into what you discover. You couldn't make it up; it might be made up; this is how it was.

His life can be followed in the seventeen, eighteen years before you actually first hear a voice, and you imagine amongst the sorted facts, painstakingly researched details and one-by-one birthdays what was happening inside his head that led to first a change of name and then the constant changes in circumstances that led to all those changes to his voice. You take in the early part of his life story – the one he was soon quick to adjust, embellish, edit, bend, erase because he had another life in mind – hoping perhaps to catch him as a kid in the middle of a revelation, as a teenager in the act of greatness, making friends with books, learning how to discover things he didn't know, noticing the absurdity or irrationality lurking beneath ordinary experience, the quiet life in Minnesota, as if this might explain something of what was to come. You might decide: here is one of those great lives that has a mystery at its centre, which began as he grew up. His real life was happening in his head, but on the outside, as he was brought to life, and planted somewhere, events transpired that pushed him into his life in such a way he started to push back.

Bob Dylan was a war baby, a child offering hope for the future and a vague sense things could still be normal as the outside world tore itself apart and fascism was increasingly, viciously sure of itself. He was born on 24 May 1941 in Duluth, northern Minnesota, in the American Midwest, a long, narrow commercial and industrial city perched on a steep hillside along the chilly western shore of Lake Superior, the largest of the Great Lakes of North America, the almost forgotten fourth American coast to the north, an almost abstracted one after the Atlantic, the Pacific and the Gulf.

Shipyards, said Dylan – thinking about Duluth off the top of his head sixty years later – ore docks, grain elevators, mainline train yards, switching yards, built on granite rock. Lots of foghorns, sailors, loggers, blizzards, the crying of gulls. It was already at the back of his mind when he wrote 'Eleven Outlined Epitaphs' in his early twenties: the rainy mist, the rocky cliffs, the Lake Superior hills. He was born into this, all those months cocooned, and then a first shock of cold air, a first wailing noise, his first great protest, as reality hit home, as alone as he would be for quite a while, eventually discovering that life obliged him to give birth to himself over and over again, to keep himself busy.

It was a world of iron and steel, under a sky of iron, a provincial city that bred hardy folk, that had stagnated a little a few decades after the time it was catching up with Chicago, once boasting it had the most millionaires per capita of any city in the world. The machines were still obediently turning, the ships were still being loaded, the trains still pulled their heavy cargo into the terminals, as though such work and effort was never going to stop, it's what made the world go round, but the wealthiest were attracted to the bigger, more glamorous cities.

As the war advanced further around the world, knocking America from its fragile neutral, isolationist position, finally convinced to take action by the Japanese attack on Pearl Harbor – 'I've been living in darkness ever since,' Dylan would say about being born the same year – Duluth life had its own internal rhythm, which never changed, as if it never would, whatever happened in the world. Babies cried, kids laughed, radios blared, mothers yelled, couples fought. It was the most ordinary place in the world for Bob Dylan to be born, but, if you think about it, the most extraordinary place, because it was so ordinary, and who would have expected it? Where else, really? He had to be born somewhere. It might as well have been somewhere so solid considering how much he would later chip away at the solid, looking for the deeper, liquid flow of things – where he would prefer to think of his birthplace as where Baudelaire lived, where 'Goya cashed in his chips', as he wrote in his *Planet Waves* sleeve notes.

Duluth was named after Lyons-born Daniel Greysolon, Sieur du Lhut, a dauntless seventeenth-century French soldier, explorer, dilettante and trader, amongst the first Europeans, the first white men to visit the area. There'd been some aborted visits twenty years earlier by other French traders without the permission of the king – Greysolon was officially sent by Louis XIV to expand French influence in North America. The French traders that made their way to this unexplored area were known as the '*voyageurs*'.

Two hundred years before Arthur Rimbaud and his obscure, wandering post-verse life as a mercenary, gun runner, circus cashier and African trader, Greysolon was some kind of self-sufficient precursor, loving a dangerous expedition, a chance to spread his wings and move further and further from home. He was also on the restless hunt for a satisfying role in life, an improvisational opportunistic adventurer and speculator with a hint of the charlatan and daredevil, only lacking the turbulent, disturbing and proto-surrealist poetry and prose Rimbaud abandoned by the age of twenty, the wild, rowdy child in him having finally died. The great elusive celebrator and articulator of fiery youthful turmoil had nothing left to say, but plenty of places to go. Perhaps Greysolon's own visionary activity, his own great lost cause, was hoping to find a northwest passage from the lakes to the then distant, largely unknown and rumoured North American Pacific coast.

In 1678, Greysolon arrived at the far western tip of Lake Superior, laying eyes for the first time on the awe-inspiring sight of miles and miles of shoreline kissing the rocky edges of a massive lake. It was his tense, pioneering negotiations with competitive local tribes including the Chippewa and Dakota, which had called this region home for over 500 years, that led to a trade agreement between the local chiefs and France. This opened the land to a number of French fur-trading posts, and the start of something unstoppable.

Legend has it that on the night of Greysolon's great break-through with the tribes, a canny, patient settling of enduring disputes, his men heartily sang songs of goodwill and triumph at their campsite, the sound swirling into the sky above the inscrutable great lake. The location named after Greysolon turned into a booming trade town that just kept growing, the spirits of machines replacing the spirits of men, until it got more or less as large as it was allowed.

Duluth would become the world's third largest freshwater inland port, about as far from the oceans as you can get on the North American continent, 150 miles north of the Twin Cities of Minneapolis and St Paul. By 1959, as a long-departed Dylan was about to set off on his great adventure, beginning in New York at the edge of the Atlantic Ocean, the St Lawrence Seaway was opened, meaning that large ocean vessels could sail the nine-day 2,342-mile journey from the Atlantic through the Great Lakes to Duluth.

Bob's father Abe had been born in Duluth in 1911, the son of Jewish immigrant Zigman Zimmerman, born on Christmas Day in 1875, who had settled in Duluth after fleeing savage anti-Semitic violence in the Black Sea port of Odessa, once an attractive destination for Russian Jews in search of a better life. In the middle of the nineteenth century, it had become a centre of Jewish life, where Jewish intellectuals, businessmen and artists enjoyed complete freedom, within reason. By the end of the century, it was a major home for modern Jewish literature and culture in the Russian Empire, where deep links were being established between Jewish and modernist, avant-garde culture. Creative spaces, theatres and cafés flourished;

writers, thinkers and political figures argued, reasoned, played, read newspapers from all over the world; and you could spot the likes of Chekhov. At the turn of the century the Russian Jewish community was the largest in the world, the vast majority of them inside the Pale of Settlement (*Cherta Osedlosti*) – a western region of imperial Russia stretching from the Baltic Sea to the Black Sea where permanent residency was permitted for Jews but beyond which residency of any sort of was mostly forbidden.

The 'pale' was an old English term from the Latin *palus* meaning 'stake' – in this sense one used to support a fence – which represented an area enclosed by a boundary. Much of Ukraine made up the heartland of the Pale, along with Russian Poland, Belarus, Lithuania and Moldova. The doomed Provisional Government, formed amidst the turbulence between the February Revolution and October Revolution of 1917, abolished the Pale of Settlement as part of a general abolition of religious and national restrictions, and a pursuit of individual freedoms.

Following the assassination of Tsar Alexander II in 1881 and a series of regressive measures introduced by his successor, anti-Jewish violence spread throughout the Russian Empire in reaction to a belief that Jews were connected to these events, and the tension kept increasing. One consequence of the failed Russian Revolution against the tsarist regime in 1905 was a particularly aggressive pogrom – officially mandated violence, even slaughter, from a Russian word meaning 'to destroy, wreak havoc, demolish violently' – targeting the Jews. This was part of a series of pogroms that had originated in Odessa in 1821, despite which they were still enjoying their enclosed freedom sat visibly outside the cafés, but they were increasingly seen as scapegoats for collapsing economic conditions and general political instability. Hundreds of Jews were killed and injured in the 1905 pogrom, at least 1,600 houses, apartments and businesses were damaged. It was the scene of the bloodiest pogrom to take place in Russian history. The mayhem spread into surrounding villages, police donned civilian clothes to join in with the violence, and Zigman like many had no choice but to leave his family and the shoe factory he managed and set out to seek safety.

After crossing border after border, never stopping to look back, passing through Ellis Island in New York, his eventual American refuge, his clean slate, his block of stone was a distorted mirror image of Odessa, a nineteenth-century boomtown on the edge of a great expanse of water a long way from anywhere else with the same brief, barely hopeful summers and long, bitterly cold winters, so cold and constant they're hard to dream away. The days would start to lose their substance by mid-afternoon.

Up until 1854, the north shore of Lake Superior was Indian country, opened up to 'white' non-Indian settlers by the Treaty of La Pointe between the United States and the Ojibwe tribe. The indigenous people were soon being shunted out of the way. During the industrial era between the Civil War and First World War, which saw the discovery of iron in the nearby Mesabi and Vermillion ranges in northern Minnesota and the arrival of the railroad in 1870, nine years after Minnesota's admission to the union, immigrants started pouring into Duluth, moving deeper into Native lands in the 1880s. They still were when Zigman arrived in 1907, finding work as a pedlar.

There were skilled Norwegian, Finnish and Swedish fishermen bringing with them Scandinavian polskas and their marching, wedding and 'pay me' tunes. Educated, professional western Europeans dragged with them their own prejudices and in-built sense of superiority, but most of the immigrants were unskilled if hard-working labourers, escaping problems in their home countries, seeking freedom and opportunity, not too aware about the native Indians losing theirs as they arrived. As part of the immigrant tradition of producing ethnic enclaves, following where others from their country or sharing their faith had settled, enough Jews came so that by 1900 the rapidly growing Duluth had four synagogues.

Abe was one of six children – Maurice, Minnie and Paul born in Russia, Max, Abe and Jake in America – of Zigman and his wife Anna, from a Turkish family called Zirghiz, who joined him after a few months, squeezing into a small apartment. The children loved to play music, playing together as a sweet little band. Zigman worked as a dried goods salesman, tried his own shoe store, but it failed, and went to work in someone else's shoe shop. He died from a heart attack at sixty in 1936; Anna outlived him by nearly twenty years.

Abe graduated from high school at eighteen in 1929, the year of the stock market crash that led to the Great Depression, which had enough negative energy to last all through the 1930s, ending with the beginning of the Second World War and Franklin D. Roosevelt's New Deal. A few got richer, wealth accreting to those who already had it; the American performance art grifters, the cheats and imposters shaking loose the chains of their identity still found the shortest route to prosperity, but most had their lives whittled away. The fear of being without cut deep into Duluth like other industrial areas, with wage cuts, job cuts, loss of social services, a decimation of all industries including rail, and a decreased demand for the iron ore that had shaped Duluth's industrial and cultural identity.

After the mining fever at the turn of the century, the Great Depression meant tremendous decline for Duluth. Abe started working for Standard Oil as an office messenger, soon becoming a junior supervisor. All things considered, it was a good company to join for an organised man who liked to take charge of things, a man of the community.

Automobile use actually increased during the Depression, at a time when petroleum products including gasoline were shipped into Duluth–Superior, known as the Twin Ports, and the Standard Oil fleet wasn't devastated by economic conditions like the iron ore and grain fleets. Abe was of no fixed class, just out of reach of the poverty that was feared increasingly viscerally, but a long way from real wealth, a sort of new American middle class depending how you looked at things. It was not a rich town, Dylan wrote in his 'Epitaphs', and his family weren't rich. It wasn't a poor town, and his family weren't poor. But Duluth, said Dylan, was a dying town.

As long as Abe worked hard, Standard Oil gave a measure of security as the Depression gouged deep scars into America. The Depression hit hard, but it didn't cause the kind of dark terror and imminent disaster that the pogroms had. Coming from a family that had fled brutal political oppression and nasty religious persecution gave you a different viewpoint on how things were. You had ancestral experience, a deep-rooted instinct for preservation, where even to live was an act of courage. This was reality, whether you liked it or not. You did what you could to survive, to keep going, to make sure your family were safe. You kept your head down. You'd learnt from the dark, devilish past not to make waves. God knows what there might be in the shadows ready to grab you and make you disappear like you had never even been here. When things turned bad, people had a terrible habit of blaming others in the worst manner possible.

Abe hoped his children would learn that sense of survival, of getting by however bad things got, keeping yourself to yourself and finding ways to look after their own destiny. As long as you survived, moved to wherever the work was, found a home, lived within your means, everything else would take care of itself. Who knew what might happen next, one way or another? One of his children might have some sort of hidden potential. There might even be a way after all to undermine the institutions that controlled ordinary people, the systems that kept them from getting ahead, to find a way to thrive in the margins. To get a foot in the door. This was America after all.

It wasn't directly Dylan who imagined Duluth life during the Great Depression, but such an imagining demonstrated how a unique, isolated and spiritual Dylan voice can emerge away from his own singing, his more personal voices. Dylan, always theatrical in how he populates a song and sets it in motion, always theatrical in his instincts as performer and persona, long fancied finding ways to represent his perceptions in a theatrical setting. In the end that meant allowing someone else to work out the details and giving approval to someone with their own vision to take their pick of Dylan songs and make a world. Dylan had made the pieces, put them on the board. He could sit back and let someone else work out a

strategy. He might never have thought of doing that by starting in his birthplace.

In *Girl from the North Country*, more than a musical in the way
'Murder Most Foul', 'Titanic' or 'Desolation Row' is more than
a song, the Irish playwright and director Conor McPherson
constructed a haunting, dream-like Duluth Depression setting using a collection of Dylan songs from across time, and
different albums, from the 1963 title song, on *The Freewheelin'
Bob Dylan* and as a duet with Johnny Cash on 1969's *Nashville
Skyline*, to 'Duquesne Whistle', taken from 2012's *Tempest*,
making another voice out of a collection of his voices, out of a
rearrangement of their meanings, references, borrowings and
rhythmical patterns.

'Girl from the North Country' is the second song from his
second album, which means it follows the timelessly ancient
and modern 'Blowin' in the Wind', immediately associated
with the civil rights spirit of the age, playing off and to the time
when it was performed but written as though by a time traveller
refusing all allegiances, easily able to slip from its immediate
moorings. Which means as 'Girl from the North Country' is a
love song, one of his prettiest, it had to be one of his greatest,
just so that it didn't get blown away by the song before with
its studiously selective, intrepid binding of tossed and turning
Biblical symbolism with the structure of a Civil War-era anti-
slavery hymn, 'No More Auction Block for Me', first sung with
melancholy, muted joy by slaves who were being freed to serve
in black regiments following 200 years of bondage.

For some of the more rigorous folk purists, Dylan's uncertain response to the questions he was asking about how long
before various social changes would take place was vague and

non-committal – he was talking perhaps about a long, soft revolution, civilisation moving slowly, even purely abstractly and individually, towards targets of freedom, justice and equality. There was no sudden revolution; there was just a change you trusted would come through your own intuition, sometimes a change that would happen just because of the way the wind was blowing. Other places where Dylan found his source for this wind include the end of John Steinbeck's *The Grapes of Wrath*, when Tom Joad explains to his ma what he's learnt it will take to see real change in the world. As he talks, his mother keeps asking him to listen to something strange outside, and he points out it's only the wind. He knows the wind. Joad's hope for the future features the sound of the blowing wind.

'The Girl from the North Country' was an immediate suggestion as to what answer was blowin' in the wind: Dylan himself and the songs he would write, featuring his responses to the disappointments that life brings and representations of his way of looking for hope and a reason to live, of dreaming of distant and otherworldly places. He took its structural spirit and the delicate threads of its melody from an ethereal arrangement of the traditional ballad 'Scarborough Fair' that he heard the legendary English folk singer Martin Carthy play when he visited England in 1962, inhaling the folk music of the time, taking in whatever he could in the London folk clubs, anything that might give him more clues about what he was capable of doing, because some peculiar form of transformative sensitivity came easy to him even if he didn't understand it.

The more music he heard, the more he could do, and as Carthy said about the first albums Dylan released after this particular research trip, *The Times They Are a-Changin'* and

*Another Side of Bob Dylan*, 'England was all over them'. Dylan knew his Americana, old time and recent, claimed to have been around the whole country, he'd soaked up the blues, was fluent in country and western swing, curious about the motion of jazz, had actually witnessed from the third row Buddy Holly perform in Duluth, three days before he died in early February 1959, claiming to have locked eyes with him, making a connection; English, Scottish, Irish roots and sources and their awkward, jagged, infectious angles of approach, with their endless convoluted stories of explorers, wildernesses, riddles, mad lovers, shysters, lost souls, missed connections, were a whole new set of ingredients. He could hear one set of chords and a particular melody, and after some unfathomable almost instant-seeming calculations, his ability to resurrect the soul of a song rather than merely recite it as heard, mixing in his own traditions and additions, he would come up with something of his own, with its own mood, its own setting and its own story.

When Dylan starts to write songs, he does so by changing songs that he likes, from the very beginning working out how to come up with the new. He writes words over melodies from other songs, like it's the most natural thing to do. In most others it would be called copying, but he is working out a form of conceptual repurposing, as though he is using a song as a found object, and placing it in a very different context – a form of deconstructing the myth of originality somewhere in between Duchampian and Warholian appropriation and the playful, or sincere, manipulation of common, pre-existing objects, and the classic folk tradition of maintaining and updating traditional knowledge. Most folk music is a product of plagiarism. You borrow a tune here, change it a little, borrow some words, add to them. Other tunes from other places are worked in, other words from other sources, and the song becomes a bright tangle of overlapping forms.

Sometimes the changes, the juxtaposition of sources with his own revelatory leap of the imagination, would be enough to open up a completely new song; Dylan was doing this before there was any sense that he might be an example of a dominant class taking the voice of the dominated. He was just channelling energy, not yet caught up with what this would mean in a world of artist royalties. By the time of his first and second albums – many borrowed songs put into a new context, which was his occult blend of ages and voices and the originality of his thoughts – it was too late for him to change his methods.

He could change the entire shape of a song, and this reflected how he himself could seem to change shape day by day right in front of you. It was hard to keep up with. One day he's big and powerful, the next day he's frail and wiry, a will o' the wisp, thin and eager, and then he's small and furtive, the day after tomorrow scruffy and sardonic. Those trying to keep up with him as he moved through time a little ahead of them, a little over to one side, were further put out by the fact that this changeling pulling in the world around him and sending it out in new forms was always wearing the same clothes. A blur of mental action, never changing costume.

Carthy had found 'Scarborough Fair' in a songbook compiled by husband and wife Peggy Seeger – Pete's half-sister – and Ewan MacColl. These progressive-minded folk artists and adventurous song hunters had been played a fragment of the melody by a Yorkshire miner who remembered hearing it in the early 1900s – it was this melody that MacColl used, with a complete text that had been published in a Leeds newspaper in the 1880s.

(The Manchester-based academic, musician and raconteur C. P. Lee attended the Manchester Free Trade Hall concert in 1965 where Bob Dylan was called Judas by a pious member of the audience for seeming to abandon the pure, authentic folk music by using electric guitars. Lee noted that the accusation, and the displeased boos that came with it, was connected to British folk music's mid-century roots in the political left as epitomised by the romantic socialist MacColl; the electric guitars of what was seen as mere pop music were an absolute betrayal by Dylan of folk music's anti-pop post-war protest energy. The surreal juxtapositions reflected nothing but the arbitrary jumble of Dylan's subconscious. What use was that? Where the hell had the principled activist gone, the more dignified performer stripped of artifice expressing collective unity and ideological anger? The man of the people had headed off in a different direction, following his inner moonlight, one where he decided to dare to be himself. He had been inebriated by protest, and now he was addicted to sensation.

MacColl in particular was scathing about Dylan's post-protest and to some ultra-modern – and effectively elitist – post-reality lyrics, the hazy, alienated self-conscious word-packed ones where Dylan follows a free-verse trail and a few ghosts of electricity, what began with Chaucer and the Psalms of the King James Bible, through Baudelaire, Rimbaud and Verlaine, Walt Whitman and Emily Dickinson to Hart Crane, Wallace Stevens, T. S. Eliot and Allen Ginsberg. It was those sort of visions that had conquered his mind, that gave him a chance to escape the claustrophobic boundaries of folk, the limitations of his background, but MacColl thought the symbolist lyrics were childish and immature, reminding him of 'elderly female schoolteachers clad in Greek tunics rolling hoops across lawns at weekend theatre schools'. Hung up on authenticity like the unstoppable collector Alan Lomax, fearing that Dylan's type of estranging language, of mystical personal revelation and paranoid fantasies might lead to political inertia, he saw a youth of mediocre talent and concluded that only a completely non-critical audience nourished on the watery pap of pop music could have fallen for such drivel.

Dylan, of his time, wasn't only coming out of the cycle of time in Bill Haley and His Comets' 'Rock around the Clock' but also the one in Eliot's 'Burnt Norton', both in their own way exploring how things are remembered through time. You see what you want to see: the radical or the sell-out, the poet turning inward or the poet 'hurt' into activism, the earnest folk straight face or the self-promoting pop posing, or all of that at once. Dylan was attracted to folk music more for its connection with magic – with the fluid mystical, the summoning of ghosts, the power to effect metamorphosis – than with any rigid, proselytising sense of social conscience. Magic could save you rather than political argument. Electric guitars had magic properties. He believed in magic, the ability as a performer to vanish and then reappear in a completely unexpected location. And, of course, he believed in verbal magic, and how well as a showman he works a crowd using words.

He didn't believe the audience member. His unflustered, don't-give-a-damn, 'I don't believe you, you're a liar' response was to tell The Band to play the next song 'fucking loud'. 'Once upon a time,' he sang, because he had a hell of a story to tell, one that had a chance of being heard forever. More magic, where Dylan's supreme value is to entertain, to fascinate, to fill us with wonder, knowing or inventing every trick in the songwriting book, whether we believe, when the curtain falls, that he was a charlatan or not.)

McColl, stuck in his own beautiful, unsullied time, had recorded 'Scarborough Fair' in 1957, and two years later the 23-year-old Shirley Collins included a sublime, tremulous a cappella version on her masterful first full-length album, *False True Lovers*, an exhaustive collection of enduring British and Irish folk tunes produced by Lomax while he was over in England. Carthy's response to one or both of these versions was to excavate a certain melancholy shimmer, to reawaken an ancient, feverish dreamtime embedded in a song written when grown-ups still believed in magical powers, which Dylan, still believing in the song as a magical spell, took even further. The magic was in how these songs never died out, how there were always those refusing to let them die away, as though they had never existed, as though nothing ever had and therefore never would.

Dylan went over to Italy, chasing after Suze Rotolo seeking blessed Bobless peace, and while he was there, inspired by Carthy's judicious gentleness, took 'Scarborough Fair' so far out into his own cataclysmic imagination it turned into something else. It was as though he could reach back into time and study the original workings of the mind, and minds, and various communities that came up with the original song and pass it through his own mind, knowledge and instincts.

'Scarborough Fair' has a tangled history but seems to have evolved out of a seventeenth-century Scottish song, 'The Elfin Knight', which was part of a movement of songs that

216

dramatised a conversation between a man, often implied to be the devil, and a woman which would result in them setting each other impossible tasks. It was a battle of the wills, a series of implausible-sounding quests. The rituals of courtship are turned into a kind of job interview. It became one of those songs, like a fetching fairy tale, that has enough interest and strength to survive for centuries.

In the erotically charged 'Elfin Knight' a girl magically wishes the knight were in her bedroom, and her wish comes true, but he thinks she is too young and refuses to be her lover until she completes a series of impossible tasks. She retorts with her own tasks, asserting her freedom, determined to have the last word. A song that begins as though it is a simple, chaste ode reflecting on lost love turns into near nonsense, carried forward by how rousing it is to sing, listing ingenious ways of imagining the impossible tasks, which was then a popular way of whiling away the time.

An early broadsheet from around 1670 describes it as having its own pleasant tune; after centuries it became Dylan's extreme version, which has a kind of transcendence emerging from someone who had achieved an extensive knowledge of 'pleasant tunes' and could produce his own by compressing memories of those other tunes into something of his own. Without knowing its long, complex history, his 'Girl from the North Country' inherited 'Scarborough Fair's' esoteric, erotic quality, its lingering traces of the supernatural, while also presenting it as a take on the development of the intensely, smoothly melodic twentieth-century pop song as a classic, resonant way of remembering a past love. One kind of articulation of courtship merges with another.

The flirtatious challenges, the test by riddles, the magical herbs for use in spells – the parsley, sage, rosemary and thyme of 'Scarborough Fair' – are gone, and Dylan's song is much more straightforwardly about a love that was, with his visitor reminding the girl of a love that once was, not one yet to come. He completes the love song that 'Elfin Knight' started out as, with his own interpretation of who is being remembered, and who is being asked to remember. He decides the essence of the song, once the extraneous detail that has accumulated over time is lost, is the enchantment of love, perhaps even the impossibility of love.

Paul Simon after his own visit to England to hear the song walked off into Simon and Garfunkel with Carthy's arrangement of 'Scarborough Fair' more or less intact – as though Carthy was just handing over the traditions of the song to the next in line, not expecting much development, or even any kind of credit. Dylan heard Carthy beautifully tap into arcane, moving history, recently discovered and transmuted by MacColl and Collins, took what he heard and turned it into something that is all at once unashamedly antique and completely modern, refined and experimental, the conversion of a song that's travelled at the far reaches of time for centuries into the fast-moving American era he was part of. He took Carthy's perceptive editing, and rhapsodic translation of the song, and made his own song – the folk tradition plus – adding his own rapidly evolving skill at constructing a song like a multi-dimensional mosaic, piecing together lines, hints, suggestions from his experience of other songs and sources.

No-one else was thinking of combining a fascination with how ornate storytelling folk songs roughly passed from generation to generation, over hundreds of years, with the slick, sincere and often sentimental songs written by the likes of Irving Berlin and Johnny Mercer. Dylan was doing this having also been inspired by the brand-new dynamism of rock and roll, creating an instant generation gap, by 1950s films, by deprived, comedic blues intimacy, by often avant-garde poetry and by the lively, compelling communication of live television.

He could put all this into one fertile, shape-shifting space, so that seventeenth-century Scotland co-existed with nineteenth-century Yorkshire, with a clean-cut crooner's closeness, a rough and ready blues verve, a rock and roll looseness, a ravaged poet's flights of fancy, a TV host's lightness of touch, and somehow a vagrant sense of cool close to James Dean and Lenny Bruce that was on the right, authentic side of the generation gap, with its own fiercely protected modernised integrity. He was drifting in from some bygone era but he was also slipping back from the future. But then, as he reveals in his songs, there is no real thing as a past or a future, just vague collections or interpretations of that continuous turmoil called 'the present'.

Dylan was using all his wide, wily knowledge of the song to write the perfect ballad because, it turned out, he could, one that would make sense at the time 'Elfin Knight' was in vogue, and one that made sense at a time when the love songs of Johnny Burnette and the Everly Brothers were becoming the love songs of the Beatles, and keeps making sense when those songs are becoming period pieces. It may or may not be about a girl from his past, his first girlfriend, perhaps, the first girl he ever loved – which of course is too sweet to be true – or someone he met as a student, or someone he was hanging out with in Greenwich Village and chasing all the way to Italy.

Maybe she's a composite of girls he's known, of girls he'd like to have known, maybe he's remembering someone who appeared in a dream. There are plenty of names associated with Dylan that have been mentioned, although I like the idea of the subject remaining anonymous, as anonymous as the writer of the original song that set this whole sequence in motion. It could be the same unreachable woman, an ideal rather than anything real, that he chased, or imagined, or even mourned for not even existing in the first place in 'Sad Eyed Lady of the Lowlands'.

'Girl from the North Country' passes through 'Lowlands', as many of Dylan's love songs do, whether written before or after, into one of the great, desperate, lonely songs about the end of love, about missing someone, about holding back and letting go, 'If You See Her Say Hello' from *Blood on the Tracks*, where agonising lost opportunity is scattered to the winds and distorted by memory.

The blood on the tracks is an internal bleeding. It's an album crowded with memories, of distant shores, of other faces, of broken mazes, of certain ruins, of empty spaces that take up so much room, with enough indelible meditations on presence and absence, on disappointment and man-made mess, to fill the world. In 'If You See Her' he lets his mind wander, but it always finds its way back to her. However far he wanders, she never leaves his heart. What he's passed through becomes a part of him as surely as anything he's left behind.

Another bewitching anonymous girl who may or may not exist has gone from his life, and she now has her independence – she has the last word. After it's all over, the narrator who is and isn't Dylan is still wandering from town to town, hearing rumours about what she's up to, putting on a brave face. He's trapped inside the irrevocable distance between the goodbye and the letting go. He's not going to chase after her, and his only message to her is to say hello – he's not going to let on what he really feels, and he'll keep it to himself, or put it in song, where his feelings, based on real life or not, belong. He pretends to love nothing but the empty road ahead.

If you have begun a playlist of Dylan songs connected one way or another by extreme heartbreak that begins with these three songs of regret and resignation, the next emotionally bare, decisively ambiguous song on the list – perhaps it's a short list, and this the final song – could be Dylan's gnarled, haunted late-life version of Richard Rodgers and Oscar Hammerstein's stately, hyper-real 'Some Enchanted Evening' from his 2015 *Shadows in the Night* album. He tenderly passes on some hard-earned words of wisdom because he's known great love, lived it and lost it, or, again, he's simply celebrating song and turning a masterpiece into another kind of masterpiece, because that's what he does.

The archetypal, grand mid-twentieth-century show tune was written when Dylan was eight for one of the first great post-war musicals, *South Pacific*, a buoyant, crooked mix of wit, farce and discreet social commentary. A 74-year-old Dylan gives it eerie, displaced weight by placing it inside his world, as he sends it deep inside his mind, his memories, into a history of the love song that includes 'Girl from the North Country', 'Sad Eyed Lady of the Lowlands' and 'If You See Her Say Hello'. He puts its perhaps pale, stiffened, middle-aged-sounding 1940s formality into the amorphous drift of time, he finds the dark-ness, the allusiveness, even an unexplained, sensual weirdness beneath the idyllic surface. The song, from another context, another world, connects with the exquisite, suffering tension of 'If You See Her Say Hello', and does things with time that Dylan would do – taking a moment, a memory, a scene, a feeling and holding it throughout a song, and for a lifetime, mixing together the precise self-awareness of the here and now and the dissolving reflections of loss with a sense of death hovering nearby. He's surveying the love of his life as darkness starts to take him. He's fixed inside a deranged interval.

It's a song capturing love at first sight, distinct, abrupt, framed as if at the moment of its suddenness, when you believe the impossible, and then taking it all in from years later, after the spark has died, after the chill that follows someone leaving, after the fallout of the falling out.

'Some Enchanted Evening' can work as a sequel – or prequel – to any of the songs of love and loss Dylan writes across time. The stranger he laid eyes on across a crowded room has become the love of his life, the girl from the north country, who he's left behind or been left behind by. The day he met her was the day he lost himself. You can never love someone as much as you miss them. Love makes no sense, and then it falls apart.

At the end of his version, somehow reaching an age only he will ever do, becoming the kind of old roughed-up romantic only he can be, where the very essence of romance is uncertainty, Dylan has gone deep enough inside himself, and inside the song, to deliver a kind of bittersweet punchline, the beginning and end of this particular fairy tale that turned into 'If You See Her Say Hello' – how to avoid the pain, the isolation and confusion that comes when love crashes to the ground and you end up dreaming all alone, and the precious memories you have fade away with time.

The punchline, or solution to lost-love woes, seems simple, but you can tell from Dylan's voice that it isn't, that it might hold within one of the secrets of life. Once you've found your true love in the mysterious, enchanted night and laughter sings in your dreams, whatever you do, never, ever let her go.

Or maybe he is really just pulling our leg.

The narrator, the messenger, in 'North Country' may or may not be Dylan himself, or another wildcat shadow of the real thing, reflecting the voyager always leaving himself and where he's been and who he's been with behind, wandering in search of what happens next, wandering in search of where to wander next. The whole song, found through an exquisitely maintained English ballad, where Scarborough Fair becomes a north country fair, is not necessarily simply about a long-lost true love, the other half of his soul, it's not another close examination of the human desire for love, it's not only about the sublime love he felt for another song – which Dylan honours by writing a sublime song. It's very much Dylan remembering with an unabashed sense of loss his own north country, a nostalgia he can't shake for innocence and the essence of being. He's thinking of home.

He's a Minnesota boy after all, and he's leaving those days behind, he has no choice, but those fleeting moments of what was once home are vanishing inside him, and the song is filled with the cold, the snowflakes falling full of ghosts, the river freezing, summer ending, the ways of keeping warm, which may involve making love, the heavy, howlin' winds – the winds that make it into his songs, into 'Subterranean Homesick Blues', where you don't need a meteorologist's help to know their direction, into 'Tweedle Dee and Tweedle Dum', where the

223

pair know the secrets of the breeze, into 'Watching the River Flow', where they have no influence on which way the river flows, into 'I Was Young When I Left Home' and the wind out there where he's going to make a home, the wind that keeps (him) moving. The ominous invisible wind whips up through the great warnings of 'All Along The Watchtower', and the wind dies down as two riders ride up as the last part of the day is already gone, urging you to make some kind of decision who and what you believe in. The wind has its reasons, and it doesn't discriminate. The wind carries us and does what it wants with us. The solemn, threatening voice of the wind and its irresistible momentum, strong enough to knead grass in his part of the world, caught Dylan's attention early on.

He will never forget where he came from, even as he races away from it, because there was nothing there for him, not if he wanted to find out where he really came from, even as he finds other places and states of mind to race away from, to find out where he really came from, even if the answer gets more and more obvious the older he gets. Away from something, towards something, which might mean nothing.

In Conor McPherson's *Girl from the North Country*, set in a guesthouse in Duluth, a series of struggling lost souls searching for some sort of salvation travel through the city bringing with them into the place of his birth the songs of Dylan. A new sequence of Dylan songs is put together in the service of this particular abstract history play, this particular emotional evocation of loneliness and community. It produces a compelling, coherent story that somehow accurately reflects transitional lives and events, demonstrating along the way how many possibilities there are for putting together a group of Dylan songs to tell hundreds of stories that all make sense as if that is what they were for in the first place. They exist on the album they were written for, taking their place in that particular environment, that familiar context, but they don't necessarily belong there. They are always ready to move, to be moved, affecting where they end up, absorbing and being absorbed by their new surroundings, ready to move on somewhere else again. They have their own kind of restlessness.

The songs take on a different life in another setting but never one that they didn't seem to suggest in the first place, and even the so-called hallowed greats like 'Like a Rolling Stone' are not only placed in this new time and space but replaced with a new arrangement, echoing Dylan's own way of turning one of his own songs almost into another – as he did with 'Scarborough Fair' – letting the life of the song, and the singer, slip away from you, taking you with it, like you are suddenly part of it. A new mystery creeps out of whatever mystery was there before.

McPherson's play is set seven years before Dylan was born, and it's as though the Dylan songs existed before he did and were being played on some ghostly, prehistorical radio, becoming part of who he was even though they didn't yet exist, part of the rich gumbo of American music culture decades before they were written along with his uncovering of old standards and the famous and not so famous songs sung by old blue-eyed Sinatra. They existed in some parallel zone to the upbeat big-band jazz artists and the Dixieland musicians that helped deliver Americans from the Depression and ease them through harsh everyday realities: Louis Armstrong, Tommy Dorsey, Sidney Bechet, Count Basie. They could be set alongside Irving Berlin,

Cole Porter, George Gershwin, alongside the singing cowboys Gene Autry, Tex Ritter and Roy Rogers bringing fun into a tough life. They would fit amongst on one extreme the sweet nothings of Bing Crosby and Rudy Vallée and on the other the hardship hobo camp songs of Lead Belly and Woody Guthrie, which led directly to the Greenwich Village folk movement of the 1940s and 1950s, and then the Greenwich Village of Bob Dylan, making his New York debut at Café Wha on a freezing day in January 1961, the city's coldest winter in twenty-eight years, with winds as biting as any coming off Lake Superior. Being from the north country, he had a winter heart, and he was ready for anything, ready to begin. The cold wasn't going to make him shrink.

The silence before Dylan has a voice is somehow filled with his voices, voices from a non-existent past he could tune into just as he tuned into songs, entertainment and real and fictional dramas that had happened. The history of the few years before he was born, when the power of songs was magnified through new mass media products, can exist side by side with the history he was born into.

'Girl from the North Country' invents some memories of bleak, defiant Duluth, some warming nostalgia for a time fighting back against time, based on Dylan songs that perhaps only existed in the first place because that's where he was born. I'm not saying that his mind would drift back to the naming of Duluth and the quixotic, diplomatic activities of the seventeenth-century French action hero who gave the place its name; to the timelessness of the rocks and the hills and the great vast lake; to the bone structure of the landscape, the loneliness of it, the dead feeling of winter, the frigid fog descending on the city even in midsummer, the stories that don't show under the surface; to the intellectuals and writers in the Odessa cafés exchanging ideas about everything under the sun, and what there is when the sun isn't shining; the discordant strains in his ancestry; the journey his brave, scared, exiled grandfather made from frightening Odessa to set up shop in thriving Duluth; all the people who have lived in Odessa and also fled around the earth; the family songs his uncles and aunts would sing; the immediate, crushing pressure of the Great Depression; the start of American involvement in the Second World War months after he opened his mouth for the first time and made a noise ... but such things must have kicked up some kind of momentum as they shifted through the generations, through time after time, rolling up like a mist across the water and penetrating his consciousness as he took his first breath. Born in Duluth with Odessa shadows right behind him.

And born in Duluth with Lithuanian shadows right behind him. His mother, Beatrice Stone – known as Beatty – was the granddaughter of Lithuanian Jews Benjamin and Lybba who landed in America in 1902, making it to Hibbing two years later.

A small, isolated northern Minnesota town on the Iron Range 70 miles north of Duluth, with winters even more inhospitable, requiring the inhabitants to be even hardier, Hibbing lies 208 miles north of Minneapolis-St Paul, 90 mostly forested miles south of the Canadian border. It's the kind of town, said Dylan, filled with country roads, where 'once in a while a wagon would come through [...] with a gorilla in a cage or a mummy under glass'. Hibbing was settled in 1893 and named after its founder, a lumber man and miner called Frank Hibbing, born in Hanover, who came to America to seek his fortune, working at a shingle factory in Wisconsin where he lost three fingers on his right hand, leaving just a thumb and little finger. He moved to Duluth in 1887 and, cutting through the wilderness of Minnesota using his skill as a prospector, soon discovered iron ore close to where Hibbing would emerge, initially as little more than a collection of tents and log cabins.

He said he knew there was ore where he was standing because his bones felt rusty and chilly. The ore he found evidence of with one dig of his trusty spade was one of the world's richest deposits, and as one of the Mesabi Range's largest mining towns the new Hibbing quickly attracted immigrants from all over Europe. Without his discovery, and the money it meant – a quarter of all the American steel ever made came from this one mine – Hibbing was too far from anywhere, on the incorrigible edge of nameless American nowhere, to have ever existed.

As Hibbing's creator, but still living in Duluth, Hibbing took care of 'his' town; he helped its development, sponsoring its water, electricity, first roads, hotels, sawmill and bank. When he died from appendicitis in 1897 at forty, a Duluth newspaper reported: 'His hand has always been ready to extend assistance to others in their distress and the worthy person never asked his aid in vain. The poor who have received coal and provisions from him when cold and hunger were knocking at their doors are without number.'

Even though Hibbing had advised a different location, the settlement slowly grew in a position above the mine, right over the valuable iron underneath, giving it the nickname 'the richest village in the world'. The deep, gaping open-pit iron mine outside the town crept closer, a man-made Grand Canyon, until by the 1910s it surrounded the town on three sides. Eventually the company running the mine was forced to accept that to get to the iron underneath it, the town would have to be moved. In 1919, 188 large and small buildings including the grand Colonial Hotel and a school were moved 2 miles south using horses, tractors, human power and a steam crawler, rolled on specially constructed wooden rails. At least one building didn't make it; the Sellers Hotel fell off its rollers and crashed to the ground. The move took about four years, and then six years later the Great Depression started, threatening Hibbing in a completely different way.

Hibbing became known as 'the town that moved', and residents loved to tell stories about the miraculous move; some said they stayed in their house as it was slowly moved inch by inch, making sure everything stayed in place, and one story told of a woman beginning labour at her old address and giving birth at the new. Residents returning after a long absence would lose their bearings when they returned. For years eerie remnants and ruins would remain of a part of town that vanished.

In 'Eleven Outlined Epitaphs', Dylan talks of how the parents of him and his friends had moved old North Hibbing to South Hibbing, leaving old Hibbing deserted and dead, with some of its sad abandoned buildings decaying in the wind, their walls covered in moss, his mother's old school 'a jagged body', and it was as though the old town had been bombed in the war. Everyone started again in South Hibbing, but the north never left them alone, and its whistling winds sliced into the new Hibbing, never leaving it alone, and, he says, he ran away, and he kept running, serving time as a refugee, eventually understanding that it wasn't the town's fault that it never gave him what he wanted.

Beatty's mother Florence had been born in Lithuania and met another Lithuanian, Ben Stone, in Hibbing, and together they ran a clothes shop serving immigrant miners in a town quickly filled with well-paved streets, shops and markets. Beatty was born in 1915, one of four children, and like the Zimmermans, they were a musical family: the singing Stones.

Hibbing's population reached 10,000 in the early 1900s, but only a handful of those were Jewish. The larger Jewish community was over in Duluth, and the Stones would often visit to meet relatives. At a New Year's party there, Beatty's Aunt Ethel introduced her to the short, reserved but very likeable Abe Zimmerman, and her eager, voluble liveliness was the perfect foil for the circumspect Abe's steadiness, the careful way he spoke.

They were married in 1934, Abe at twenty-two three years older than his wife. The Depression was nowhere near giving up its merciless grip on minds and lives and despite Abe's steady work at Standard Oil, it would be another six years before they felt ready to start a family. Abe reached management level, and they rented a two-storey house on a hill in Duluth overlooking the port and the lake.

Beatty gave birth to their first son at St Mary's Hospital near their home along Avenue East. One thing she immediately passed on to him was her direct blue eyes, and a hooded way of looking as though she was both sizing people up and keeping her distance, which her son would get to appreciate when he needed to act, as he often would, as if he was a blazing part of something, but also indifferently apart. Within a few days their son was already claiming two identities – there was Robert Allen Zimmerman, destined to be a Bob, a Bobby, a Dylan, and there was the Hebrew Shabtai Zissel ben Avraham, Shabtai because he was born on a Saturday, the Sabbath.

Because Abe met Beatty, and on American soil at that, Bobby was around to learn the kind of lessons that can only exist being part of an American immigrant's family, and to start singing when he was four years old eagerly involved in the entertainment at family parties. He wanted to sing for his grandmother Florence, born in another century, sometimes looming more than God, with lines on her face tracing the story of generations. She seemed to have travelled such a distance to get where she was. Simply he wanted to sing, he felt a deep need, I feel a need to say this, and in the middle of the party's hubbub, he demanded attention, complete quiet. Whenever gifted, nervy, bossy Bobby was asked to sing at parties and events, he made sure everyone was paying attention. If he was going to do it, he wanted it to be taken seriously.

He was a hit, not nervously reciting a nursery rhyme but heartily singing 'Some Sunday Morning', a song being played on the radio taken from an Errol Flynn western, *San Antonio*, where a reformed rustler tracks down a gang of cattle thieves and tries to reform a crooked dance-hall girl. A second song was called for, and he was ready with Johnny Mercer and Harold Arden's 1944 'Accentuate the Positive', one of his early party tricks, which features Jonah in the whale and Noah in the ark, a character called Mr In-Between, and the message to eliminate the negative when everything looks so dark, signs and symbols that seem to have left their mark on Bobby.

By the time he was ready for school, two blocks from home, the Second World War was over, and the shipyards around Duluth that had had a new lease of life building hundreds of ships for the American navy and coastguard after all but fading away during the Depression were shut down once and for all. Bobby got a baby brother, David, in February 1946, but even as America revelled in the triumph of winning the war, developing the atomic bomb, ready to lead the world, everybody doing what they thought they were supposed to do, they were powerless to stop a disabling, life-threatening, highly contagious disease which attacked the nervous system, leading to weakness and even paralysis.

Nineteen forty-six was the year of polio – leading to ten years of cyclical epidemics forcing great change on American life – of quarantines, closed churches, cancelled festivals, shut parks, graduations held over the radio, and Minnesota was the centre of a particularly aggressive outbreak. Abe Zimmerman was stricken with the disease, a fit, mobile young man reduced to a terribly weakened version of his former self, often in pain, never himself again even as he worked hard to resist the post-polio effects. He walked with a small limp and put on a brave face. This is how he was during most of Dylan's childhood. 'The illness put an end to his dreams,' Dylan would recall.

You needed help to deal with the way your sure, untouchable dad slipped into another state, to set the disconcerting everyday aside, the help you can find in songs, in films, by sliding into daydreams, where Dylan felt he belonged, where he could pretend to be somewhere else, even someone else, and steal away from a more ruthless, interfering reality. Solitude never bothered him; quite the opposite.

Abe was forced to take time off from his steady job at Standard Oil, and after a few months he was let go. Needing help from family, in 1947 the Zimmermans moved to Hibbing, where Beatty's family still lived, including her Yiddish-speaking mother, and Abe's brothers Maurice and Paul had a business, Zimmerman's Furniture and Electric. Abe joined the company in 1946, and Bob worked there as a youngster, helping with deliveries, watching with a certain discomfort how his uncles would ruthlessly chase down customers that owed them money.

The Zimmermans were part of a modest Jewish community in Hibbing of about 300, casting Dylan early on as something of an outcast, a normal boy but quickly developing a little odd-ness around the edges, setting him up as a loner, the kind that starts to write poetry, including a neatly rhymed one for Beatty when he was ten. Bobby hoped she would never grow old and grey and already there was death, and cemeteries, and aban-donment on his mind – he'd be six feet under without her love.

She wouldn't die until the year 2000, outliving Abe by thirty-three years, remarrying to a man who had various small businesses, in land, investment, recycling, a little bit of this and that. She lived a cosy, unspectacular family life a long way from where her son's was as he became, again and again, Bob Dylan, but she was still his mum, as ordinary and sweet as any, even during that period in the manic mid-1960s between picking up the electric guitar and crashing his bike. They were friends when he was a child, and they could still be friends even as he became some kind of myth, sometimes teetering on the edge of collapse, and she was fretting over the details of bar mitzvahs for cousins and more distant relatives. She proudly saw him as being in show business, smart at doing what he did, taking a lot of care, and over the years, as he faced up to his mum while he lived out secrets and lies as Bob Dylan, as the world tried to work him out, and elevate him higher and higher, or ignore him and resent him, she was a constant glimpse of another reality, awkward but undeniable. Even she came up against his reluctance to explain and share. After a while, she learnt to stop worrying about what he was up to, about what the press were saying, and discovered it's best not to ask any questions about that side of his life. That's his business, his way of making a living. She didn't want to interfere, but she continued to connect him with a before time in Hibbing, which he'd escaped so successfully it's amazing she still existed to remind him that he was once the boy who wrote her a sentimental Mother's Day poem.

A year after the poem to his mother, a less dramatic, slightly awed Father's Day poem for his dad suggests a sporting man who played golf and had a handball trophy. When his dad got mad, said Bob, he thought it best to keep quiet. Abe encouraged him to join the Boy Scouts, but he didn't last long. He rode his bike up to the hilltop overlooking the open-pit iron mine, but he was less and less the outdoor type. He liked to make things out of words, and even though for a while his parents thought he'd grow out of it, he never did. At eleven, twelve, he was already beginning to spend a lot of time in his room, alone it seemed, but not in his mind. His mind was beginning to fill up.

*

He landed in a town built on metal that had once been moved to a new location, leaving shadowy parts of itself behind, parts that crept inside his imagination. He arrived in a town where the iconic Greyhound Bus System started in 1913, when after one or two failed businesses a 26-year-old Swedish immigrant, Eric Wickman – formerly Martis Jerk – and his partner Andrew 'Bus Andy' Anderson learnt that most iron miners were too poor to afford to own a vehicle. They started carrying workers between Hibbing and a mining town 2 miles away, Alice, squeezing fifteen passengers into an eight-seater touring car, a 1913 Hupmobile looking like a tent on wheels, charging 15 cents a trip. Wickman started to use it after failing to sell it in the dealership where he worked. Long distant motor buses didn't exist when Wickman and Anderson invented intercity bus travel, which then became interstate travel, helping integrate the nation.

Their regional company eventually became the national Greyhound with their sleek lines and grey paint, resilient enough to survive the railways, the Model T and even the stock market crash. Greyhound turned into one of the great American success stories with one of the American Dream's great brand names, up there with Coca-Cola and Disney, a significant part of a collective national perception, glamorising their passengers and the country they travelled across, as if they could be heroes on mythic journeys, even if the reality was just being exhausted after gruelling, filthy fifteen-hour rides.

Greyhound buses appeared almost as stars in their own right in classic movies, notably in *It Happened One Night*, *Breakfast at Tiffany's*, *Hud* and *Midnight Cowboy*, and turned up in songs looking for America by Simon and Garfunkel ('America'), the

Allman Brothers ('Ramblin' Man'), Creedence Clearwater Revival ('Lodi'), the Lovin' Spoonful ('Never Going Back'), D. A. Hunt ('Greyhound Blues'), the Drifters ('On Broadway'), Chuck Berry ('Promised Land' and 'Alabama Bound', where the 'Hound breaks down and leaves him stranded in downtown Birmingham) and Bruce Springsteen ('Johnny Bye–Bye'). In Robert Johnson's 'Me and the Devil Blues', you can bury the singer's body after he's dead and gone by the side of the highway so that his spirit can catch a Greyhound bus and ride wherever and whenever. In Bob Dylan's momentous 'Last Thoughts on Woody Guthrie', there is a line about needing a Greyhound bus that doesn't bar any race, a reference to the segregated buses and bus stations in the South that were still a terrible, apparently unsolvable, problem in 1961. He wants a Greyhound bus that doesn't judge you because of the way you think, look or act.

Cocky, joyously crazed, self-styled King and Queen of rock and roll Little Richard, born Richard Penniman during the Great Depression in 1932, worked in the café at the Greyhound bus station in Macon, Georgia, in the early 1950s, washing dishes twelve hours a day for $10 a week to support his newly widowed mother and eleven brothers and sisters while in his mind he worked on splicing together pounding boogie, imploded gospel and jump blues. He was still there in 1955 just before he sent an ultra-lewd, raucous demo of 'Tutti Frutti' – a blatant tribute to anal sex – to Specialty Records in Los Angeles, looking for a deal after years getting nowhere. The world wasn't ready for him, but that didn't stop him.

In 1955, Specialty happened to be on the hunt for their version of the 25-year-old Ray Charles, who was fervently

236

marrying the blues and gospel and retooling spirituals, using sacred techniques in secular songs, on the way to opening the road to rhythm and blues and soul music. Finding and funding Little Richard, the label got a lot more than they bargained for, which included fire, brimstone and an ecstatic, unbridled self-confidence so unlike anything else on the planet he was destined to make a slippery difference to the future of music, psychically moving the air around him to such an extent it energised the next generation or two of rock and roll stars, immediately striking Dylan and leaving a dent, crackling via Lennon, Jagger and Hendrix to glam, Freddie Mercury, Bowie, Michael Jackson and Prince. The sheer mouthiness, the pure extravagance of his mind, dance as the hidden language of the soul reached through to the flamboyant self-publicising house styles of James Brown and Muhammad Ali.

Little Richard's awesome, energising battle cry 'A-wop-bop-a-loo-bop-a-wop-bam-boom' that set him and his first single, the cleaned-up but effervescent 'Tutti Frutti', in motion came to him in the Greyhound kitchen. There had been plenty of songs that sounded like the beginning of rock and roll before it, claiming some sort of crown, but this was perhaps the first rock and roll lyric, the creation of a new language beginning with pure expression. Maybe he was describing the new music's rhythm, or he'd taken the random syllables from the Pentecostal services he'd been to in his youth where believers spoke in tongues and did the holy dance, but he liked to tell the story that he was fed up with the pots and pans his boss kept bringing him to wash. He didn't dare swear at his boss, so he came up with this spectacular, haywire incantation, which became a cry of freedom complete with exultant high whoops he lifted from exuberant gospel singer Marion Williams; originally, the phrase ended with a 'good God damn'. For some, the call to arms made total sense, and it was clearly what he was after, what witchcraft he was advocating. Those who thought it was plain nonsense were missing out on some incendiary sorcery. They weren't going anywhere, and change was only possible through movement. And of course a lot of that movement meant sex.

Richard also dreamt up the wild, tearaway passions of 'Good Golly Miss Molly' and 'Long Tall Sally' in the same kitchen, drawing on the energy, secrets and dreams of passengers travelling through, coming in and moving on, heading home, or going somewhere new. The rock and roll of Little Richard was the quintessential symbol of how America by the 1950s had become a place of movement and connection; it was the soundtrack to immense national flux, an explosive reflection of the furious energy of post-war America, the optimism, disillusionment, soul-searching, horniness, hatred, boredom. The music that was coming to life in the 1950s, the ever-evolving mutant melting together of styles, sounds and rhythms, reflected how the expanding routes of the Greyhound bus were criss-crossing the country and generating all sorts of motley interconnections between people, spirits and places.

Beat's Big Daddy, Allen Ginsberg, had worked as a baggage clerk at the San Francisco Greyhound terminal in 1954, and wrote a poem about his experience, 'In the Baggage Room at Greyhound', watching millions of the poor and those on the margins of life rushing around from city to city, getting where they needed to get, to see their loved ones, run away, hide, hope, find work, and he weighed up the loneliness and endless activity of America as he loaded suitcases onto what he called 'an aluminum box of human blood'. This was the America cloaked in solitude and always on edge that Dylan would write about, rolling on from Little Richard and Allen Ginsberg, infusing the postwar American landscape with a surrealist sensibility.

Young Bobby Zimmerman started his own travels, his own looking for America, first of all by heading away from where any action might be, which of course put him into the sort of comfortable but static place that even someone well loved from a stable family with a solid education would eventually need to leave. A place you might be born, and where you end up dying against your will, if something doesn't come along – possibly some scream of rage from the depths of the nation – to change your point of view, to urge you on.

Beginning in Hibbing like the boundless American Greyhound, he found himself in a small unhurried town on the ominous edge of the wild, small enough for more or less everyone to know each other, relying on each other to build an important, protective community spirit, almost an ironically prepared version of a classic, flag-flying, all-American town populated with decent people who came from all over, but now wanted nothing more than to fit in, to not stand out, to find their own level of dignity. It had a busy main street and the Greyhound bus now travelled a lot further than its first 2 miles, but nobody was going anywhere. Many would only get to know one narrow strip which they kept walking back and forth all of their life.

It could seem like a government experiment in creating the

perfect, flawed American small town, which someone might want to study from within. There was plenty of boom-and-bust work because of the iron ore, so that money came and money went, meaning nothing was ever entirely settled, nothing was ever certain. Nothing was guaranteed in life, even as America increasingly sold itself to the rest of the world as the place to be. You still needed to pray, or whatever your equivalent was, you still needed to pledge allegiance.

There were European immigrants bringing with them determination and a little leaning to the socialist left, a variety of well-stocked shops, and as part of the rebuilding after the town was moved the company that owned the mine financed a business district with civic hall and a high school completely out of scale with the surroundings. It was the company's way of keeping people in such an unlikely out-of-the-way place — invest in social services, and mostly in education.

The four-storey Hibbing High School was built in the shape of a capital E deliberately to be a castle in the wilderness, dramatically outlined against the sky, described at the time as 'the richest gem in Minnesota's Educational System' and later as 'the school with the golden knobs'. The intention was for it to become a landmark more than merely a school. Inside there were marble staircases, mosaic-tiled floorings and a number of looming murals tracing Minnesotan and national history, featuring Columbus discovering America and the signing of the Declaration of Independence. Everywhere you looked, as soon as you entered, there was some sort of historical statement, the presence of history and American importance, as though the students would notice this importance, like it meant anything in their lives.

240

In the library, as well as statues of Lincoln and Washington there was a dark, immense mural 60 feet long, a rural modernist influence on Dylan's own paintings with all their lonely railtracks stoically heading down memory lane. Made by North Dakota-born local artist and etcher David Tice Workman, *The Iron Industry* follows the process of converting iron ore into steel: extracting the raw product, stripping away the earth to reveal the ore, steam engines hauling the ore, carrying it on ships from the Duluth-Superior harbour to the steel mills of Detroit and Pittsburgh. Sixteen life-size figures represent some of the forty different nationalities that settled in the area.

The school came complete with an opulent 1,828-seat auditorium modelled after the Capitol Theatre in New York City and featuring giant cut-glass chandeliers imported from Belgium, hand-moulded ceilings, nine dressing rooms, a green room straight out of Broadway and four massive pillars featuring four female figures representing music, art, drama and literature. It stuck out there in Hibbing like an opera house in the Amazon rainforest.

The company's lavish investment in education as part of their strategy to create an illusion of affluence in this cold small town meant that it paid good salaries to teachers at their public schools, to bring the best teachers to a remote area they might otherwise not have considered. This led to a polite, inspirational poetry-loving English literature teacher, Boniface 'B.J.' Rolfzen, being at the school when fifteen-year-old Robert Zimmerman – quiet, serious, maybe a little superior – was in the eleventh grade, sitting in the front row, getting close to the source of Keats, Shelley and Byron, the gilded entrance to the infinity of Shakespeare, not saying a word during class – saving them up – but doing a lot of listening. Poetry was coming to search for him, which you'd never know looking at him.

A normal boy, really, living a normal life, nothing special, padded out with some stubborn baby fat, but there was a focussed, faraway look in his eyes, like he was seeing something outside the range of the rest of the Hibbing kids mostly heading the same way, thinking the same things, world–weary before they'd left school. On the quiet, despite wearing everyday shirts and jeans, he was unravelling as an exotic in his environment. He'd have to go.

In the incongruous Hibbing castle listening to B.J. quoting the likes of William Carlos Williams – 'Time is a storm in which we are all lost' – he had a feeling what he was hearing might come in useful, or perhaps he was just impressed seeing such a performance – from a teacher – right in front of him. This was the sort of teacher who would visit graveyards and read the names from the gravestones because he loved the sound of the words, and the words still had life even as their owners didn't.

It wasn't clear what B.J. was talking about, but it sure sounded persuasive. In a funny sort of way Dylan knew about it anyway, but it was good to hear the authors' names, and get a sense of how it all authentically fitted together, if only to know how to pull it all apart, and piece it back together his own way. And these were important times, if Nebraskan writer Willa Cather was right and the basic material a writer works with is acquired before they are fifteen. At fifteen, you can already be burying your youth under your self.

The skittish, unshackled *"Love and Theft"* album, songs linked to each other and to an outside world Dylan snipped things out of, was released as if it was meant to be – and of course because it was just one of those weird links in time – on 11 September 2001, the day of the attack on New York's Twin Towers. It includes one of those songs as remote within the more familiar Dylan canon as Hibbing is remote from the rest of America; the last time he played it live was 7 December 2007, in Toledo, Ohio. 'Floater (Too Much to Ask)' is a slinky shuffle of a song with a violin from black-and-white movie heaven that you could have heard in Hibbing in the 1930s and 1940s, possibly some oblique take on a local murder, a reminiscing outlaw waiting to be arrested, sung by someone who's just sung 'Accentuate the Positive'.

Its melody is taken from one song, which Bing Crosby had sung, and the words come shaken from a novel, which was a concern to some onlookers, as if Dylan was scared of the blank page, of an empty mind, but it ends up as clearly an original, feverish, perspective-shifting, pattern-seeking Bob Dylan daydream. It's Dylan savouring the power and possibility of his preservationist imagination, lying in order to get to the truth, part of the album's interconnected tour of twentieth-century American popular music – which he scrupulously loves and steals, or unscrupulously absorbs and mutates – and reflecting how he likes to reflect on the everyday and the mysterious, somewhere between autobiographically building himself into a story and being a plain old if sometimes secretive storyteller, hiding inside some tall tale or another, surrounding himself with the spontaneous thoughts, words and feelings he came across wherever he came across them.

He's thinking about something, and to find meaning, or not, the listener can go in any number of directions, depending on the mood they're in on any given day, and where they are in their own thinking about Dylan. It might be one of those Dylan songs that revels in language for its own sake, that loses itself inside language, how it can make a world that resembles this one but has its own logic and marvels. From there, some images might emerge, as if the song stands for something real.

The song could be about Hibbing, about some of its people, some of whom he's related to, not least because it's about nowhere in particular, which can then become everywhere. There are back alleys, buzzing bees, a cold rain, boats for fishing, a new grove of trees, pinewood burning, and then suddenly he's at school, the school bell is ringing.

As the sweet, resonant language keeps turning, and vicarious memories keep floating past, too quick to pin down, he swings close enough to what seems a glancing memory of his English teacher, B. J. Rolfzen, and the seat Dylan would sit in to hear about some heroes. Dylan sings how it's good to get close to your teacher if you want to learn anything. (Thirty-five years before *"Love and Theft"* at his father's funeral, on one of his rare trips back to Hibbing, Dylan came across B.J. at the family home after the ceremony, and he was Bob Dylan at about the time of *John Wesley Harding*, so he really was Bob Dylan, eyes full of language, with more or less a new mind, making an art form out of evasiveness, but to B.J. he was still mumbling, even tongue-tied Robert, and he made a point of letting B.J. know he taught him a lot. Without words, he was nothing.) After mentioning his teacher, he switches to some flirty back and forth, straight out of 'The Elfin Knight', between Romeo and Juliet, who in one version of all this he first heard about from his eleventh-grade English teacher, opening a few doors

244

in a place the song implies where people got out anyway they could. Maybe by making a wish.

'Floater' could be a song from inside the mind of someone who believes he once lived in a place like Hibbing, who had the sort of memories of a time and place, of times and places, that have been planted in their brain. A song that is part of some experiment in constructing an America that can be randomly blissful, a kind of paradise, it can be a place where things are easy and then things are hard – you just have to see how it goes – and it can be a place of nightmares and disasters, the sort of horrors that need songs, and meditative variations of the blues, to deal with, to feel safe and secure. It's a song about how words that land out of nowhere like sunlit rays, like summer breezes – God's whispers – have the ability to hold back the dark and throw a force field around depravity and disruption – or at least give you the hope that they can fight back against adversity, even fight off illness and death.

Boniface Rolfzen's belief in the power of words and his zealous enthusiasm for and knowledge of poets and poems, for Robert Frost – 'I am not a teacher but an awakener' – for William Carlos Williams and Sylvia Plath, may or may not have contributed to his pupil's love of language, or is that particular rumour just part of the idea that this town was designed to be the town it was, which involved it being the place Bob Dylan, of all Americans, would find himself as he began to build himself and some sort of legend from scratch, implanting memories of himself into the lives of others? He had to begin somewhere, learning things for what might have been no reason at all.

*

Bob had played the piano since he was six, on the family instrument the attentive Abe and Beatty had bought hoping it would pique the interest of their two boys. David picked it up easily, all the way to classical and showing a real sight-reading skill, but a less disciplined Bob got frustrated and quickly lost interest in formal learning. He ended up teaching himself the basics, as he did on the acoustic guitar he got in 1952, around the same time his parents bought one of the first televisions in Hibbing once their cost was dropping.

The TV set took a position in the room the Zimmerman brothers shared, swapping comic books vividly illustrating literary classics like *Moby-Dick, The Iliad, The Pit and the Pendulum* and *Hamlet*. In the Zimmerman household, with parents gently encouraging their children to think a little higher, be a little better, the Classics Illustrated adaptations fulfilled their brief of introducing kids to literature as though they were actually reading comics – whole universes opened – but television was something else.

It was a new language to learn, a new world to be interpreted, and Bob as one of the first TV kids picked it up pretty quickly – getting a first attack of addiction, to something that so easily dulled and sharpened reality, the kind of addiction that blew up for the baby boomer generation in the '60s. Bob, the older, stronger brother, took charge of programming. Black and white TV fuzzily brought to the centre of his thoughts singing cowboys like Gene Autry, the real-life nation-building cowboy stories of *Death Valley Days* helping consolidate primary American values, suspiciously idealised happy families with their dopey dads, and comedians like Red Skelton, Milton Berle and Jackie Gleason helpfully laughing at any old thoughts.

There was also the 1870s Dodge City of the realistic-seeming *Gunsmoke*, which started as *Gun Law* on the radio in 1952, and then moved to television in 1955, the second adult cowboy series on television after *The Life and Legend of Wyatt Earp*, initially shown on a Saturday night. In *Gunsmoke*, the laconic, morally decent Marshal Matt Dillon, a quiet, flawed peacemaker dedicated to the law, was played by the 6 foot 7 James Arness, recommended for the role by the production's first choice, John Wayne. Arness himself was from a family of Norwegian descent, raised in Minneapolis, Minnesota.

On the radio show, he introduced himself with these words: 'In the West there's only one way to handle the killers and the spoilers. And that's with a US marshal and the smell of gunsmoke ... the story of the violence that moved west and the story of a man who moved with it. I'm that man, Matt Dillon, the first man they look for and the last they want to meet. It's a chancy job, and it makes a man watchful ... and a little lonely.'

Dodge City was presented as a chaotic frontier town packed with roughnecks, card sharks, drunks, prostitutes, evangelists, homesteaders, buffalo hunters, bullies, baddies, drifters and sundry low-lifes, a dangerous place not because of the reasonable folk who lived there, but because of the troublemakers who came from outside. Dillon would say it was like 'pitching a tent in a lion's den' and he was drawn to the dangerous town because someone needed to preserve law and order, to make it clear how good was good and bad was bad. Fans would love the villains as much as, sometimes even more than, the solid, law-abiding citizens. Dylan shared an interest with many western lovers in the dangerous, morally complex edge of things, the honest thief, the tender murderer.

Dodge City reminded Americans of the lawless, violent country the new America had left behind, how quickly it had evolved into a civilised society. The murderous past was celebrated, the Wild West town where justice could be found in all sorts of ways, but only from a place of apparent, even cosy, security. Law officers were still necessary, because, oddly enough, so were the guns that in an America twisting around itself ended up for a lot of its citizens on the side of good. Americans will go to any lengths to make sure no-one kills their spirit even if that means killing each other.

Bob loved the show, one of millions who liked Dillon's thoughtful, inscrutable style, his solitary search for peace and justice, and he read all about how Arness himself was a self-styled drifter, leaving home at eighteen, hopping freight trains, walking with a slight limp after a wartime injury. Dillon was portrayed as a voice of reason, and you needed those wherever you found them. Also as he got on with his job, he didn't seem to be all there. His attention, a lot of it, seemed to be some-where else, somewhere he himself didn't know where. Dillon was condemned to try to create meaning in a world governed by a tragic imbalance of chance and determinism.

Bob also got an early sense of the effect of land on people; how landscape shapes language, how parts of the country – and he was surrounded by some, all the wind and waves, the blue shadows, smooth rock tilting into the lake – can seem as alive as anything.

TV was just beginning to pick up speed, about to overtake cinema as the dominant entertainment medium in the United States. It worked like a dream; it couldn't fail. By 1955, TV ads even included commercials for television sets, pushing the idea that to satisfy the needs of the entire family, a second set was necessary – the very beginning of an increasing fragmentation of media and messages. But if you wanted to keep up with the accelerating American movement since the Great Depression, since the Second World War, cinema was still where you looked. Cinema reached the darkest, most rural corners of America.

Hibbing had plenty of movie theatres, and by the 1950s, after a decade of more conventional, straitlaced wartime representations of men and women and conformist, patriotic American values, there was no room for nostalgia; youthful desire for change demanded exciting, challenging anti-heroes. Paul Newman, Marlon Brando and the leader of the pack, James Dean, replaced the Tyrone Powers, James Stewarts and Robert Taylors. Misfits were in vogue, filled with frustrated purpose and confused volition, casting doubt on the vague optimism and inhibited obedience of the Eisenhower era, which was also the era of McCarthy with his anti-communist hysteria, the time of the men in their grey flannel suits. Things were unsettled under a surface of plenty, one of those times where the climate is ripe for progressive ideas.

Post-war life was affluent and convenient, but a hyper-vigilant new generation could sense that this was fragile, that despite appearances nothing was certain. Everything seemed planned out for them, but they didn't make any of the plans. They didn't want to be told what they knew.

All-instinct replaced all-American; leather jacket, jeans and T-shirt gave young men their own coded outlaw style, nothing like their parents. Brando, nearly thirty, introduced the brooding, rebellious presence of the bad boy, and a visible, in its own way radiantly articulate, inability to articulate feelings of angst. What Jackson Pollock was doing with painting and Jack Kerouac was doing with writing, Brando did with acting – giving a face and a silhouette to a new form of spontaneous, contagious post-war energy. He was also acting how Dylan would write songs – finding the ingredients to make his character from various sources, taking what he needed and getting rid of what he didn't, distilling everything down to its essence.

Coming straight off the stage plays *A Streetcar Named Desire* and *Julius Caesar*, Brando featured as tough, detached, chaos-loving motorcycle gang leader Johnny Strabler in László Benedek and Stanley Kramer's 1953 film *The Wild One*, glaring from underneath a tilted cap, arrogantly sizing up the squares of the world that needed sorting, with a clear contempt for the banal, judgemental authority of the straight world. Asked what he's rebelling against, he snaps back: 'Whaddya got?'

Thirteen years later, after Brando's attitude, his genius at looking and challenging and just being, had imprinted itself into rock and roll and wider American culture, Andy Warhol's 7-foot-high silkscreen print *Four Marlons* repeated a still from the film illuminating Brando, confident, beautiful, seductively sure of himself, leaning on his own Triumph motorcycle, which he used in the film. It was part of a series Warhol began in 1963 with *Silver Marlon*, idolising his sexuality, forever holding him when he was young and at his most conventionally attractive.

Warhol looked closely at Brando looking closely at the mood of things, and both of them were looking at America, at sex, at fame, in a way at Warhol himself, who was preserving, upgrading and worshipping a slightly out-of-date image of rebellion – by 1966 modern images of rebellion were now on the covers of records like *Blonde on Blonde* and the Mothers of Invention's *Freak Out!* – placing Brando in pop art stainless glass somewhere between sex god and god-like.

In the early 1950s, Brando had this look in his eye which made it clear he didn't believe that America had the biggest apples in the world, better cotton, the fastest and most beautiful machines, no unemployment, and of course that the American president was the best leader in the world. The way he would just stand, drink a beer, look at his hands, showed he didn't believe in the collection of new post-war myths Americans, mostly the white, superstitious ones, were clinging to. He hadn't become a slightly mad victim of some insidious brain-washing. And others were beginning to think a little about that look in his eye.

In 1954, *White Christmas* and *Rear Window* were the most popular films of the year, but *On the Waterfront* was winning the Best Picture Academy Award, and its star, Brando, the Oscar for Best Actor. In 1956, the big-time Biblical *Ten Commandments* and the opulent, easy-going travelogue *Around the World in 80 Days* were the two most popular movies, but the film at number three was the oil melodrama *Giant* starring James Dean, with a look in *his* eye that said he was a little unsure about things, and maybe America didn't exist, it was just a name you gave to an abstract idea.

America itself was split between great new prosperity and growing Cold War anxieties, between socially controlled conventions and neglected, marginalised otherness, and in Nicholas Ray's *Rebel Without a Cause* (1955), James Dean played petulant, inarticulate troublemaker Jim Stark, cigarette hanging out of his mouth, part of a world teetering on the edge between conformity and rebellion, representing the new restless youth craving their own refuge from society. Ray shifts traditional perspective by seeing things through the unusual viewpoint of the youngsters, who inside a day live a whole end-of-world-seeming life of emotions, break-ups, rivalry, fears, laughter, mockery, drinking, love, romance, fights, death. They're trying to hold on to something that is slipping through their fingers, and they don't know why, and there's no-one around to help them understand, to navigate a brand-new form of existence.

Dean is as modern as Brando, groping towards something terrible or divine, born into chaos, adolescent Nietzscheanism in a nutshell, shrinking into himself, spinning mystery, body gestures all off the cuff, hard to read. He gives nothing away, but clearly has a lot on his mind, and this generates the kind of shaded cool that teenagers with all their secrets and shame could instantly identity with.

The film opened four days after the 24-year-old Dean died in the car crash which instantly froze him as an eerie, permanent symbol of youth rebellion, perversely adding some lustre to the abstract America ideal, a key to its identity, quickly matched in real life by Elvis, who took the ambiguous energy, sexual fluidity, mental tenderness and sly humour – even to those in the know some dangerous magic – into pop music, into where rock and roll connected with possibility and the American Dream. 'Ain't nowhere else in the world', he said, 'where you can go from driving a truck to a Cadillac overnight.'

Bob Zimmerman saw *Rebel Without a Cause* at fourteen in the winter of 1955, Dean already resurrected as celebrity myth, and immediately attached himself to Dean as the ultimate juvenile romantic Stark, with his vivid red jacket almost assaulting the beige blandness of his home, his ravishing awkwardness, the displacement between him and his classmates, the search for somewhere to belong. He seemed to come from a similar family, Stark's dad not unlike his own, stuck inside his deliberate, old-fashioned, passive ways, looking for respect especially from his sons, the edgy, alienating weirdness simmering under the surface melodrama chiming with his own life.

The messages were received and understood, especially by someone who had been cursed with a double dip of pessimism and soul-sadness, inheriting it from two of the gloomiest, most doomed tribes of all, the Russians and the Jews. The whole world is against you. Expect the worst. Either you are with those who know secret things, or you are alone. There are so many people who shut themselves away who would open up quite wonderfully if only you were interested in them.

He wasn't the only teenager who took as gospel the teen drama of *Rebel Without a Cause*, but he would get to see it in Hibbing's Lybba Theater, opened on 1st Avenue in 1947, named after his maternal great-grandmother and owned by his uncles Max, Julius and Sam Edelstein. Seeing *Rebel Without a Cause* and other great and not-so-great American movies of the time in what was effectively the family cinema – a key component in Dylan's personal research and development department – added to its contagious intensity. His uncles' cinema accounts for his enduring love of Hollywood movies from the 1940s and '50s.

He could quote chunks of *Rebel Without a Cause* with his pals, loving the line Dean/Stark uses when he asks his dad for some help in how to deal with life. He's told he'll see things differently in ten years' time. 'I don't want an answer in ten years' time. I want an answer *now*.' Dylan had his own sense of wanting answers now, which could manifest itself in sudden, almost violent ways. Circumventing the idea of being a musician who could read music, following his own leads, his own methods of creating sound, he would play the piano with some gusto, which was exaggerated when Little Richard and piano-pounding Jerry Lee Lewis came along, piling up his Brylcreemed hair on the top of his head like his heroes, so that he was known to almost physically attack pianos at the houses of friends, in the school talent shows, jump on them, break bits of them off, like he was so angry with something, maybe with where he found himself in life, in the world, getting something out of his system that seemed antithetical to the more inward-looking boy people were used to seeing. The urge to destroy was also the urge to create, but what the hell was it doing, dressed up like this, in Hibbing?

It was all a bit Jekyll and Hyde, one half seeming too much in control, and then the other half acting totally out of control. Part introverted loner, part uninhibited showman transfiguring, treating, staring down loneliness.

Getting his head around the piano and guitar intensified his solitary instincts, but it also meant his way of making friends. He wasn't the type to go out of his way to make friends, but he would almost randomly come across kindred spirits around town, through music and films. He started playing with those who also played instruments, forming a beginner's band rehearsing in the little garage attached to his house, the Golden Chords, in honour of the unusual chords Bob was beginning to find on his piano and guitar.

The Golden Chords would play the hectic southern rock

and roll and the brooding blues they could pick up on their radios late at night, particularly beamed in from KTHS in Little Rock, Arkansas, more urgent signs of life getting through to them in their chilly, still isolation on the edge of a massive hole in the ground, songs breaking through the iron range, the surely cursed forest, taking the roof off the little town shot through with inevitable America they'd been consigned to. Outside reality started to rain in on them.

By the mid-1950s, as well as Marlon Brando and James Dean, this meant Fats Domino, Chuck Berry, Hank Williams, Muddy Waters and, screaming from up there on high, Little Richard making it clear that the erotic and the exotic go hand in hand and that the love for exotica can be an imaginative projection of a sexual desire.

Bob spent more time in the local music shop, Crippas, long hours there listening to records in the sound booths, flicking through sheet music, getting his bearings, charging his purchases to his father's account, acquiring knowledge before many even understood that all this crazy-sounding new music was about knowledge as much as anything else. He was quick to transform his pleasure into knowledge, and knowledge was a kind of madness that he relished. Songs were becoming more significant for him than his surrounding reality.

Rock and roll hadn't even got a history yet, but Bob in insignificant Hibbing was already becoming a historian, taking responsibility, adding to that unspecified oddness an awkward distance that locals less tuned into the greater values of rock and roll or the blues were soon noticing. Something was getting into his bones; he could feel it just like Frank Hibbing had felt the buried iron underneath his feet getting inside him.

At the back of his mind, Bob was working on songs that wouldn't appear for years, even decades, grabbing stuff left, right and centre, already preparing for the journey. Taking it from Crippas, from the Lybba movie house, from Dean and Brando, from the radio, from television, from his English lit class, and from places no-one else ever had any idea about. He was storing information, some of which wouldn't materialise until *Rough and Rowdy Ways*, until the great playlists of 'Murder Most Foul' that pierced the darkness. He'd think about things for a few moments before he wrote them up; sometimes he'd think about things for thirty or forty years before they became a song, every song which can be threaded back to when he was at school, becoming an expert at daydreaming, imagining his life was different from what it was, starting to stand on stage and see where performing might take him.

Listening Bob got some knowledge about the harmonica – a treasure trove of spices – and there were the great harmonica players to savour, like Sonny Boy Williamson, with a name and a birth date no-one's ever found out, which Bob started to figure is as it should be, Sonny Terry and Big Walter Horton, playing on the first record on the Sun label that brought Elvis into play. Bob bought his first harmonica at Crippas, and ordered his first harmonica rack, which wasn't part of the everyday stock. He was getting ready to pack his knapsack with essentials, including a jacket just like James Dean's, and with more specialist equipment.

He was already thinking of a new name to scrawl on that knapsack, because a new name meant he could be anyone he wanted to be, a new name led to 'Books are for people who wish they were somewhere else' from Mark Twain (Samuel

Langhorne Clemens), 'The mind of man is capable of anything because everything is in it, all the past as well as the
future' from Joseph Conrad (Józef Korzeniowski), 'My guitar
talks best when I'm playin' and singin' the blues' from Lead
Belly (Huddie William Ledbetter), and 'A-wop-bop-a-loo-
bop-a-wop-bam-boom' from Little Richard (Richard Wayne
Penniman). Even James Arness, who was for many no-one but
brave, single-minded Matt Dillon, had changed his name, even
if it was just a little alteration, the Norwegian Aurness becoming the all-American Arness. It didn't need much to make a
difference, to slip into someone else.

Of course, there was the hope when you were Jewish that
some camouflage might disarm bigotry at a time when early-
twentieth-century suspicion of the foreign born still festered.
There was also an old Jewish superstition that to give a sick
person another name could change their luck and save them
from the ill fortune stuck to their old name. And what in the
end did he have in common with Jews? He didn't even have
anything in common with himself.

Jewishness, though, was as difficult to pin down as he would
be. As a kid, part of an extended Jewish family, with a certain
Jewish pride, he went a few times to a Jewish summer camp
in Webster, Wisconsin, run by an Orthodox rabbi, singing
along on guitar and harmonica with his fellow campers. He
dutifully followed his parents' traditions when he was thirteen
and studied enough Hebrew so that he would make a good
showing at his bar mitzvah, an estimation that a boy achieves
manhood at that age and is now able to join the public reading
of the Torah, the Law of Moses. He had an ear for the rhythm
and read it well, at ease with the exotic sounds, without fully

understanding the underlying meaning; poets often utter great and wise things which they themselves do not understand. It may be that a mysterious white-haired rabbi turned up under strange circumstances just as Dylan needed a rabbi to teach him his lines, and then disappeared after a few months like a ghost, or it may be that he was tutored at the only local synagogue, the Agudath Achim Synagogue – which had been part of the Hibbing move – by Rabbi Reuben Maier, who was suitably impressed by Bob's application.

The archaic ceremony became a formalised ritual in the Middle Ages, a powerful emotional link to Judaism even as the first- and second-generation immigrant Jews looked to assimilate into America. Shabtai Zissel's ceremony was a mix of religious formality and American display – Beatty as president of the local chapter of Hadassah, a Jewish women's volunteering organisation, and Abe as president of the B'nai B'rith lodge, at the centre of Jewish life in Hibbing, meant 400 people attended, out of 500 invited, much to Beatty's delight.

Bob and family celebrated his attaining manhood in front of quite a crowd at Hibbing's grandest hotel, but eventually his rebelliousness against Jewishness was his way of being a Jew – in the tradition of the non-Jewish Jew, like Spinoza, Trotsky, Marx, Rosa Luxemburg, Freud, Ligeti and other Jewish humanists with overlapping and co-existent identities, living at the edge or in the shadows of their countries, alienated from mainstream society as a Jew, and then through natural inclination from the Jewish community they were raised in. These non-Jewish Jews couldn't restrict themselves to ideas that were religiously or nationally limited; their Jewish background was critical to their becoming radicals and revolutionaries, but they couldn't reach their dream of universal human emancipation within the confines of the Jewish tradition.

Defining his own fluent identity, the Marxist Polish historian and social revolutionary Isaac Deutscher wrote in 1954, the year of Bob Zimmerman's bar mitzvah: 'The Jewish heretic who transcends Jewry belongs to a Jewish tradition.' Even the heretic can remain connected to what they reject, holding true to their moral compass and value system, fulfilling fundamental disruptive Jewish ambition by breaking free of its tight boundaries and taboos, taking with them if nothing else a certain underground humour, the humour of survival in the midst of all sorts of adversity, and a deep sense that the world is not what you see, that beyond everything you see is a more important reality, and behind every explanation another explanation. But before anything else, before there was any transcendence leading to profound artistic upheavals, Bob was heading towards show business, where a change of name would be an advantage even for a Jew with a brilliant mind.

Everywhere you looked, especially in the 1950s, there were examples of actors in the old studio system taking the Jew out of their names – Edward G. Robinson from Emanuel Goldenberg, Tony Curtis from Bernard Schwartz, Jerry Lewis from Joseph Levitch, Eddie Cantor from Israel Iskowitz, Kirk Douglas from Issur Danielovich, Lauren Bacall from Betty Perske, Al Jolson from Asa Yoelson. Even Doris Day had been Doris Kappelhoff. Lenny Bruce was once Leonard Schneider, but he wasn't really trying to come on all goy – the 'Lenny' gave the game away. The real need was ease of pronunciation, something innocuous that made sure as soon as you were introduced there wasn't a problem. The problems could come later, for other reasons, especially if your sensibility exploited the idea of being some form of changeling.

Once upon a time ... because it's my turn to tell the story biased towards what I want it to be, following those muddy deer prints wherever they go ... quiet, unobtrusive Robert Zimmerman, as American as an all-round average B student, easily bored when something didn't interest him, but causing no problems, joining no side-burned gangs of delinquents, made some noise when it came to playing music in the regular school talent shows. Rock and roll with all its sudden wows had turned his head in his first years at high school, and he saw something in it that no-one else around him could at the time. If there was a school show, he always wanted to be involved, it was surely the law, showing a belief in something he didn't display much day to day, something he pretty much kept to himself.

He'd got an electric guitar by the time he was fifteen, a $39 Silvertone ordered from Sears, Roebuck; it was hard to play, made your fingers bleed, you had to be serious about the electric guitar to ignore the cuts. He'd wear it round town like a necessary accessory, and the move from acoustic to electric matched the move he'd made from a kid's bike to a Harley-Davidson motorbike his parents bought him, spoiling him so that there were parts of him that never grew up, which was a blessing and a curse. His Harley mostly led to minor crashes and occasional close calls with passing trains and loitering kids, like he was getting some gentle warnings. In his *Planet Waves* sleeve notes from 1974, it's these accidents suggesting a certain recklessness that he's referring to when he mentions a 'fear of getting killed on motorcycles'. Motorbikes and electric guitars were destined to cause him trouble.

Seeing him up on the stage in the big hall shocked those at the school like B.J., used to him being a little taciturn, a shade wary, especially in an eleventh-grade performance at a school talent show that anticipated the post-folk volume he unleashed around ten years later. His bandmates were hooked up to guitars and amplifiers meaning as much business as teenage boys ever can. Bob, taking things seriously, wanting to be heard, combined his band's amplification and microphones with the sophisticated sound system in the plush school auditorium.

Bob and his boys started playing as soon as the curtain rose, in this ridiculous pretend temple of dreams, to an innocent audience that included the principal, school governors and local dignitaries. The volume was turned all the way up at a time when few would have fully appreciated what amplification could do to music, what raw power it could summon, and the monstrous, distorted sound that came from the stage as the group imagined they were equalling Little Richard and Jerry Lee Lewis sounded as though the precious building was collapsing, as though music itself was disintegrating. The gruesome metallic detonation seemed to be rising up out of the great iron hole of Hibbing; maybe the town was on the move again.

After a few minutes' confusion the hall's sound system was cut, leaving Bob and band to struggle through at lower volume, illusion shattered, delusions exposed. The stunned small-town audience, a few sending out some boos, got to hear his singing voice, a white boyish stab at blues bawling, which already seemed to have his future voices from 1960 to 2020 scratched into it, the ones he would use to warp actual circumstances into something else. It was a hell of a howl, like he didn't know where some words were meant to end, and he was scowling like he'd got a little too close in his fantasies to surly Dean and searing Brando, wearing his cheap leather jacket like he'd lost all sense of reality. Who could take that seriously? How dare he think he could sing? Who did he think he was? His adolescence was really giving him some problems.

Sometimes you have to steer away from the crowd in order to be a better person. It's not always easy, but it's right. And sometimes doing the right thing feels good, even if it does end up in a trip to the principal's office.

Next day at school, mad electric would-be rocker Bob was back to being mute, obliging Bob, sat in his chair at the front, left of centre, as though butter wouldn't melt, perhaps brushed with a little smirk, fancying himself a villain dancing on the edge of chaos, a little high, if a little hurt, imagining what people had been saying about him. He kept thinking about that new name he needed, to escape the distracting local and foreign skin of Zimmerman, and because his real name was his mortal name. He needed a name that represented this other fluctuating self, the one he is inside or when he's on a stage, which as far as he was concerned was becoming his real self. He was toying with a name that he thought could work, something that would help him with his voice, his appearance. It was short, plain, to the point, not too far from 'Dean', the name of someone who once said he was a freak user of words, not a poet, a name that also happens to sound the same, but spelt a different way, as the last name of the mythically pure and fair American lawman in *Gunsmoke*.

262

This 'freak', Dylan Thomas, had written a poem, 'Light Breaks Where No Sun Shines', which would make sense to Bobby in sunless, cagey, ghostly Hibbing, in ravaged, boarded-up, randomly abandoned Minnesota, a poem generously describing the effect of hope on a person when there seems nothing ahead but hopelessness. It sounds like it should be declaimed from a cliff top or inside a deep wood or from a bridge as a long, lonely steam train churns underneath, whistle calling no-one and nothing in particular. The poem spins between the ancient and the modern, rhythmically piles up quasi-Biblical images of light, water, stones, soil, bones, blood and flesh, talks of hope bringing energy to a young heart, fertility to a place of sterility, enabling you to reach the stars.

It was written in 1933 when Thomas was nineteen, tramping after Blake, immersing himself in the King James Bible, a self-styled Welsh Rimbaud, spurring the interest of T. S. Eliot and Stephen Spender, keeping a photo of Walt Whitman above his writing desk, paving the way for the driving beats of the Beats; he was known to be a bit naughty, impressively troubled, with a scandalous, hedonistic fighting spirit, lashing out at the polite gestures, authority figures and surface lies that prop up so-called ordered society, and he looked the part. Born in 1914 in Swansea, ugly, lovely like Hibbing, he was named after a minor character in a collection of medieval Welsh tales. His headmaster father with his own unfulfilled literary ambitions made the choice, pretty much inventing Dylan – pronounced in Welsh as 'Dullan' – as a Christian name.

Dylan was a pre-Christian name, meaning 'son of the wave' or 'born from the ocean', connected with the mystery of water and the rivers of dreams that would eventually flow into

Thomas's imagination. His middle name was Marlais, the name of a river, but Thomas, naturally fond of self-mythologising, liked to claim it meant 'prince of darkness'. When he wrote poetry as a youngster, reading indiscriminately 'with my eyes hanging out', he admitted he wrote endless imitations, but he never thought of them as imitations. He considered them wonderfully original things, 'like eggs laid by tigers'.

In 1953, after fame, love, loss, affairs, debts, after years of Celtic hard drinking, as though he had a death wish and was drinking himself to death, the poet who had written 'Do not go gentle into that good night. / Rage, rage against the dying of the light' died a neglected, squalid death in New York, the causes named as swollen brain tissue, fatty liver and pneumonia. He died in a coma while his body was being bathed by a nun. A New York undertaker dressed his body with a gaudy new suit, which caused a friend to comment that Thomas wouldn't have been seen dead in a suit like that. The darkly romantic fantasies and rumours of self-destruction, guaranteeing legendary-poet status, immediately started swirling, a reputation quickly settling over him in death. The prince had been doomed all along and crashed to the earth at just the moment when the electronic media were aligning with print culture in a new kind of creation of cultural heroes, a post-war kick-starting of the survival myth that could be traced back to Western outlaws like Billy the Kid and Jesse James, to blues singers like Robert Johnson. *Après* Dylan Thomas, and James Dean, and Marilyn Monroe, and Buddy Holly – and Bertolt Brecht if you are so disposed – *le déluge*.

When Thomas read his poems in New York in 1950, invited on an American tour by the Young Men's and Young Women's

Hebrew Association, greeted like a pop star, he was introduced as someone who had emerged 'out of the druidical mists of Wales'. In pictures staring into the camera like he was taking on the world, loving a tragic pose, he had a tumble of unruly blonde hair blowing in the wind.

Did B.J. bring the poem to Bob's attention, revelling in the awry bursts and odd matchings of words, patiently picking apart its puzzle, ignoring the sniggers in class when the candle between the thighs is mentioned? Or did it somehow make it into the spiel of one of the late-night DJs bringing some civilisation into Bob's bedroom from the distant Twin Cities, about to play the anonymously written gothic-gospel 'Let Your Light Shine on Me' by the gravelly, graceful gospel-blues singer and pioneering self-taught bottleneck slide guitarist Blind Willie Johnson? He used an old pocketknife or a gold ring to play slide, playing agile, transporting call and response with his own vocals, and was known to preach from the pulpit holding his guitar. Ry Cooder built much of his guitar sound around Blind Willie's, basing his soundtrack to Wim Wenders's *Paris, Texas* on Willie's 'Dark Was the Night, Cold Was the Ground', where he faced up to another night with no place to sleep, Cooder calling it the most soulful, transcendent piece in all American music.

Dylan took the resounding guitar, the harsh, purifying voice washing away the dust from his soul and the long-suffering, existential gospel of Blind Willie straight into his debut album – naturally as he was only twenty it's his death album, because all his beginnings and endings were happening at the same time – adapting a sparse, observant spiritual Willie recorded in 1927 as 'Jesus Make Up My Dying Bed'.

Johnson's lament, uncoiling from a song inspired by Psalm 41 and taken from an early eighteenth-century hymn book, was his debut 78 rpm single on Columbia. Formed in 1889 as The Columbia Phonograph Company and originally selling Edison phonographs, the label had a field unit that travelled to smaller towns to find new talent and found Willie in Texas begging on street corners and singing songs of salvation in mission halls. His record did well enough to outsell the label's segregated 'race records' star Bessie Smith on their 14000-D Race series – they had a Hillbilly series as well – but the relationship didn't go any further. (The 14000 series was originally the 13000 series, but 'race music' buyers didn't like the number 13.)

Columbia had got what they wanted out of the transaction, and Johnson returned to singing on the streets. At the end of his life, in 1945, aged forty-eight, after a lifetime of hurt and faith, his house burnt down, and he spent his last few months living in the ruins.

The Bessie Smith and Louis Armstrong wing of the 'race records' phenomenon between 1920 and 1940 was an anomaly, and even then illiterate Bessie got the fame but not the royalties; most artists pioneering radical new sounds in blues, jazz and gospel came and went with little fanfare and after their brief turn in front of a microphone, a brief glimpse of the capital, technology and distribution monopolised by white business, were more or less thrown back into the gutter.

Seven years after he died, Blind Willie got a little fanfare, some small honour for his discoveries and technique, making an uncanny, revelatory appearance with another song on Folkways Records' monumental 1952 *Anthology of American Folk Music* – folk, blues and country, eighty-four ballads, social music and other songs recorded between 1926 and 1933, every one of them helping to change the shape of the universe, which included positively interfering with the mind of Bob Dylan. This deep, panoramic survey of rock and roll themes, energies, desires, pleasures, love and despair, existing before there was such a thing as rock and roll, passed through fired-up, investigative Bob Dylan, in the process of bending history itself, into Led Zeppelin. They turned 'Jesus Make Up My Dying Bed' into a radiant extended example of their demonstrative, reverential white blues – Willie clearly having had an influence somewhere between the technical and the mystical on guitarist Jimmy Page's fate as a musician – and of course took all the writing credit.

Dylan's influenced and influential arrangement was called 'In My Time of Dyin'', the title Led Zeppelin used; according to the album sleeve notes he'd never sung it before – and he hasn't sung it since 1962, at least in public – and couldn't remember where he'd first heard it. It's an early example of how his abstractly collaborative subconscious absorbed everything he came in touch with that interested him, and which he made immediate and/or delayed use of.

He may have only been twenty, but he received messages transmitted by obscure, devout Blind Willie when he was thirty, a wizened, experienced thirty, and Dylan could somehow possess his magnetism, his imagination, breathe in his spirit, and have it appear in his voice. It wasn't impertinent imitation, it was more a form of elemental recognition. Or maybe how he transformed one piece of work into another was a form of having visions; you could hear his hallucinations, which themselves were hallucinating.

He sounds closer to his deathbed than being an eccentric, diligent white Jewish kid from small-town Hibbing, but raging a little, burning and raving at the close of day, turning his singing and performance into predetermined theatre. He sounds grown up, even as he never really grows up. He's always the same age inside. The sleeve notes also note that his version of Willie's knife to play the slide part was Suze Rotolo's lipstick holder.

Both the poem 'Light Breaks Where No Sun Shines' and the song 'Let Your Light Shine on Me' seemed at the mercy of words, in love with words, in a way Bob understood, and who knows in what part of history they really belonged. They were both a mystery in all sorts of fantastic ways, coming from lives that seemed beyond belief and that needed a lot of checking out but which you could clearly trust. Dylan would always deny the Dylan he was came from the Dylan of Dylan Thomas, but I could never bring myself to believe him, and I learnt over the years that just because Dylan denies something it doesn't necessarily mean it isn't true. And sometimes things become possible if we want them bad enough. Whatever satisfies the soul is truth. Fiction reveals truth that reality obscures.

The darkness being lit up in the song and in the poem, the light flooding in, got tangled up in Bob's mind. Imagine if it was the poet singing the song, tossing in his own sense of over-the-top rapture, playing guitar as surely and vigorously. Dylan Thomas with all that succulent, triumphant language singing Blind Willie Johnson with all that evangelical intensity. It wasn't much of a stretch of his intoxicated imagination to think of himself being someone like that, and a new name happened to come to mind, one that instantly connected him with literary immortality, and even with a legendary lawman standing up to injustice, doing the best he could to come up with some temporary fixes for chaos.

One answer to who the hell he thought he was.

# SEVEN

## BORROWED TIME

To keep up with Bob Dylan, now he's been named, with no strings attached, perhaps it's simply a matter of opening the door and heading outside, finding the room to roam, in order to escape being contained and cut off from all that life that has ended up making the world something to believe in. If the first step doesn't happen, neither does the journey.

Out on the road, in my mind, checking the moves and routes of Dylan, I'm travelling with a plan, booking various places and venues, following a map, if only the map of my own madness, but leaving myself open to unforeseen detours, to be side-tracked by all kinds of curiosities, characters and mysteries, and twists and turns in the river. Leaving home again and again, shaking off the cloak of many cares, taking things personally, so that routine experiences become new all over again.

I'm travelling to be steeped in history, to expand the space that surrounds me, to broaden my horizons. To multiply. Travelling for the journey, for the events that unfold in time. Travelling for the accidental meetings, the unexpected connections, because the world can be a small place, small as a pebble, yet as large and as alone, understood in a flash, misunderstood a lot of the time, and you see what a tiny place you occupy in the world.

Travelling to places that call to me, that seem familiar and expected, and to places that knock me off balance. Travelling because the world never ends, as you lean forward to the next crazy venture beneath the skies, tramping a perpetual journey, often winging it, going without the latest iPhone, hungry for reality, sailing into an unknown spring, hauling on frayed ropes, moving about free and unanchored, not towards something but away from something. Wandering away from the world's somewheres into our own nowhere, all things tending towards the eternal or what we imagine of it.

Travelling, because writing a book about Dylan demands that you do, that you travel into him, and through his mind, from swerve of shore to bend of bay along his imagination, which exists as a preview of life's coming attractions, filled with lunatics, lovers and poets, idols, villains and tricksters, judges and jukeboxes, with good stories, freedom songs, cautionary tales and cosmic laws, his head constantly spinning with riddles and rhymes, a man of extremes skipping in a moment between heaven and earth, between yesterday and tomorrow. There's a long way to go, so much to see, a lot to learn.

I travel to defy imposed boundaries and limitations, things that only exist in the minds of tedious people. I travel to places out of restlessness and yearning and spill a little blood but leave no tracks. I travel out of frustration with the familiar and with mundane moments. I travel to see, to find out, to pass through, to heighten my senses, to take delight in small things, to conquer, to feel less cocooned, to find other souls and other states, other lives, and, you never know, if you're lucky, or heaven knows damned, to return.

There are some places that you know you will never return

to, the *mélancholies du voyage*, for Gustave Flaubert one of the most rewarding things about travel. Travel to leave your body on a distant shore. To be at the centre of the world and yet to remain hidden from the world. Travel to cease to be alone, to come across places that are like fabrics of enchantment piled to heaven, every change of scene a pleasure of some sort. Sometimes, the circus arrives without warning. No-one told you it was coming. It is simply there, when yesterday it was not.

Travel to hear in the late afternoon of time ghosts with names you know, to hear the rain the trains the planes the wind the sea the moon the sound of time itself whisper in my ear, urging me on, helping me out; the world is a book and those who do not travel only get to read one page ... wherever you go becomes a part of you ... the journey itself is my home ... escape the things that harass you not by being in a different place but by being a different person ... travel is fatal to big-otry, to prejudice, to narrow-mindedness ... the really precious things are thought and sight, not pace ... the wanderer does not have a final home, a certain destination, he keeps on drifting from place to place ... home is not a place but an irrevocable condition ... bad or good as it happens to be, this is what it is to exist! Don't be sorry. What's the worst that can happen?

Travel like Bob Dylan, taking care of his name, his cos-tume, his voices, as the rain starts falling, hard, travel with his cravings, fits of temper and fears, his hermit spirit, checking on his ancestry, smiling at the absurdities of life that suddenly make complete sense, smiling because he's been reminded of the immensity of fate. Nothing tragic about that; it is what it is.

Travel like Dylan, celebrating the right to be a vagrant, chatting with Byron, strutting and fretting with Shakespeare, asking Marlene Dietrich how close they are to Montmartre, carving across the nation on a train with Charlie Chaplin because anything is possible on a train, staring at the bag in Abraham Lincoln's hand, making a way for the wind with Yoko Ono, sawing Houdini in half, lying down in a bed of dust, keeping his place with Oscar Wilde, visiting a seedy little town on the Santa Monica Bay with Dante, holding hands with Duke Ellington, searching for who knows what with Virginia Woolf, playing a jukebox with Edgar Allen Poe, spying unicorns in the garden of reason with Nina Simone, cocking an ear and keeping an eye open with Rosencrantz and Guildenstern, eating a mouthful of sand with William the Conqueror, praying aloud with Dame Julian of Norwich, presenting Jacques Derrida's *Specters of Marx* to Cate Blanchett, gun running in Africa with Rimbaud, sharing scraps of memory with Salman Rushdie, hanging out in the stars with Rilke, enjoying some random trivia with Chekhov, staring at Titian's *Entombment of Christ* with Fiona Apple, listening to Beethoven's 'Eroica' Symphony with Somerset Maugham, dropping in on Sylvia Plath's 1950s New York, catching the sudden look of some dead master, borrowing Blind Lemon Jefferson's guitar, spending time in prison with Kafka, discussing Christianity with Fidel Castro, dropping in on seventeenth-century Salem, Massachusetts, getting to know 'hanging' Judge Blood, piling battered suitcases on the sidewalk with Jack Kerouac, turning vampire with T. S. Eliot, stealing whatever feelings, fables and phrases he can under cover of darkness, reading Proust and suffering a little heartburn.

Travel like Dylan, agreeing with Mozart that someone of ordinary talent will always be ordinary, whether they travel or not, but someone of superior talent will go to pieces if they remain in the same place forever; agreeing with Kurt Vonnegut that bizarre travel plans are dancing lessons from God. Travelling for travel's sake, not to go anywhere, but to go, not to seek new landscapes but to have new eyes, to find what was always lying ahead, always finding a past he did not know he had, always saying goodbye. It was time to go; always time to go. You go down new streets, you see houses you never saw before, pass places you didn't even know were there before. Everything changes.

When things change, especially for the worse, when the shit hits the fan, when people really start to believe the end is nigh, it helps to have someone who weirdly seems to be in control of the situation, even if they have no official credentials and sing songs for a living. Someone who always seemed born to travel, bored and excited between security and disorientation, and always came out the other side with at the very least a response or two, and the kind of good advice that actually comes from someone who acts as though he has no personal interest in the matter. A major change in the state of the world, a confusing, frightening historical out-of-sync shift is just something else he has come across in his life, which is neither here nor there, but which sure whets the imagination, and encourages a passionate suspicion about the destiny of the human race. After all, why should things be easy to understand? The world's a puzzle; no need to make sense out of it.

Suddenly, something happens that for many people is the worst event in their life. There are some last unclouded happy moments, something we quickly begin to remember as Normal before everything falls apart. Survival itself seems threatened by insurmountable problems. People feel lost, they have no idea what to say or feel or do or think, they become messes and it looks as though they will remain messes. The universe, it turned out, really does have no sense of obligation even when faced with the fact that humans exist. The light seems to go out, as though the sun might set permanently, the ground shifts under our feet, there's an insidious unseen enemy, the future is not what it was.

But there is someone who is ready if only in their own life to pass on some advice, some clues about how to relish an easy life but find the strength to endure a difficult one. Someone who, it becomes clearer as they live longer, was always ready in their own life for whatever came their way, deciding that the fact that life has no meaning is a reason to live – moreover, the only one. This someone then got on with making meaning, ready for action, ready to communicate that what is happening is in many ways just one of those things, and life goes on, what else is there, even if suddenly there is so much change that the very nature of what it is to be human has profoundly altered. We seem doomed, but then, we always have been, but that doesn't mean you stop thinking, or dreaming, or hoping. It doesn't mean you stop looking to art, poetry, writing, music for some guidance, as well as some distraction, and consolation, and – you never know – some sort of solution. We are at death's door, at least we seem to be nearer death's door than ever, even if we have only just started our life, setting out on an adventure that will contain other adventures, as many adventures as you can find, before your time's up.

It doesn't mean you stop writing songs and singing, even if

about how life is a perfect graveyard of buried hopes, an endless field of dead Christmas trees, and the future is a dark corridor and at the far end the door is bolted; when someone is in despair it means that they still believe in something. Even in despair as the night trembles and the earth might stop spinning you can lose yourself in action. A monster has grown that will devour us all. Yet we must fight it. Using words if nothing else to tame the pain if nothing else. Expectation lives on.

As John F. Kennedy once said, and Al Gore loved to say, as though they were incorrectly quoting Bob Dylan incorrectly quoting someone else, the Chinese use two characters to write the word 'crisis'. One stands for danger, the other for opportunity. In a crisis, be aware of the danger – but recognise the opportunity. (The second character more accurately means 'change point', but that clearing up of some wishful thinking ruins a good story. It also appears that the supposed Chinese curse 'May you live in interesting times' is not from any known Chinese source; the closest equivalent expression is 'Better to be a dog in times of tranquillity than a human in times of chaos'. Dylan found himself right in the centre of interesting times, this chaos and conflict, which day by day brought new objects of interest, and also new objects for anxiety. A lifetime of burning in every moment. Think of the songs that could come out of that, if you were paying attention, and you believed in the truth of the imagination.)

Imagine that with Kennedy in the same room at the same time, Hunter S. Thompson, part of a group of advisers, interjected: 'The Edge. There is no honest way to explain it because the only people who really know where it is are the ones who have gone over.' Standing in the shadows there is someone who went over the edge and returned to sing the tale. Sometimes, he whispers, or is it a growl, you need a little crisis to get your adrenalin flowing. We might die out, become extinct as a species, no-one left to remember Aristotle or Cleopatra, or we could rise above the limitations of our condition through an evolutionary leap.

Suddenly, in 2020, such thoughts were almost making their way onto the 24-hour news cycle amongst all that panic and fear and frustration, all that reality-television-shaped spectacle, all that fake news and threatened democracy: a rampaging virus, apparently with its own mind; the foul subtractions of the Covid dead; the war on laws; the shifting data; the burning trees, the polluted skies, the toxic air, the wind swirling without recollection, the green leaves shrinking before the hot breath of furnaces, an ocean of ashes, nature having the last laugh; the floods, murders and ghost towns; the deserted streets with dust suspended in the air; the trampled fields of battle; hooded hordes swarming; women suffering at the hands of men; all the trash and trashing of Trump, with his herd mentality, the Devil as Mr Wise Guy, the sentimental celebrity as autocrat, the moron as performance artist, misogyny as a form of recreation; charlatans and bloodsuckers grabbing power, denying science, fearing and scorning the all-American descendants of immigrants and revolutionists, all that bamboozling American bombardment; a race between education and catastrophe; a modern audience clutching cheap gods; the soiled slapstick of bonkers barbarian Boris Johnson, all that English vile rage and melancholy moaning; the mindless vandalising by those in power of whatever norms, whatever standards, were left alone by the virus; the to-be-and-not-to-be of masks and social distance; the splintering of countries; the enforced solitude; the empty theatres, stadiums and arenas; the tortured dissolving of the numbed normal; all that chaos and division, the riots and shootings, conspiracy theories, disinformation, cancelling and cat-calling, the culture wars, social bubbles and social media babble; all that disinformation being facilitated by the shadier side of modern technology, the trolls and bots and hackers, squabblers and racists and influencers and pundits and ghosters and monument topplers, one fucking thing after another, a heap of broken images. Doomsday calling. Days are numbered. Reality denied comes back to haunt. Demise is imminent. How does it feel?

There is someone, somewhere, who has always been agile in his deliberately ambiguous way of embracing explosions of chaos, happy being able to despair, because being aware and being in despair sometimes coincide. Someone who was brilliant at apprehending events, and their effects over time, someone who on the sly was a specialist in the sudden, sometimes terrifying turning points of history rooted not only in wars or political shifts but also in the very fabric of human character. Someone who always knew that on the calendar there was always one thing for sure: a storm. A storm was coming. This someone, an American and a gypsy, arbitrary daydreamer, fucked-up fantasist, exquisite and listless, scurrilous and sublime, hypocrite and hypothesiser, unattached and detached, this attentive passer-by with a cycloning brain, mind glowing into words, into cool reason, thumbing through Rimbaud and borrowing from him, igniting the imagination, meaning what he says, literally and in every sense – he felt this developing storm without fear as he strode through his life from end to end, from paradise to hell, and hell to paradise. And he was here to be the I in the storm. And when that storm had passed, another one was immediately due.

All of this becomes part of the story of this someone, this decentred, renamed Bob Dylan, and it becomes part of his story even as it began in the very different twentieth century, in the middle of a world war, in the late 1950s and early 1960s, let's say 1961, when he reached twenty. If you allow YouTube to show you how things are and were, that's when you can first hear the thin, thieving voice of keen, nervously alive recording artist Bob Dylan, the activated folkster wildling with a baby face he can't wait to grow out of.

He's already giving up on the idea of being normal, already shooting off his mouth, already doing things differently even as he is recycling others without a qualm, clearly considering the idea of copyright and plagiarism an annoying seventeenth-century invention. You can hear him sing in early performances. You can't yet see him, but if you could, you'd see that his eyes are already lit up with warning. Very soon, that warning will get more urgent. And if you keep on saying things are going to be bad, you have a good chance of being a prophet.

This music of the apocalypse was established as soon as he materialised in the 1960s, and has been refined and warped ever since to suit the times and the state of his burning, or retreating, or evangelical mind; he teases out, loses himself in, actually tours the end of civilisation, recording in vivid detail a world in ruins, getting the measure of absolute extinction, sometimes even lecturing his fans that they are heading for hell if they don't repent.

Most of Dylan's songs, for all their boldness and beauty, are about a dark, darkening world buckling and cracking under pressure of imminent disaster. They have often featured a disastrous atmosphere that made more sense in 2020 and a rampant collective catastrophe than it did even during previous troubled times, where they originally came from, when there were assassinations, and resignations, and civil wars, and protests, and deadly international conflicts, and terrorist attacks, and festering corruption.

Dylan, years back, had already guessed this, even if only abstractly, which is perhaps why sometimes he seemed to be making crazy decisions – about who he was, what he was doing and why, where he was heading, what he should sound like, who and what he should believe, where the hell was that new dawn he thought was coming. The spiritual dimension of his 'better', more acceptably classic songs sometimes seemed to be absent, or just inhabiting a different kind of present. He had a lot on his mind, all that trauma coming our way, adding to haywire history, and if he couldn't get it out of his head and into his songs, it just sort of weighed him down, and made the decisions he had to make about his songs and the life behind them a little harder than he would have liked. Sometimes he was wounded, lost in the desert, blinded by the light, not so sure anymore that there was another voice left in him. It's not surprising.

He charged again and again into impending doom, into the chaos of social upheaval, into Cold War dread, into American mass confusion, into the churning precariousness of his own mind, the dubious state of his faith, into the accumulating equations and persuasions of popular culture with a deep sensitivity towards the hovering presence of, generally speaking, the end of days. Whether the end was coming through environmental or economic or nuclear destruction, he had been thinking this from when he was twenty – 2,000 in wizard years – writing a song for Woody Guthrie and lightly remarking about a torn, barely born world that was breathing its last. It wasn't long before he was telling us that we had a fight on our hands in 'The Times They Are a-Changin'', which was sung by others in pretty ways as though it was a fair symbol of hope and resistance, but which for Dylan was about a country, and a world, being smashed apart. Deal with that while you march for peace.

His life, and his work, his songs, through the prism of a devastating 2020, became something else, but still what they always were, because his life ended, or neared its end, as the world itself flirted with an ending, or certainly changed into a very uncertain version of itself. You cannot fully understand the events, uncertainty and mayhem, the shuddering sadness, of 2020 without experiencing Dylan's songs, which themselves have become more intense and destined to outlive him and rock and roll because they were written in time for when the world slipped off the rails, contents spilling everywhere. He was writing about threats, fears, obsessions, the grim charade, the powerless, persecution, ignorance, chastisement, thunder and lightning, borrowed time and a borrowed world, how the world is always going to break your heart, from the moment he started. There he was in 1961, taking his time even if the world was due to end at any moment, or slip back into the Dark Ages, steering towards catastrophe and untethered insanity, putting his faith in songs to survive the fallout. However things end, the moon will keep shining, the song will keep rhyming.

In 2020 it was as though the reality of the world itself – which previously ran in very separate ways from the far-off visions and disordered sensations of a Bob Dylan, continually disrupting set stories, alerting us to alternative dramas, calling into question all kinds of beginnings and endings – had moved closer to where he found, or placed, himself. Reality lurched nearer somehow to his totally hallucinated universe, his enshrined alienation, his constant, seductive invitations to give up the rational mind, his songs that mirror the unreality of what *is*, even as for many they are only rock songs or, even lower down the pecking order, only pop songs. His rock star persona, his pop star years, the talked-up mystic drifter, the poseur as living legend guarding his privacy: all these were in turn a series of masks, a just about socially acceptable front for what was really weird about him, and the weirdness he was holding in reserve. At the core of the hidden life was a need for signs. The signs in 2020 everyone was needing.

Dylan, continually wanting more from language, forecast a world gone irrational and was around to see it come true in all its untruths, a world raving deliriously and chopping up history in a way that once seemed to belong only inside his songs. Equilibrium was abandoned, the hold of natural and societal laws was loosened, trust was slaughtered, every day featured a traumatic encounter with death, disease and televised demons, and it was stateless legislators, these individualist rebels like Dylan, the artists usually lost in their own worlds, committed to their own form of free speech, wanting really to be in a minority of one, who we had to rely on for stability and even safety and to help us invent secure new realities and plot our survival. We were not in 'the real world' anymore, we had shifted over into the kind of reality Dylan conjures up in his songs: fractured, febrile states of mind, a shattering of grace, even a new kind of violence, which seemed beyond and far-fetched, featuring scenes from Dante's inferno, a stretching of the everyday into something transcendent and impossible, a wild and distant planet, but which now seemed to be where we found ourselves, tumbling against our poor ruined will through a jumble of haywire events and assaults on the senses.

No-one knew what the hell was going on – which seemed to suit Dylan down to the ground, both the part of him that was always happy to get stuck into some pitch-black existentialism and the part of him that loved the literal time he was born into even with all the horror, the horror. Not least because of all the characters lodging in his mind, sharing the raft, thinking for themselves, with their stories and quirks, and glories and destinies, their marvellous ways of sizing up the big bad world, finding ever more ingenious ways to tame it, to get it on side. All that history to understand, all that past to study, a past full of life.

Since the beginning of 2020, everyone has become another, as Arthur Rimbaud proclaimed he was in order to become modern before the modern, and the Beats and various fugitives followed through, and then Bob Dylan took it over, giving the idea plenty of voice, of voices, poet as exile and witness, as entertainer specialising in the fleeting moments of liberation. Everyone is extremely different to how they were before Covid-19 interrupted things, becoming part of some cruel, unthinking intention to rewrite history and our role in it. We have become another, but not like Rimbaud, as some conscious anti-social transformation of personality and his own destiny, nor through the gadgets and mechanisms of social media; we were forced into this being another, into separation, into the isolated, locked-down self, adrift amongst many, with all the anxieties that came with it, with having all the freedom in the world promised by the controlling technological companies and suddenly more or less no freedom at all. Access to numerous worlds, and somehow enslaved at the same time.

Dylan's teeming, tumultuous, apprehensive, wildly paranoid songs about lost souls, mercurial impulses and the ghosts of ideas, these constant dramas of instability and insatiability, smashed together blasted boogie and the last human on earth, Lord Byron as he depicts himself in 'Darkness'. (An apocalyptic vision of Byron's from 1816, when an astronomer had predicted that the sun would burn itself out by the end of the year. Swirling ash and strange weather caused by an erupting volcano in Indonesia had crossed north-eastern America and northern Europe, bringing gloom and cold, increasing darkness and an unnerving drop in global temperatures. Panic ensued, a general sense this might lead to the end of the world, and 1816 became known as 'the year without summer'.

Byron's poem emerges from the New Testament, out of Matthew 24:29, depicting a blackened-out sun, where Jesus predicts the apocalyptic events leading up to and during the time He returns to Earth. Jesus describes twelve signs that will occur before He returns to save humanity from destruction. There will be false Christs; there will be wars and rumours of wars; there will be famines; there will be pestilence and widespread diseases; there will be earthquakes in new or different locations; there will be persecution, hatred and killings of Jewish people; there will be many people who are easily offended; there will be widespread betrayal; there will be widespread hatred; there will be many false prophets that shall deceive the masses; there will be widespread injustice, immortal behaviour, crime and unholiness; there will be a coldness or indifference to others instead of love.)

Dylan's songs didn't lose any of their power in the middle of a stunning, unexpected dress rehearsal for the apocalypse as events in 2020 refracted Byron's terrible darkness and Matthew's blunt prognosis, with the added ingredients of social media, comment boards, Google, a deranged mean-spirited leader and a remorseless, ricocheting 24-hour news cycle. He knew he hadn't been the first to have all these portentous feelings; he knew such fearful, ominous thoughts went all the way back to the apple in the garden. His most hyper-alert, acutely frantic songs had already been examining and imagining the end of the world, explaining what would happen in a world filled with so much information, division, dread, fragile self-awareness, serpentine threats and contagious violence of thought. It's why there were so many selves, all named Dylan, each with their own voice, expressing their own visions and revisions, always maintaining an interest in the world, their own take on what might have been and what has been, and what was coming, again and again.

The songs made more sense than ever in a world that overnight made no sense at all. They were, apart from anything else, a response, a reaction, to an angry planet filled with souls made aware of possibility, seeing it all quivering on the edge of being destroyed. Whatever else they were about, and another list of one hundred is needed here, starting with imaginative freedom and ending with being in the middle of a nervous breakdown (or something), they were about endurance and celebration in the face of catastrophe.

If you don't believe me, time for a playlist of his apocalyptic songs about the apocalypse by someone who on his own could fit into a musical genre called apopalyptic – apocalyptic pop songs sharing themes with Biblical texts, the impending abolition or maybe purging of life as we know it, the immediacy of death and the final judgment, a strong emphasis on a moment of truth or vision, a moment in the here and now in which choice and commitment are demanded. Dylan with electric guitar and leather boots pointing the way addressed the listener just as the Bible did the reader, in heightened language, with esoteric symbolism simmering underneath the surface, urging a yes-or-no answer to the views and actions of the revelation being described. The intense confessions and bitter weariness of the blues were tangled up with stern, stormy Biblical tones, shuffling one with the other to explore a dark future. Dylan issued commands and threats in order to make people realise the urgency of the situation, where their very souls were threatened by a modern world that just kept getting more modern, and prosperity and convenience were just as likely to lead to insanity as to any kind of paradise. If you don't watch it, sang the skinny touchy pop prophet under a radiant halo of hair on commercial records you bought in your local shop, you might be lost forever in the apocalyptic wasteland. Dylan used pop songs very deliberately to 'lift the veil'. He did not come as potential saviour. He just had a point of view, cynical, soulful, with a nothing-to-lose truthfulness.

For Dylan, the waters were always dangerously rising, the river was within us, heavenly bodies were shaken, and sensing the torment of others he was always handing out warnings. You could use a Shakespeare quote as an epigraph to the playlist, 'When sorrows come, they come not single spies, but in battalions': 'Highway 61 Revisited', 'A Hard Rain's a-Gonna Fall', 'All Along The Watchtower', 'This Wheel's on Fire', 'High Water (for Charley Patton)', 'Stuck Inside of Mobile with the Memphis Blues Again', 'Everything is Broken', Let Me Die in My Footsteps', 'The Groom's Still Waiting at the Altar', 'Slow Train', 'Tryin' to Get to Heaven', 'Talkin' World War III Blues', 'Gates of Eden', 'It's Alright, Ma (I'm Only Bleeding)', 'Desolation Row', 'Thunder on the Mountain', 'Ain't Talkin'', 'Trouble', 'Band of the Hand (It's Hell Time Man!)', 'Things Have Changed', 'Drifter's Escape', 'Not Dark Yet', 'Pay in Blood'. The songs were ahead of the action, which is what made them so radically exotic and spectacularly inscrutable, so above and beyond their time, in the first place. Dylan's electrifying energies, the multiple consciousness of his songs and his relentless performing of them were translated during tense infected times in 2020 into a concatenation of contemporary experience, an expression of complex urgency, even as they were pieced together using steady, well-worn traditional forms like country, Irish outlaw balladry, folk, gospel, blues and old-time rock and roll.

But he understood as a scholar and a ruffian a lot about roots, about the background and sources of the music he used at the heart of his music; he understood the source of country music in the oral tradition, the urgent gossip and local philosophy, of immigrants from Europe, especially the Scots Irish who populated the Appalachians in eastern Tennessee, paralleling plantation blues and Protestant church music. He knew that the stories begun back then still needed to be honourably told in ways that still made sense once there had been Pete Seeger, Bertolt Brecht, Little Richard, the Beatles and Nina Simone – hell, even during and after the kind of lacerating crisis that could only have landed in the twenty-first century. He knew so much, as though he had actually been in St Louis at the time, about how pianists in backrooms of bars along the Mississippi joined snatches of tunes and voices into a single composition, the stitched-together snatched-together 'rags' being energetically produced as a reflection of the moods and floods of the river becoming jolting tunes that would wash up into early jazz.

And then he released an album of original songs that no-one saw coming, just to keep up to speed, as if to indirectly confirm how his songs beating with the heart of the past were somehow from the future. He was still on the time travels he began at twenty, down the road from when he was a teenager, but now approaching eighty, having slipped around the back way into the twenty-first century, regularly taking cover in the songs of others, his memories of Sinatra, his own repertoire that he liked to play around with, even turn inside out.

*A new Bob Dylan album! As if there wasn't enough weird stuff happening in the world,* the bystander, the critic, was bound to say. He took the opportunity to pounce like a philosopher, an undefeated champion, with a prophet's warning cry, on the state of the world.

The new or perhaps old-as-new, even old-as-time, songs sounded like he'd known what was coming sixty years later back in 1961, when for the sake of this particular history, this particular, personal documenting of his routes from one place to another, he started to find his voice, or at least was finding a first voice, deciding how to sing, a first way of being heard outside his own head. There was already a hell of a lot going on inside his head, and then in one voice after another. He was hearing voices, and soon so would we.

Before he officially had an understanding he had a kind of understanding. He was already blurring some lines, between rural folk, the talking blues, western swing and classic blues, mixing up an elastic social conscience, 'woe is me' and cracking up one way or another, switching them all around, coming up with something only he knew. Playing tricks on tradition. Moving the blues somewhere else, moving folk and country somewhere else, moving a combination of the blues, country and folk and his particular thing somewhere else, and continuing to do so until he turned up in 2020 with where he'd gone forty, fifty, sixty years after he first emerged with this jaunty, tormented, inside-out knowledge of storytelling folk, confessional blues and his own instincts, and how to take them to other places, again and again, twisting and turning, his blues, his folk, his inventions, expanding his ability to sing in different styles so that he could sing different types of songs and keep them true to themselves, 'til death them do part.

And as much as there was a new voice to contend with on this new collection of songs, yet another addition, all of his other voices came along for the ride, to round things up, a ghostly choir of Dylans showing how, wherever he'd been since the early 1960s, footfalls echoing in the memory, as though he was remembering all the actions and reactions as composer and performer that had brought him that far, whatever style he'd adopted, he was always where we found ourselves in 2020 – on the edge of a cliff, where there is no secure foothold, and we're menaced by monsters and fairy lights. Risking enchantment of one sort or another.

Interesting times, you might say.

There was of course plenty of shining, dreamt, interconnecting history written into *Rough and Rowdy Ways* – into songs, not textbooks – and much of that history was about Dylan himself. The sort of history that doesn't repeat itself but that does rhyme. Written by someone who if he does believe in anything believes that we are what we remember, what we know. The less we remember, the less we know about ourselves, the less we are. There was his telling of the history of the human spirit and in there as well a history of his spirit, which just happened to be retrospective and prophetic.

It works if it is the final Bob Dylan album of original songs, one end to his history, the final memories of a survivor – even if it isn't – because it can easily be read as containing all of Dylan in one place, and actually that does include whatever else is to come; all his working, thinking, writing, playing, keeping score and singing washes up inside it, as though every time he made a record, made a change in style and appearance, followed a new direction, modified the myth, extended the terms and conditions, corrected a few defects, picked up a new set of clues and found a new voice, there it was at the edge of vision, already taking shape. And as it took shape, all his other albums along the way took shape around it. These songs were always following him as he wrote, rehearsed, recorded and sometimes performed the songs that made him what he was, sung not necessarily to win the applause of the moment – although that would be nice – but to be a possession for all time.

For someone who began all over again and again, the surprise album contained a sense of all those beginnings and was still a beginning in itself. All those early sparks, the first flickers of an idea, those kernels of thoughts as he learnt his craft, learnt from experience and earned his spurs, had ended up here, all worked out and fully grown. It becomes a good place to make some relatively final judgement about his recording career, as long as you're ready to admit it could all change again.

It exists as a natural continuation of where he's been and what he's seen, but it is also a panoptic summary of his moves and allegiances, his guide to navigating perilous times. It turns out that for someone who was always in the process of changing and replacing himself, always keen on releasing his greatest self, he hadn't thrown away any parts of himself. He could piece himself together as in 'My Own Version of You' where he pieces together a history of sense and a history of some sort of creature, a new species, an ex-lover or someone he's got his eye on, maybe even an extreme entertainer who also happened to be drenched in sticky history and who's written a song about history as a document of civilisation and a document of barbarism with a twist of the heretic.

He reports that he can see the history of the whole human race, and it's a horror story, it's a fantasy, it's a constant emergency situation, and fools rush in, and some people you can trust and some you really can't, but you do what you can to improve your mind, make the acquaintance of Marx and Freud. Things can get sour, but you've got to laugh, even if it all ends in tears.

As Dylan shows in 'Murder Most Foul', history goes backwards and forwards at the same time, dust swirling in the air, rising up and rising down, and that's what happens to Dylan on *Rough and Rowdy Ways* – as he comes to the end of the trail, you can sense the very earliest Dylan moving into view, Bobby as a boy coming to his senses, drawing his own map, wondering how history might remember him, even though he wouldn't have been able to put it in so many words. You can hear a faint trace of Dylan beginning to use his first voice just as in those early days you could hear deep down a phantom anticipation of the voice he would have sixty years later, two different ways of finding out what he's got to work with as he looks around him and looks back, wondering what we are left with after all that's happened.

On *Rough and Rowdy Ways* you hear where he is more or less around now, in some sort of current moment, and you hear overlapping phantoms of himself that have come along for the ride, and every life he's brushed against, as he stands at various points of his life checking in on how he's been keeping body and soul together and getting on with his mind as time just keeps speeding up even as on occasion it seems to slow down. You hear him as he has sounded in every year he's been singing, every year he's made a record, and you hear him at the end of his life, two decades into the twenty-first century, sounding connected to when his voice was first recorded, first taken into time, at seventeen, thirteen years after the Second World War.

# EIGHT

## ON THE THRESHOLD

His voice can be heard for the first time in 1958. It's still very much a prehistoric voice, not yet his first, a voice on the way to other voices, the voice of someone in the process of working himself out, changing names, changing faces and the story of who he was and where he came from.

He's messing about with a tape recorder with a Hibbing schoolfriend, John Bucklen, son of an amateur musician, from the other side of the tracks, a friend you could call close at the time. They spend time at each other's houses, in John's house listening to records on his sister Ruth's record player. Jamming with John, Bob hunched over the family's white piano, he creeps closer to writing his own material, sampling chunks of songs and adding his own ideas.

For a while, before they drifted apart, their pop-fuelled fantasies were intimately intertwined. They were both part of temporary groups – the Rockets, the Satintones, as if a name change might make a difference to their ability to attract attention, even a star spotter. Bob was the more eager of the two, getting them onto TV in Duluth, not afraid to hustle a little. If he didn't hustle, nothing was going to happen.

They would mime in front of a mirror to 'Be-Bop-a-Lula', leather-clad Gene Vincent's reconfiguring of 'Heartbreak

Hotel' with a bit of Carl Perkins, wearing Vincent's signature blue denim cap. It was as though this was how James Dean would sound if he could sing, more than Elvis, Vincent's immediate inspiration, because he possessed something more menacing, tense and melancholy. The voice was tough, tender, sad, swooping, livid, his eyes lifted to the gods as he suffered real pain from his crippled leg.

In 1956, rock and roll was starting up, knocking obstacles out of the way, but the business was still dominated by bland, almost pulseless, music stuck in the past, by the sexless lulling ballads of Pat Boone, Patti Page and Perry Como, with voices so smooth and straight they went everywhere but important. Vincent could handle a sweet, luscious ballad, just like Elvis could, both adding a sprinkle of carnal gothic romance, the dead-cold edges of the truth, and this eased his way onto the radio, but it was the gaunt, driven punk that got under Bob and John's skin.

'Be-Bop-a-Lula' had the aching, insinuating sound of 'Heartbreak Hotel' and the idea of the syllables of the title seemed related to the 'a-wop-bop-a-loo-bop-a-wop-bam-boom' of 'Tutti Frutti' (all three songs released in 1956), the transmission of a secret code straight through to those in the know like John and Bob, teenagers in tune with the slang, with words put together for fun and something deeper, which made them feel they belonged to something all their own. Hit rock and roll records started to create slang from the very beginning, the kind of slang created by the downtrodden and marginalised, a language of the streets, every new generation of susceptible, identity-anxious adolescents getting its own slang.

Bob and John taped themselves as though they had their

own radio show, a few minutes of song and talk and larking about. The self-conscious but revealing chat between Bob and John gives some detail of how Bob was paying close attention to music that was shrewdly critical and analytical, and also approaching music with a sense of play – an attitude, both formal and informal, serious and light, that would make it into his approach to writing songs.

As it should be in a story that can often seem written from above and beyond to be the perfect, incomplete beginning to the life of Bob Dylan, possibly based on the truth, the choice of songs was unusual, the kind that would appear on his *Theme Time* radio show, and the conversation had some strong knowledge and opinion from Bob, who was definitely in charge. They tried out hard-working Bronx doowop duo Robert and Johnny's 'We Belong Together', a minor pop hit around the time of the Hibbing recording, lilting midway between dreamy and dreary and later sung by Richie Valens, and 'Buzz, Buzz, Buzz' by the doowop vocal group the Hollywood Flames – who'd been the Turks, the Jets, the Satellites, the Pelicans and the Sounds, seeking their lucky name – which reached number eleven in the US pop charts in 1957, and which naturally begins 'Buzz, buzz, buzz goes the bumble bee'. Great pop songs were often novelty songs, because everything had to be new, trivially or transcendentally, to keep up with the livid new living pace of America itself.

There was a lot of Little Richard in Bob and John's bedroom show, because the year before he'd had six chart songs in the USA, making American pop music harder, funkier, blacker, queerer, despite having had to tone down, even turn into a vaudevillian cartoon, the illicit desires, the dandiness, the black speech patterns in order to break into the mainstream. What he didn't tone down was his physical dynamism, enough to subvert a racially skewed cultural landscape, and make visceral contact with teenagers like Bobby Zimmerman yet to make their minds up about race, gender and sexuality.

On the mad-packed dead-on two minutes of 'Jenny, Jenny', which Bob and John vainly attempted to capture, Richard's all banshee speed, blast and squeal, melted down by his own energy, bringing freakish carnival hoopla to rock and roll, the carnival a place where there was no difference between black and white, man and woman, even up and down. The railroad rhythms that had underpinned American music in the twentieth century, putting the percussion in work songs, spirituals, folk, blues, jazz, bluegrass and country, were now racing away with themselves, chasing Richard's unruly, emboldened urges, so that the song can only finish by crashing to a shattered, pleasured end. John didn't think Bob had done it fast enough. Bob was convinced he had. This swift, blurred first manifestation of a Bob Dylan voice – if we imagine in his head he'd made up his mind about a new name – includes a het-up tribute to Little Richard.

Bob talked about Little Richard's 'expression'. When you sing, he said, you gotta have some kind of expression. He was asked to give his reasons – in under twenty-five minutes, which suggests John was used to hearing Bob give some long know-it-all lectures on music – why rhythm and blues was his favourite music. It's something he couldn't explain, but when it's good, you get chills up your spine, when it's good you want to cry. He talked about how all the big popular stars of the day got their songs from the little groups, about Ricky Nelson copying

Elvis, but Elvis copied too – he copied Clyde McPhatter, he copied Little Richard, he copied the Drifters. John wasn't so sure: 'Name four songs that Elvis copied from others.' 'Rip It Up', 'Long Tall Sally', 'Ready Teddy' and one Bob couldn't quite remember. Bob was definitely a Little Richard guy.

In the 1959 Hibbing High School yearbook, Bob Zimmerman, not quite yet Dylan, trying it out a little on John to see how it fitted, maybe getting the pronunciation wrong, wrote that his ambition was 'to join Little Richard'. (Other 'clubs' he wished to join were the Social Studies Club and the Latin Club.) He'd been collaborating with other musicians he found in Hibbing, including one who had written a couple of years before in his yearbook entry that he wanted 'to be another Elvis'.

Ric Kangas was a couple of years older, and also had ambition to be a songwriter. In 1957, he too had tried a little amped-up rock and roll in the grandiose high school theatre, looking for a reaction with a new Elvis song, 'All Shook Up', written by Otis Blackwell, who'd also loaded up Elvis with 'Don't Be Cruel' and 'Return to Sender', and supplied Jerry Lee Lewis his outrageous raging theme tune for tortured sinners, 'Great Balls of Fire'. Ric and Bob, an unlikely pair, before they drifted apart, drove around town in Ric's Ford, drank, chased girls, played a few talent shows and parties, failed an audition or two, and shared a liking for Hank Williams and the usual new rock and roll arrivals, while Bob introduced Ric to more of his new finds, including the Coasters and Jimmy Reed. In May 1959 in Ric's bedroom, they started fiddling about with a monster-sized reel-to-reel tape recorder and a pretty good Shure microphone, and the three songs Dylan/Zimmerman performed became one of the earliest Dylan recordings, amongst them a possible first sighting of an original song, 'When I Got Troubles'. It became the earliest recording of his to make it onto an official release when it appeared as track number one of Volume 7 of the Bootleg Series, the soundtrack to the Martin Scorsese documentary film *No Direction Home*.

A single voice emerges out of the void, ready to move in all directions, where anthemic political songs are sung as love songs, love songs sung as ghost stories, folk songs sung as soul songs, pop songs sung as nineteenth-century novels, country songs sung as dreams, blues songs sung as postmodern novels, cabaret songs sung as bluegrass, mystery songs sung as hymns, ballads sung as garage punk.

The last track on the soundtrack – featuring music not in the actual film – is from the Manchester Free Trade Hall – remarkably, a mere seven years later, in 1965, the other side of a few switches in style, a few changes of voice, a few contradictions, a taking on of history – when he's being called a Judas. He hurls himself into the maelstrom and snarling vengeance of 'Like a Rolling Stone', jumping off a cliff because in those years since he taped some tentative teenage musical sketches in Hibbing, he'd grown some wings, he'd learnt some moves, he could hear the whirl and roar of the crowd in the vortex of life around him.

Back in time, on the ground, building up some courage, he hesitantly crept through the ninety-second 'When I Got Troubles', singing low to himself as if he might be just strumming some favourite Delta blues chords and adding the odd line he'd taken from somewhere, trying to add a little grit to what is more a distracted if rough-around-the-edge croon than a raw blues moan. It's the perfect first sighting of the sound of his voice, because it's next to nothing, which means you could read whatever you want into it.

There's no clear sense of where this original song came from, although it will have come from somewhere. Maybe he'd heard the Sister Rosetta Tharpe version of the blues standard 'Trouble in Mind', written by Richard M. Jones, the producer of the beautifully transformative Hot Five and Hot Seven recordings made between 1925 and 1928 led by Louis Armstrong. Maybe it all started with Charles Brown's 'Trouble Blues', or Muddy Waters' 'I Be's Troubled' or 'Trouble No More', evoking the basic themes of loss and sorrow. He took the word 'trouble' into his song, and little else, thinking there should be more blues songs with 'trouble' in the title, the perfect word for a blues song. Songs about spiritual and physical weariness, about feeling troubled and wanting to escape the present, nourished the blues. The only response to the suffering was to leave, to travel, to dream of a better life.

He'd use 'trouble' a few times down the line: just 'Trouble' on its own on 1981's *Shot of Love*, the third album in what became known as his born-again trilogy – although shot through with the first signs of a return to secularity – the song imagining a world, a universe, without God. He thinks of the trouble that would cause. God likes to cause trouble, whether he's around or not.

Thinking that this new sectarian, pompous-seeming Dylan meant that he had changed one too many times – had over-preached – many fans imagined a world without him. Their free spirit, the eternal rebel and emancipator of worlds, had slipped into the dark ages. His fans were suddenly his enemy, even if he did say he loved and forgave them. 'I told you the times they are a-changing and they did,' he told one audience. 'I said the answer was blowing in the wind and it was. I'm telling you now Jesus is coming back and He is! And there is no other way of salvation.' His modern, absurdist, existential consciousness seemed derailed by an orthodox old-world conscience, he stopped freely moving back and forth between the two, which didn't seem very rock and roll, didn't seem very Dylan. At least, not very Dylan if you weren't paying attention.

He got into trouble for suddenly trusting so frankly the word of Jesus Christ, for surely getting on the wrong train; Jesus promised his disciples three things – that they would be completely fearless, absurdly happy and in constant trouble. Dylan relished trouble; he lied about his background, he abandoned social consciousness, he turned electric, he seemed to be his own god, he dropped out, he went missing, he turned to Christ. There was always somewhere and something to turn to, often just as he was at his most beloved, his most acclaimed, that would give him something to fight against. Trouble couldn't be avoided. You either went looking for trouble, or it came looking for you.

Maybe it's something he picked up from the hardy folk in Hibbing; tough situations build strong people in the end. Some wondered what his poor mother thought of his conversion to Christianity, a friend remarking she was probably sitting shiva for him at home. Allen Ginsberg once asked Dylan's mother what she thought about it. She said, well, he sang about Jesus, but they came from a neighbourhood where everybody liked Jesus. 'I like Jesus too.' He was a tough, determined, thoughtful Jew with an extremely sensitive moral compass, probably too sensitive. Dylan burning up, or burnt out, taking it seemed to a new faith was something else she didn't want to worry about, and in a way just another part of his take on show business. His performance was based on being born again, and again, and again, out of the America he believed in.

Perhaps his turning to Jesus could be seen by long-suffering relatives as a positive move away from the chaos there could be in his life, around the time a major relationship fell apart, or when he got seduced by the various forms of excess that came with fame. He was reading the Bible now not so much to get lines and ideas for songs but to get some guidance. 'Not in carousing and drunkenness, not in sexual excess and lust, not in quarrelling and jealousy. Rather, put on the Lord Jesus Christ, and make no provision for the desires of the flesh' (Romans 13:13–14). 'There is a way which seems right to a man, but its end is the way of death' (Proverbs 14:12).

During his years of religious imperialism, as the '60s freak turned Jesus freak, musing more than usual on the fiery word of God, Dylan still believed he knew what he was doing. He still believed he existed; he was just examining magic, faith, the mystical and ultimately music from a different point of view, using the sort of Biblical sources and imagery he always used as a poet, just a little more passionately, more dependently, less like an atheist, with more unambiguous feeling, and more appearances by the Lord, and sometimes Satan, Dylan showing a little respect for his talents. He was acknowledging the debt rock and roll owed to religion, and how Little Richard, Elvis Presley, Johnny Cash, Jerry Lee Lewis and B.B. King all attended Pentecostal services as impressionable teenagers in the 'Christ-haunted' South, watching the flamboyant, charismatic

leaders with their fiery, mysterious stage presence and swinging hymns played as though God were a cosmic hipster. The
energy of Pentecostalism gave them ideas. Religious zeal, the
flow, energy and transformation of Pentacostal ritual ecstatically generating a sense of the presence of God made it into the
bloodstream of rock music.

By the end of the 1970s, time racing forward, rock's fundamental sources seemed a long way in the past, and any notion
that there was a perverse even subversive religious element in
how rock and roll had come to be had long dissolved. Dylan
hadn't forgotten – once he knew anything he wouldn't forget
it – and his religious years connected with that as much as a
new belief.

The Bootleg Series boxed set of performances, rehearsals
and studio outtakes from that three-year missionary period was
given the title *Trouble No More*; it refocussed what at the time
was received as stolid and sanctimonious as an inevitable, valuable, even crucial part of Dylan's idiosyncratic and enigmatic
evolution, another more explicit example of Dylan starting
afresh anew, detecting and rewiring more links to American
musical tradition – in this case, gospel music, his ultimate concern perhaps more than the Gospel itself – looking for hope,
craving the miracle of regeneration, the maintaining of civilisation, in whatever form it takes. The function of prayer is not
to influence God, but rather to change the nature of the one
who prays. He's had a complicated spiritual history.

A bleak, desperate, difficult song written by Dylan actually
called 'Trouble in Mind', like the Richard M. Jones one that
Nina Simone and later Johnny Cash would end up performing,
was the first song recorded for the first album in the born-again

trilogy, *Slow Train Coming* – it didn't make the finished record, maybe because the whole song is about being at breaking point, about feeling flawed, fallen and imperfect, not the best place to start work, but you can hear it on *Trouble No More*.

His early, provisional Hibbing use of 'trouble' was spooky, faded like a precious field recording of a moment in time almost lost forever, and nothing special at the same time. He just couldn't bring himself to let go, or at that time didn't know how to, and was gently circling the idea he had any kind of serviceable blues voice, feeling his way towards the gospel structures he'd use later whether he was singing folk, blues, pop, country, rock. He knew that the blues is easy to play – as Jimi Hendrix would say later – but it's hard to feel.

He was already experimenting, trying to zero in on that elusive, fundamental feel, getting his friend to record him so he could hear himself and work himself out. But even then it wasn't just one voice; others were already beginning to circulate.

Another taped performance gets called by Ric Kangas 'The Frog Song', because it's Bob tapping into the madcap energy of Clarence 'Frogman' Henry, the light-hearted Professor Longhair and Fats Domino-influenced New Orleans-born rhythm and blues/rockabilly entertainer. His theme tune was the Louisiana stomp 'I Ain't Got No Home' where he croaked like a frog and sang in a high falsetto like, he said, a girl. He once said he started singing like a frog in school, to scare the girls. Bob's whimsical version at eighteen years old already shows he was prepared to do all sorts of maybe ugly-sounding things with his voice to inhabit a song, to tell a story, to shake up reality. It took a bit of seeking and blundering to learn.

He was learning how to hide his sources, and sometimes how to keep them in the open but completely transcend them – you don't have to necessarily conceal your thievery. It's like he knew about something Jean-Luc Godard hadn't even said yet: it's not where you take things from, it's where you take them to.

Nothing is original. He learnt to steal from anywhere that resonated with inspiration and fuelled his imagination. He devoured old films, new films, music, books, paintings, photographs, poems, dreams, random conversations, architecture, bridges, street signs, trees, clouds, bodies of water, light and shadows. He chose things to steal from that spoke directly to his soul, which is what makes his work authentic. Authenticity is invaluable; originality is non-existent.

He hadn't lived a lifetime of experience before he started writing songs that seemed to suggest he had lived a lifetime of experience. He got his experience from the experiences of others, from all the songs and books and films and poems he devoured, as though this was as real as day-to-day reality. He got his experience from objects, from the weather, from the landscape, from bumps in the night, from the personalities, passions and moods of friends, colleagues and strangers, and he took from songs and books in the same way – as if he wasn't stealing anything, just picking up experiences, combining the efforts of others, learning something else about being alive, about the idiosyncratic joy of just living. Every experience was a form of exploration. When the image is new, the world is new.

He perceived these feelings as intensely as those that first had them – perhaps they too hadn't thought of them first or experienced them for real. His experience was rooted in pure imagination, in pure sensation, places he'd never been, people he'd never seen, discoveries he'd never made, and perhaps he was one of the very first to assimilate all the stimulation and information suddenly flowing through media channels, because America had turned into another planet, and he had a mind to take it all in, process the data and interpret it all because someone needed to make sense of it all. Someone needed to preserve law and order. Life happened to give him whatever experience was the most helpful for the evolution of his own particular consciousness, his ability to impose a pattern on his experience. What are the odds…?

Don't ask me how – don't ask him how, unless you happen to get the chance – but he was ready for everything, ready as he left school to sound the depths of his own being, developing a habit of looking askew at the world, even as he just looked like an unremarkable eighteen–year–old heading to university, starting out for the first time or maybe for the millionth.

Midway between Zimmerman and Dylan, he became someone else, if this is the truth, in the summer of 1959 after graduation, working as a bus boy in the Red Apple café in the Fargo-Moorhead area on the border between Minnesota and North Dakota, about 200 miles from Hibbing. A member of the then–unknown sixteen-year-old rockabilly singer Bobby Vee's band, the Shadows – Vee, né Robert Velline, was a Fargo boy, making music with his older brothers – was in a local record shop, Sam's Record Land, and out of the blue a blue–jeaned someone with dark curly hair introduced himself as Elston Gunn, mysteriously stressing the three *n*s in Gunnn. The first name might have been his take on Elvis, and he might have spun the surname out of Judy Garland's real name, Frances Ethel Gumm, because after all she was a Minnesota girl, born in Grand Rapids, less than 40 miles from Hibbing – and her parents ran a movie theatre, like his family, so they were kind of related. The taking care of business of Elvis and the Miss Show Business of Judy.

He'd heard it said, as you do, that Vee and the boys needed a pianist, and keeping a straight face confidently mentioned he'd just been playing some shows with Conway Twitty, formerly Harold Lloyd Jenkins, named after his great uncle's favourite silent movie actor. Working at Sun Records in 1957 with Carl Perkins, Jerry Lee Lewis and Johnny Cash, needing a more marketable showbusiness name, Harold got the Conway from a town in Arkansas and the Twitty from Texas. He'd had a number-one hit in both the USA and the UK in 1958 with the doowop devotional 'It's Only Make Believe', dripping with Elvis, to the extent some thought it was Elvis using a pseudonym. Playing with Conway Twitty sounded like enough proof of 'Elston's' credentials, and why would he lie, so they auditioned him, and he actually played pretty good in the key of C. Later, they realised that was the only key he played in.

He was a funny guy, Vee liked and hired him, bought him a plaid shirt so he fitted in, paid him the $15 they were all getting. When they went to fetch him to take him to a show that night, he didn't have his own piano, as they assumed he would. He played the gig anyway on a venue piano so out of tune he ended up reduced to handclapping and a bit of sing-along, trying out another voice. He was OK, looked at home on a stage, he could have been a Shadow. In the end, he couldn't afford his own piano, they couldn't afford to pay him, he told unconvinced friends back in Hibbing he played on a minor local hit by Bobby Vee and the Shadows that sounded a little Buddy Holly and the Crickets, and Elston Gunnn faded away.

Bobby Vee had a tragic preview of the big time a few months earlier when his band helped fill in for Buddy Holly at the 3 February Winter Dance Party Tour show in Moorhead, which Buddy never made. The chartered four-seater plane that had been hired to fly Holly and fellow performers to Fargo on the way to Moorhead crashed, and he died instantly along with Ritchie Valens, the Big Bopper and the pilot, Roger Peterson – the day the music died, days after Bob Zimmerman witnessed one of Holly's final performances. It had been a gruelling tour, and cold, cramped bus journeys between venues led to musicians succumbing to flu and in one case frostbite. Holly asked for a plane so that he could avoid another cold, tiring bus trip, and it took off after midnight from Clear Lake, Iowa in freezing conditions, almost immediately crashing into a cornfield.

The Winter Dance Party Tour carried on. A local Moorhead radio station asked for local bands to help out, and young Vee and his two-week-old, unnamed high school band volunteered. Vee came up with the Shadows on that shocking night when someone asked their name before they went on stage. They played the six or so songs they knew to an audience lost in mourning thought. They didn't get paid.

A couple of years later, Bobby had a hit with the barmy, bouncy 'Rubber Ball', a formulaic song on the cusp between cute and kitsch co-written by Gene Pitney at the Brill Building in midtown Manhattan, which had become a pop song factory, peaking in the early 1960s. Bobby became a pretty, sanitised, very willing pop star in neat suit and tie, and his ripely melodic next song, 'Take Good Care of My Baby', also written at the Brill Building by Carole King and Gerry Goffin, confirmed him internationally as a polite, bright, scrubbed clean, clear-singing teen idol, the kind taking advantage of rock and roll's perfect specimen Elvis being drafted into the army and shorn Samson-like of his quiff and sideburns, his intoxicating magic powers immediately drained.

In 1962, walking through Greenwich Village, Vee saw a record sleeve in a shop window with a picture of someone he knew as Elston Gunnn. Bobby and Bob, the band brothers that never were, found themselves on opposite sides of a vast pop divide between the light and frothy and the deep and serious that Dylan was widening all the time, but always connected by an invisible thread. Sometimes, if this is true, as they got on with their separate careers, Vee's career a bouncing ball, Dylan's altering the course of music history, wherever they were in the world, wherever they were in the charts, they'd think about each other at the same time.

# NINE

## LEGEND HAS IT

After he packed away Elston Gunnn, Bob moved to Minneapolis in September to attend, more or less, the University of Minnesota during the 1959/60 school year. He arrived with the appearance of someone still snagged by the worlds of *Rebel Without a Cause*, *The Wild One* and rock and roll, wondering what else was out there in a city like Minneapolis, one of the twin cities bisected by the Mississippi River at the beginning of its journey, meandering through Minnesota's pine forests, before flowing south through nine states to the Gulf of Mexico, through the cities of St Louis, Memphis, Baton Rouge and New Orleans, the dividing line between the Eastern United States and the American West. When the river meets the ocean, its memories meet the memories of the ocean. Radio stations with a few exceptions would use the river as a dividing line for broadcast call signs, the first letter of a station's call sign a K if it was west of the Mississippi, W if it was east.

Interviewed in February 1962 on *Folksingers Choice*, a New York City radio show broadcast on WBIA, as a still obscure unusually wisecracking and fizzing folk singer a few weeks before his debut album – using the opportunity to cloud the details of his humble beginnings and add some tall tales, which included the years he skipped school to spend time with a travelling carnival – Bob Dylan said he moved to Minneapolis because it was 'about the only place you didn't have to go too far to reach the Mississippi River'.

He was sort of joking. He was beginning to produce his slippery, distracting, distancing, even playacting interview voice – which itself contained other voices and characters, the multi-self constantly shedding the past, the writer not having much to say, just watching the river flow, comfortably stuck in a limbo between reality and fiction – the voice he would pursue for a few decades, which sometimes he had trouble believing. But he was also taking it seriously. The river was calling out to be explored, one way or another. The Father of Waters, the grandest river in the world, had first been explored by the chess playing Spanish conquistador and brutal conqueror of Peru Hernando de Soto, who reaches the Mississippi in 1541, one of the first Europeans to head deep into what is now the United States. When he died a year later while searching for gold, his men buried him at night in the river to protect him from his enemies.

When Bob left Hibbing in 1959, he was heading towards the Mississippi as much as he was going to university, right at the edge of the river. On one hand, off to university was the apparent normal route for someone of his age from his family, heading out into standard, well-signposted middle-class America, and joining in with the predictable ebb and flow. On the other, it was the beginning, amongst constant beginnings, of a travelling-light trek into an America he was imagining, a world of yesterday, tomorrow and fantasy. Things already were not what they seemed. He went to university, he ended up at the Mississippi. From there, more than from the lectures, everything he needed for now could be found.

He wasn't at the right end for the Deep South source of the blues, the folk music of former slaves living in the Mississippi Delta, the interconnected secular and religious cultural patterns of thousands of African-Americans in a desperate situation, trying to survive a world that kept trying to destroy them, but he was getting closer, physically as well as psychically, to the building-block DNA of blues, gospel, soul, R&B, Little Richard, Elvis and beyond. The travels of newly freed and runaway Black men and women during the Civil War inheriting spirituals that combined African music and European hymns saw the gestation of what became the blues, and a few performers from the middle of nowhere made music that was too powerful to ever be killed off; it just kept coming until it was so successful it wasn't the blues anymore.

The river shows how everything is connected. The river is everywhere at the same time, at the source, at the mouth, at the ferry, at the current, in the ocean and in the mountains, everywhere, flowing across borders because rivers know the secret. A river pays no attention to boundaries. Water finds a way to get where its going. The water provides a constant thread of connection and dependency. The river keeps the imagination flowing.

He was moving closer to the river where down south emerged the sole bluesmen, wandering songsters who could travel and play anywhere as long as they had a guitar and a harmonica, where the early musicians with their infectiously captivating wild notes and tales of woe accompanied travelling doctors, musical companies, comedians, magicians and circuses. He could slip into their slipstream in his imagination, even if he didn't look the part, just to see where things go. This was what he was studying, to keep on flowing, to think like a river, to change like a river, widening and deepening, sometimes eddying back on himself, bursting his banks when there was too much life in him, sometimes drying up from lack of rain. The river moves at its own pace, and sometimes it may have no direction.

How lovely and how strange a river is, fugitive and elusive, an unbreakable stream of consciousness, a magic, moving, living part of the very earth itself, always changing and always on the move, always flowing, always different, always there, and he'd follow the Mississippi, one of the world's great rivers, like the Nile and the Amazon, flowing as freely as it did, coursing through the land and ploughing a valley of his own. You keep following your own way.

He moved into the Sigma Alpha Mu Fraternity on the university campus and made a few liberal arts classes, but he was searching for different sorts of information and stimulation and looked for his own unofficial classes, his own improvised centres of learning, which meant looking for like-minded souls and the locations they inhabited, to continue the inexplicable connectedness he'd been making with places, people, music, art, ideas and entertainment. Almost as soon as he'd moved in, he'd be making his way back home after a night out seeking sustenance just as other students were getting ready for class. In his own way, he was studying hard.

His fraternity house was not far from where University Avenue crossed what was then Highway 61, another great symbol of how America constantly moves into itself and leaves behind a trail of ruins and monuments. He was right there where the highway crossed the Mississippi, which put him closer to the centre of his obsessions. The road is a place of endless possibility, but the moments on the road are always transient in nature.

Known as the Blues Highway because of the blues musicians born and living along its routes, with the southern half connecting Memphis to New Orleans, Highway 61 ran 1,699 miles from New Orleans to Duluth through regions and cities making up a key part of American cultural consciousness, and then on high cliffs along the lake towards the Canadian border. The northern end now to the north of Minneapolis, it was part of a numbered highway system linking the whole nation, leading to unity between north and south and allowing people unable to afford trains to travel wherever they wanted. An escape from southern segregation, it enabled migrants from the Mississippi Delta and below to journey north via Memphis to Chicago, one highway away from 61, and bring the blues with them. Cultural significance moves along the highway because of the travelling musicians, Muddy Waters, Howlin' Wolf, B. B. King, stranded no more, spreading the word, their verbal rhyme play, their inheritance of west African trickster folktales, the complaints of souls boiling over with bitterest anguish. Chicago became another home for the blues, waving its sadness like a battle flag, absorbing the dust and sun of the south, electrifying its sorrows and unspeakable memories.

Bob in Hibbing, and then in Minneapolis, was at the wrong end of Highway 61, but not in his mind. The blues started in some field, in some plantation, in some prison, in some mind, some imagination, some trembling soul, on some sweltering road, and it got mixed up with jazz, gospel, church, country and rock and roll, and it started in his mind, and got mixed up with his music, giving it tartness and irony, authority and tenacity, a respect for the force of life, for life itself. He's part of Highway 61, which cuts through American music, running alongside the great river, it's part of him, it ran all around and through him as he grew up, into his voices, into his guitar playing, his harmonica, his early records, his later records, into the very nerve centre of the blues, which is connected to his own central nervous system. Hibbing is just a road trip away, Minneapolis just a river ride away, from the music that soaked America with the blues, soaked the rest of the world, helping him see how catastrophe and celebration, joy and pain sit side by side.

As he made up some stories that made him seem more from the southern end of the Mississippi and Highway 61 than the northern, he'd claim he'd travelled with some of these blues travellers, he'd been anointed with their warrior energy, seen them play live in Chicago when he was eighteen, nineteen, and in his mind he had, and as far as he was concerned that seemed as real as anything. His evasive, far-fetched version of events, reflecting his fantasies, which felt as legitimate as day-to-day life, certainly made him seem more interesting – to himself – than any normal tales of high school and family life.

There are blues songs written about Highway 61, by Big Joe Williams, by Sunnyland Slim, and one by Mississippi Fred McDowell, '61 Highway', imagining that the southern end is so rough and unpaved, even the Greyhound buses don't run there. The south is different from the north. It's behind in many ways. The only way to get out of the Delta is on the back of a horse.

There was no chance Dylan wasn't going to create his own Highway 61 myth, not so much because he was influenced by the blues, but because he knew he could do something with the tunes and tone that made it his own, because being without being is blue, and it wasn't so much about black and white as tragedy and comedy, it wasn't so much a case of breaking the chains of slavery as breaking through the constant negative hassle of everyday existence.

'Highway 61 Revisited' is the title song of his sixth album, released in 1965, where Dylan, still generally seen as some sort of a folk singer, one who led protest marches at that, even if he wouldn't be seen alive at one, didn't play the blues as some shallow white commercialised dilution, or even an energised, glamorised tribute. He looked for where the blues would be if it was still evolving and shifting shape, connected to all the books he'd read and remembered and heard and crammed into his head. He wasn't pretending to be black; more than anything he was pretending to be himself, because we are what we pretend to be, and the blues was part of that.

He was travelling at a hundred miles an hour, feeling he could scrawl his name across the face of the world, racing within a few months from *Bringing It All Back Home* – split into an acoustic side and an electric side, where he began to have searing, post-protest pop hits with 'Subterranean Homesick Blues' – to *Highway 61 Revisited*, overtaking those that had made him put his foot on the accelerator, especially the Beatles and the Stones, adding rock to folk so that what he did was now folk rock, knocking the folk off so that it was just rock, and then following so many omens, hunches, signs, responding so instinctively to the flux of the world, he broke out of it being rock before anyone else even had a chance to fully see where he'd got to and what he was up to. Even at the speed he was moving, trying to keep up with himself, he kept receiving new information about how to proceed, so he was constantly changing his mind about where he was and who he was, sometimes it seems midway through a song, even half-way through a line, pursuing the twisted currents of his thoughts.

The people he was working with at the time, seeing this blur of activity in the form of a musician, tried their best to keep up with him, mostly hoping for the best – which is just as he likes it. It's those who sometimes don't have an official role in the studio as a track is recorded, those who end up on a track much to their surprise, sometimes not even playing their instrument of choice, whose contribution to a song often ends up being for Dylan the element that elevates it above the ordinary, that nudges it a little closer to that near-impossible sound he hears in his head, the sound he remembers when he first heard the blues, hillbilly, folk and rock and roll records he loved, a sound that may well not have been there in the first place.

He often can't explain what he's after, not even when it happens, and it tends to happen by chance as musicians and colleagues try to understand his mood, his movement, his inner workings. He never quite gets to that sound in his head, but the search for it is compulsive. The search is what drives the endeavour, even when sometimes it feels he's had enough. The search remains his task, which keeps him on the road.

He was imagining a blues that kept evolving and absorbing influences from the here, there and everywhere he was making his way through, refracting the changing nature of its hybrid-ised beginnings, its original complex mutation, rather than acting as though the changes that made the blues in the first place, from a collection of sources that were physical and meta-physical, technical and emotional, musical and historical, sonic and psychological had come to a halt, frozen in time. His blues, his folk, his rock and roll, his country was never simply playing the music like most others; it was always strained through his inflamed imagination, even if it then worked its way back into what the music then became. By making his own particular imagination, his own particular Mississippi River and Highway 61 part of the source material of these particular genres, he hit on something and became part of their history, an integral part of their dynamic.

Dylan's 'Highway 61 Revisited', sung on the recorded version with a fierce calm, a detached raucousness, with sirens blaring, like they did on the highway when he was a kid, makes its way through the history of everything, including not least his own place on the road, with the history of everything he was compiling in his head. It motors from his birthplace down to the start of the American music that he connects with from his time and place.

Bessie Smith died in a car crash on Highway 61. Robert Johnson sold his soul to the devil at the crossroads between Highway 61 and Highway 49. Elvis grew up in a housing project on the Memphis stretch. These are the facts, but Dylan had other ones in mind, some of which were nothing of the sort, and there are facts to come after the song was written that the song seemed to be heading straight towards: Martin Luther King would be fatally shot in a motel in between the Mississippi and Highway 61. Long stretches of the road are empty, forlorn, as if in mourning for what has gone missing.

People left, creating a ghostly beauty after they'd gone. Some remain, yearning for a more vibrant past, but reluctant to abandon the place called home.

The song begins with an attitude – all over the album it comes from – that it will begin wherever it wants, so because the Highway was pretty much the beginning for him, then pretty much it is the beginning of everything. 'Revisited' begins with the beginning, with 'In the beginning', with Genesis, with Adam and Eve, God talking with Abraham, Abraham the name of Dylan's father, Abraham sacrificing his son Isaac, as if hallucinogens triggered religion in the first place, and ends with the end, with politicians gambling with nuclear war, inviting an inferno, bringing on the end of the world as a twentieth-century entertainment event, featuring a cameo from Satan, playing his own games, Robert Johnson's soul safely filed away.

It's a road of opportunity, because it takes you to places of inspiration, but it's a road where anything goes, where fights are fought, lives ruined and dirty stuff happens, hate and pain, folly and bewilderment, accidents and arguments, hurt and humiliation, like a road to hell. It's a road that will take you places, but be careful what you wish for. Be careful what you pretend to be. Our fate cannot be taken away from us.

All of this happened in Bob Dylan's head, filled with pieces of what he remembered, madness and dream, anxiety as the dizziness of freedom, so it happens on Highway 61. Which in the end is just a song he's written, where he's the great plot twist, because he's the one making it up, he's put himself in the story, as an observer, as a reporter, bearing witness, taking the stand, studying motives, sending a letter of intent, because one word led to another, as it always must, and it's another of his songs that is about words as much as anything else, and what connection they may or may not have with your real thoughts, and it's about someone dealing with a life amidst ghostly incidents, a life that's all it's ever going to be, if that.

By the time he wrote the song, he'd travelled the whole highway, metaphorically, rearranged it a few times, and revisited it as a place that can take you everywhere, make you see further, realise that fear is the main source of superstition, and one of the main sources of cruelty, and to conquer fear is the beginning of wisdom.

As he arrived in Minneapolis in 1959, he was still on some kind of schedule, building his confidence, checking in with serendipity, thumbing lifts in his mind, close to the real Highway, closer to where it was in his head. It's a tricky thing to map, but that's the point.

Elvis was in the army, Buddy was dead, Little Richard was renouncing rock and roll as the devil's music, lowering the tempo and slipping back into church, asking God for forgiveness for his demonic music. The Russian launch of Sputnik in 1957 was a clear sign of the apocalypse he had helped cause, a message from God that wanted him to turn his back on rock and roll. Music had been moving so fast, it had to be moving somewhere else, rock and roll already a thing of the past. Dylan was already beginning to chase sound like it was going out of fashion.

He was in Minneapolis for a reason, and within a matter of weeks, he found it, an acoustic guitar now part of his travelling equipment, because a piano was too much trouble to take with him on the road, and his electric guitar meant he needed a band around him. Before he famously went electric in 1965, he went acoustic in 1959.

An acoustic guitar meant he could find a venue, of which in a university town there are plenty, and just get up and play, and it made him a folk singer, which can also mean a blues singer, any kind of singer, of his own songs and the songs of others, which very quickly started to bleed into each other. The revelatory moment was when he heard in the sound booth at some record shop *Odetta Sings Ballads and Blues*, a couple of years after its release in 1957 – the acoustic debut album by the regal, operatically trained Odetta, twenty-six years old, born deep at the beginning of the Depression, during the repressive Jim Crow era, using just the one name well before Cher, Prince or Beyoncé. The album had the ornate, opinionated power and force it was dangerous for a black woman to have at the time, at any time, especially one wearing her hair cut short into a natural Afro, but she raised herself above enduring, menacing racial realities and existed on a different, timeless plane, where the songs rooted in devastating black grief were about and for everyone.

He heard her on his particular Highway 61, he might even have come across her in 1960 when she passed through town and delivered some words of encouragement to the eager fan, when he was young enough and tender enough to feel he'd been given a sign. Hearing her, he recognised a fellow musical historian, learning about music by playing it, someone else theatrically putting themselves together from blues, jazz, gospel and folk, but also arias, art songs and lieder, as though Mahler and Muddy Waters were walking through the hard rain hand in hand, white euphoria merging with black realism. She effortlessly combined black and white traditions without compromising either and she had a delicately dynamic, dynamically delicate way of playing the guitar that got called 'the Odetta strum', which made him think it was all he needed as part of his performance. As though creating a template he would follow on his debut, her debut album included spirituals, blues, prison songs, lullabies, slave songs and sea shanties. When Bob the discriminating cosmic receiver craving comprehension hears something that makes a connection, he immediately thinks of a way he can use what he hears, how it will fit into what he wants to sound and be like.

Her voice helped him realise he could have a voice, even if he wasn't trained like she was – in fact, restrained by the pretty, repetitive exercises she was compelled to practise, she broke out of her training into something entirely her own, enabling her to move through raw, rougher styles without leaving herself behind. She'd got a voice that's like no other voice, almost too much at times, crashing down from the heavens, mighty, wounded and unconventional, because the opera singer she'd have trouble becoming because of the colour of her skin turned to singing songs that emerged out of the fight against racism and a resistance to the financially exploitative and predatory culture of the time, articulating the fury and frustration she felt, the anger and helplessness. It was a voice that said in all sorts of ways: *I will be heard*. It would be heard because the voices that inspired and encouraged her needed to be heard.

The classical music she was singing as a teenager in the end had nothing to do with her life; she started singing what she called 'liberation songs', channelling the pain and perseverance of her ancestors and peers, challenging the insidious power structure even when she was a nobody, fighting for justice and equality. She used song to teach and preach in a way that meant she became a vital voice in the folk movement of the late 1950s featuring Woody Guthrie and Pete Seeger, and out front in the alliance that followed between the folk singers and the civil rights movement.

She came out of the sincere, formal and trusted grandeur of Paul Robeson but led to the defiant flamboyance of Janis Joplin. She was somewhere between the militant entertainment activism of show business subversive Harry Belafonte and his belief, inspired by Guthrie and Lead Belly, that song could drive genuine social change, and the empowered, empowering church-inspired soul singing of Aretha Franklin, with her own tremendous range and her single-minded way against all odds of shaping her reality. And Odetta was between Lead Belly's field holler, his feeling for time and his raw, agile guitar playing, and Bob Dylan.

Her voice created all kinds of intense drama, and even though his voice was worlds away from her voice, it gave Dylan clues about how he could use it to present songs as dramas, as events, as living testaments, as things that got so close to you they touched your skin before you even heard them. She sang the blues, without sounding inauthentic, but didn't sound like a blues singer traditionally sounded. She had her own rhythm. She understood how melody had a mind of its own and how hard it was to hold. She wasn't afraid to raise her voice. She took sides. She told the truth in public, even if people weren't quite ready to hear it.

Dylan could sing the blues not necessarily sounding like a

blues singer was apparently meant to sound, and he realised it didn't matter. From Odetta as much as anyone he learnt how to measure the rhythm of his vocal phrasing and let the sound of his voice take care of itself; for him, the meaning of a song is a combination of the words and the rhythm, which puts each word, each syllable, into a world of its own. Just his voice, open to the elements in his very own way, and an acoustic guitar, attached to some kind of innate charisma and something you've got to tell people, and this is how he could get moving, get away with it, travel along the highway, down the river, out of and into history.

Once folk dropped out of fashion – not least because Bob Dylan the folk singer with a fine regard for the resources of tradition wasn't really a folk singer, more someone resisting tyranny and oppression pursuing his own individual indignation, his own eccentric meaning – Odetta wasn't cut out to keep up to speed with what was happening next. Dylan of course, not being one thing or another and thinking for himself, had other voices he could change into, other selves.

He could make another change in double-quick time because his songs were never 'political'. The only thing that was political about them was the atmosphere in which they came into being. He preferred to be at odds with political trends of all sorts, following the road, the river, towards the existence of realms to which political impulses and forms do not extend. Or not, as the case may be.

At the start of 1965, two years after she sang 'Oh Freedom' at the great Martin Luther King Jr March on Washington, the year of Dylan's melodramatically received switch (back) to the electric guitar, Odetta sang an album of songs by the performer she had abstractly mentored, and metaphorically handed an acoustic guitar. *Odetta Sings Dylan* was released the same month as *Bringing It All Back Home*, as though the Dylan camp – Dylan's manager, Albert Grossman, was also her manager – was organising a certain elegiac summary of his more specifically folk period by one of his favourite singers, and one of folk's most vivid interpreters. It was a kind of discreet anointment, a formal celebration, at about the time he shot himself somewhere completely different, as if he really was killing off the folk singer and enacting a kind of resurrection, which would get the world talking, or at least, that part of the world paying attention.

Perhaps, through the voice of Odetta, there's a hint of the Dylan that would have kept on being the Dylan he had been leading up to until 1965, an early, prime example of the other Dylan voices that exist that are not actually from Dylan. This alternative Dylan is a Dylan that never was, that only had about three years in prime time and was then stuck in the same channel through the next few decades, a beloved but parked-up legacy act. It would be an entertaining, ingenious Dylan, old and wise before his time, responsible for a few indelible modern American standards, possessing an epic way with words, but a Dylan fixed into the folk era, entombed in his own stardom, his own initial self-creation, in exactly the way he continually fought to escape. An artist forever associated with the stunning and stunned Kennedy years, with that changeover period between Elvis and the Beatles, a period that took in 'Blowin' in the Wind' and 'The Times They Are a-Changin'' and climaxed with 'Mr Tambourine Man', before the loaded beat groups and emotional, introspective singer-songwriters politely thanked him for his service, for revealing some of his secrets, and took on the challenge their own way, leaving him where he was on the road, waiting for a lift that never came.

Odetta as this ghost of Dylan future covered songs arranged for a small band that he had recorded without a band, and long before it was completely clear how important Dylan was going to be seen to be as a songwriter and as a performer. Already she was doing to his songs what he would later do, and what he was already doing to the songs he covered – never taking the recorded versions as anything other than a guide to interpretation, as the beginning of another song, a door into the next world.

She didn't go to extremes, even as her folk went further than most folk could at the time without spilling into the folk–rock that Dylan was instigating, but she did enough to make it an Odetta performance, no mean feat considering the weight and power of the songs she sang. It means that even as she released one of the very first albums of Dylan covers, before doing so became a more obvious rite of passage, before anyone had really noticed how much death there was in his songs, she sealed herself off into her own time and space as one of the greatest readers, and rewriters, of Dylan, one of the great other voices of Dylan, as if this was part of her destiny once she had made the 1957 album that helped him work out his own immediate destiny. Her mesmerising 'Masters of War', where the world holds its breath, almost written for her, or for her to do with as she would, is as perfect a taking over of a Dylan song as Jimi Hendrix's 'All Along the Watchtower', Al Kooper and Stephen Stills' 'It Takes a Lot to Laugh, It Takes a Train to Cry', Nina Simone's 'Just Like Tom Thumb Blues', Fairport Convention's 'Percy's Song', Bruce Springsteen's 'I Want You',

Judy Collins's 'Daddy You've Been On My Mind', Richie Havens' 'Just Like A Woman', Joan Baez's 'Love Is Just a Four Letter Word', Them's 'It's All Over Now, Baby Blue', Bryan Ferry's 'A Hard Rain's a-Gonna Fall', Tom Verlaine's 'Cold Irons Bound', Nick Cave's 'Death is Not the End', Patti Smith's 'Wicked Messenger', David Bowie's 'Tryin' to Get to Heaven', and Elvis Presley's 'Tomorrow Is a Long Time', which he came to through the Odetta version.

Surprisingly, singing Dylan in 1966 was part of Presley's route back from the sorry, hollow theme movies he'd been making since he came out of the army that tragically separated him from where music had headed. He was missing out, getting lost to the world, and he sings 'Tomorrow Is a Long Time' as if he's sending a message out from his loneliness, from behind the cinema screen that was now screening him off from his public even as he lived out stupid, joyless fantasies all over it. There is a world where it helped him back to life, pushing him towards the resurrecting Comeback Special of 1968, where loose in tight leather he finally stepped out of the soulless movies and their dismal soundtracks, breaking out of the cage his manager had put him in.

Dylan wrote a song about the meaning of life and love and music and beauty, another one of his sublime lost love songs, maybe actually telling us something for real, from his real life, no half-truths, no misdirection, beginning on a crooked highway, from a time as the Russians loomed when life seemed more fragile than ever. It also exists as if he knew the kind of pain the exiled Elvis was feeling, trapped as a has-been, cut off from a world he helped invent, as sad as anyone can be; he can't see his reflection in the waters, he can't express his pain, he can't hear his own footsteps, he can't even remember the sound of his own name.

And when Dylan wrote about the beauty there is in a silver, singing river, then Elvis could easily be that river, the singer he said when he heard him for the first time made it feel like he was busting out of jail. Elvis sings it from deep inside a lost, lonely America, where the capital city is Las Vegas, a place Dylan doesn't have to go because Elvis does. Elvis sings it, gathering everything up he knows, or at least what he can remember, as though he knows he hasn't got far to flow before he joins the ocean.

The more traditional Dylan fans, those particularly alarmed when his voice scattered into a million burnt pieces decades later, would love how Odetta – and Elvis – with her formal training enunciates each word of each song with all the respectful, clear-singing care in the world, any hint of sarcasm, irony, hostility, danger, impatience or croak cleaned away in an honouring of the words' beauty and insight that Dylan never felt himself. They were his thoughts after all, and he didn't necessarily want to have to keep repeating them the same way, whereas Odetta was expressing them as something seriously special that needed to be held up to the light, and sometimes examined with a kind of awe.

Those disappointed fans would have loved these sensitive, probing and sparsely literal arrangements of 'Baby, I'm in the Mood for You', 'Long Ago, Far Away', 'Don't Think Twice, It's All Right', 'Masters of War', 'The Times They Are a-Changin'', 'With God on Our Side' and 'Mr Tambourine Man' to be the ones that fixed them as part of the canon, give or take the slightly suspicious way Odetta turns 'Mr Tambourine Man', at the time relatively obscure, into a wandering, weary lament of nearly eleven minutes. It's as though she needed the time to work out where the song was going, where Dylan himself was going, because the lament is for the Dylan that was no more, for the end already of him as the tambourine man. He'd used the song to leave where he'd been, as a bridge from one part of his Highway 61 to another, disappearing into himself, into his next song, with a voice only he knew was coming.

There is a world where Odetta could have kept singing songs from many of his different stages as long as she lived – which would have meant up to *Modern Times*; she died in 2008, a few weeks before she hoped to appear at Barack Obama's inauguration – even those songs from when he was in whatever state he gets into when he feels dried up, exhausted, overwhelmed, jaded, washed up, when he's not feeling it, lost en route. Each of his songs, the songs that followed him as he followed the road, existed to be lifted up and placed back into the traditions he came from where they never looked out of place. She sang the songs as though they were part of her carefully selected repertoire in 1957, so in some dimension they existed before Dylan had even written or recorded them, like how in Conor McPherson's *Girl from the North Country* his songs seemed to come from the 1930s, ready for him to find later.

Dinkytown was the natural place for Bob – Zimmerman flickering in and out, on the way to being over and out – to find somewhere to sing songs standing on his own, stepping closer to finding his first voice, to writing the kind of songs a sincere solo singer with acoustic guitar dreams about writing, songs that will become a part of America. A small commercial and residential district next to the University of Minnesota's east bank campus, Dinkytown was where the book and record shops were, the lunch counters, the basement venues and the coffee shops with a small stage in the corner. It was a little bohemia, a provincial Greenwich Village. No-one knows for sure how it got its name; the sensible ones say it comes from the days when small trolleys and railcars, known as 'Dinkys', ran through the area, and some like the idea it was simply because it was such a small part of town, or that there was a theatre so small, with only four rows, it was called the Dinky.

Up to his eyes in self-discovery, Dylan disappeared into the transitory community of students coming and going over time and slipped easily into the local folk scene, a developing network of underground musicians, misfits and poets connected to a new wave of radical politics as the Beats were morphing into the hippies. He made contact with the sort of thinkers, university intellectuals, fellow travellers, record lovers and stoners that would be useful in helping his education, and also useful when it came to remembering their time with and around him that they couldn't really remember, or only in a different version from someone else's. As Zimmerman became Dylan, out in the open, there are different points where it seemed to happen, depending who you ask, what you want the story to be.

He slipped into the history of Dinkytown, quickly escaping the unappealing fraternity house and moving into a small, no-frills apartment, which students following him in years to come would talk about, even if no-one knew for sure where it actually was, somewhere on 4th Street, above the back alley of a drug store, with enough room for people to sleep on his floor after a night spent listening to records like listening itself was a creative act, the creation of some kind of magic potion, a way of moving a few more miles towards the source of everything.

By October 1959, telling the manager, Dave Lee, his name is Bob Dylan, acting like he's just made it up, a sudden moment of inspiration, he was singing in the Ten o'Clock Scholar on 4th Street to a crowd probably made up of other musicians. It seemed a real kind of place, and the name Zimmerman didn't seem as real to him as the name Dylan, which he'd been calling himself in his head for months, getting used to the moment he would move from one self to another, becoming once and for all what he had practised pretending to be.

He got a residency there for a few months, played in various rooms and folk clubs with names you'd expect like the Purple Onion, appeared with good, strong local musicians like Spider John Koerner, Tony Glover and Dave Ray, built up some repartee, visited John Bucklen back in Hibbing at Christmas, his news full of Odetta and his new role as folk singer. He got caught a couple of times stealing records, and his parents were called out to sort things out, presuming once they'd settled him back in college that he'd grow out of his youthful passion and concentrate on his studies. He kept studying hard, but not the way they wanted.

The set list of a gig he played on 1 June 1960 at the Purple Onion presents Dylan the serious folkie developing his repertoire: a whole host of resonant traditional songs he'd found for himself – 'Go Down You Murderers', 'Sinner Man', 'Another Man Done Gone', 'Everytime I Hear the Spirit' – and via the performances of singers like the crystal-voiced twenty-year-old Judy Collins, whom he opened for on a trip to Denver, 'The

House of the Rising Sun' and 'Maid of Constant Sorrow'. He was on the trail of traditional songs, which he could walk right into and stake a claim to, using a voice on the way to his professionally recorded voice that we get to hear on more rough, local tapes recorded so that he could hear for himself how close he was to getting the voice he heard in his head. He was experimenting with his feelings.

Dylan agreed to be recorded by a teenage enthusiast with another of those early bulky reel-to-reel tape recorders who fancied recording some of the Dinkytown musicians, even as others the teenager wanted to capture above Dylan passed on the chance, not taking it seriously. Dylan wasn't particularly being noticed as standing out from any of the other folk singers, but he had a greater sense of self-improvement. Dylan recorded some songs at his latest, ground-floor apartment, and the twelve songs, lasting about half an hour and recorded over a couple of hours in a small party setting, became known as *The Minnesota Party Tape*.

It's an example of pre-voice non-rock-and-roll Dylan, carefully singing more traditional songs, 'Red Rosey Bush', 'Johnny I Hardly Knew You', 'Streets of Glory', 'Roving Gambler', a Jimmie Rodgers yodel song, a handful of Guthrie's and a daft minute-long improvised talking blues, 'Talking Hugh Brown', rightly abandoned. If it now sounds a little like a slightly undercooked Bob Dylan impersonator, that's because at the time, September 1960, he was a slightly undercooked Bob Dylan impersonator, impersonating himself, those voices he had in his head only heard by him, not sure how smooth to sound, how rough, still working all sorts of things out, but already possessing, or being possessed by, the kind of deliberate, volatile phrasing that would make it through to his first albums and wherever he went after that.

Perhaps on these sorts of early tapes, grab bags of experiments, sketches, try-outs – taking traditional songs that have the fingerprints of others all over them and adding his own, not yet adding the wrinkles of time to his singing, the adapted grit of the ancients, the accents of other times and places – there is a sense of the actual untampered sound of his innate, warm handmade singing voice, the one that peeked through later on the country crooning *New Morning* album, on the nutty, knotty nostalgia of *Self Portrait*. A song from the tape called 'Rambler, Gambler' appears on the *No Direction Home* soundtrack, before a November 1961 – so about a year later – version of 'This Land is Your Land', Woody Guthrie's retort to 'America the Beautiful', where he's found a way to beat and break his voice up a little, like he's seen things, knows things. But as rudimentary as the Dinkytown home recording is, as cautious as he is, not expecting the recording to become part of a greater history, it is definitely Bob Dylan, beginning to sing for others whatever they may think, moving out of his head, crossing time.

There is a particular clear witness to one living moment where Zimmerman became Dylan, although he might have made everything up and Dylan later just went along with it, loving the unreliability of it all, because here was the perfect loopy character to be the outlandish freak, the charming guru, the surreal consultant with a gift for the gab and a fancy for a little on-the-hoof mischief who'd got for Bob a whole new set of recommendations, contacts and tips. The sort of roaming, loose, playful character from a weird old America that Dylan's always been on the lookout for, a decent, deviant American spirit from before there was even an America. This new arrival on Dylan's Highway even had his own origin story, how he left his home in Minnesota to join a carnival where he used to talk people in: 'Freaks, geeks and curiosities, the strangest and most unusual people on the face of the earth. Step right in!' Then he heard something was happening in San Francisco.

This ultimate scenester, Diamond Dave Whitaker, a couple of years older than Bob, was like a Beatnik Zelig, there in the background in whatever American city was having a cultural moment whatever the decade, hobnobbing in the 1950s with heavyweight poets like Kenneth Rexroth, Lawrence Ferlinghetti and Jack Spicer, there front row in the audience as Ginsberg read 'Howl', as Kerouac read *On the Road*, as Gregory Corso read *Elegiac Feelings American*, as Richard Brautigan read at Blabbermouth Night in North Beach, San Francisco, where you could let out whatever was on your mind and poetry was read to jazz. This was where the urban, spiritual East Coast Beat, often teetering at the edge of comprehensibility, aligned with the reborn, apocalyptic, satirical and bardic American romanticism of the San Francisco Renaissance, closely related to wilderness past, the sensibilities of both feeding into Dylan.

Diamond Dave kept on keeping on through the protests, the Diggers, the Merry Pranksters and the Summer of Love of the '60s, the punk of the '70s and '80s, as one generation replaced another, becoming an ageing countercultural legend relating how he first met Dylan and helped him on his way. You might not have believed him until Dylan introduced him larger than life in *Chronicles*.

Whitaker had travelled back to his hometown after some Beat time on the West Coast, some exotic time in Paris. A friend of his bumped into a raggedy, restless Dylan with some vague, sulky thoughts that he wasn't meant to have a mundane existence, looking everywhere he could for signs of life, needing some sort of a fix. She knew exactly who he needed to meet and sent him over to Whitaker's house. He knocked on the door, complete with acoustic guitar, and when the door opened said: 'I hear this is where I am meant to be.' They fell into a conversation like they'd been talking for years, and this is the point where Dylan was introduced to marijuana, because it had to happen that his induction was with a local Svengali who'd smoked the stuff with Jack Kerouac, who'd first tried it with the soft and sure saxophonist Lester Young, who'd got the idea from Billie Holiday, who'd shared her first smoke with Louis Armstrong, a pioneering pot evangelist famous for his cigar-sized joints.

Armstrong was known as the king of the Vipers, an inside club of stoners in the 1920s when pot was still legal, when it seemed to him just another herb like the ones his mother picked by the railroad tracks in New Orleans, pretty natural because it grew naturally, put there by God. This one had a heck of a buzz, though, a hundred times better than whiskey, made him forget the bad things, made his already elevated jazz better and better, the conversations about it – the nuances of a drum beat, the riff of a piano, time starting to slow up and act like crazy, the influence of the blues – more intense. After Diamond Dave passed on the message to Dylan, happy landings, his eyes were soon glazed and happy, he felt a few more boundaries dissolve, activated a few astounding new trains of association, the bright blessed day, the dark secret night, and a few years later, as part of the trading chain of pop culture command, Dylan was introducing it to the Beatles with his blessing and probably Louis' as well.

When Whitaker heard Dylan mumble that he hadn't been reading much lately, his guitar taking up a little too much of his time, he handed him a copy of *Bound for Glory*, Woody Guthrie's embellished, fanciful but searingly frank autobiography published in 1943. Guthrie was born in Okemah, Oklahoma in 1912 and the book is set in an America rising up out of Twain, Steinbeck and Kerouac, a Depression/Dustbowl-era story in between the two world wars about an institutionalised mother, a broken family, grinding poverty, boyhood jinks, odd jobs, aimless wanderings, riding in, on and under freight trains, bumming rides, travelling on foot, learning to use the guitar, throwing his hat on the floor and singing for his supper, scraping a living, playing picket lines, hobo camps and various skid row dives.

It begins and ends with Guthrie riding in a crowded boxcar as he heads somewhere between nowhere special and the heart of America, which is always just out of reach. (Todd Haynes begins and ends his prismatic filmic evocation of the lives and minds of Bob Dylan with two of his different Dylans, guitar in hand, boarding a train and settling into a boxcar.) If there's ever a hint he might settle down, that he might take the easy option, he feels the outside world calling, the road beckoning, the next train out of town is all he wants. The book roughly, toughly cuts up the adventures and experiences, the loss and regret that Guthrie turned into songs of resistance – 'I've seen plenty to make up songs about,' he wrote – and which turned him into an independent-minded political performer championing the hard-working poor. He was following through something William Faulkner once said: 'Never be afraid to raise your voice for honesty and truth and compassion against injustice and lying and greed. If people all over the world would do this, it would change the earth.' Steinbeck concluded that Guthrie symbolised the American Spirit.

He acts up a little, suggesting he doesn't consider himself a writer, just 'a little one-cylinder guitar picker', even as he tells great stories that use the artistry of a novelist. He disguises the kind of radicalism that is treated with suspicion in America with a solid display of down-to-earth common sense. There's a deliberately maintained difference between performing Guthrie the travelling truth teller, making a mockery of those in power and attacking oppression and hypocrisy across the country, and everyday, erratic, playful, deceptive Guthrie. He learns about the value of image – even for someone apparently so aggressively unfiltered – from the early twentieth-century protest singer Joe Hill – born in Sweden as Joel Hägglund – bringing un-American socialism into songs of revolt.

Joe Hill's an edgy, challenging singer, he's something of a miscreant, possibly a murderer and definitely executed by firing squad as if he is, but most of all, above the performer and the man, he's a myth, even before his death, the ultimate symbol of working-class resistance. The myth you manage to project, that's then projected on your behalf, overwhelms who you actually are; it takes over. The myth can for better or worse carry your music.

Guthrie gets an offer to make some regular money singing sentimental songs and comedy ditties in a posh New York club, the Rainbow Room on top of the Rockefeller Center, but he hasn't got the heart for it, he's got too much soul, and he prefers to swing back to the streets and sing for union workers and soldiers, angry rabble-rousing songs about underdogs, down-and-outs and people's struggles that needed to be sung.

Dylan devoured *Bound for Glory* in one setting, a vivid, revealing history lesson that isn't in the usual textbooks, Guthrie as harsh-voiced vagrant minstrel enacting the kind of wanderlust he could only dream about, setting a certain grim, deviant vision of the triumph and tragedy of America to music. He didn't read it as a book tragically documenting hard times and suffering and recording the rise of folk protest but as a self-help pamphlet for those looking to build a quintessential American life.

As much as anything it's a guide to how to become mythic; how to seem to come from a long-ago past or have no past at all. He wanted to learn from this character who wanted to learn. Dylan found in Woody Guthrie a carefree vagabond examining his own conscience, as knowledgeable about Kahlil Gibran, yoga and Confucius as he was about standard American idealists. Guthrie had been fixed in place as the simple, earthy, heroic, compassionate political writer with biting wit and a contempt for privilege, a leftist saint, but Dylan saw him as someone fluid and nefarious, frustrated and mercurial, issuing startling reports on the nature of the universe, a working man in how he manufactured realities.

*Bound for Glory* is the tale of a folk outlaw living a life at the opposite extremes to Dylan's safer, small-town one, and to get anywhere near to the homespun authenticity of Woody Guthrie he had to come across like he was from that kind of life rather than the one he'd had. He read the book like a script, and imagined it carrying on with someone like him as the main character. Guthrie jumps on a train setting out to wherever it's heading, but it's Dylan that gets off, carrying on Guthrie's duties, dressed for the occasion, the celebrating of the human spirit with something of himself added in, a whole cosmos of influences, a vast body of information from darkest Russia and brightest Rimbaud to loud rock and roll that Guthrie didn't have, which meant eventually Dylan would go places Guthrie could never make, never know. Guthrie's songs switch and stretch out between agitated fantasies and scalding reality, roam across empty, glorious landscapes real and all in the mind, and it makes a lot of sense to Dylan, with his own liking for articulating credibility and stretching credulity. It's the haunting, teasing, illusive Guthrie that Dylan loves, the one that said even though his job was the here and now, this week, this month, this year, there had to be a timeless element in his songs. 'Something that means tomorrow will not be gone with the wind.'

Whitaker said that when Dylan sat down to read *Bound for Glory* he was shy-eyed Robert Zimmerman and when he stood up, a little unsteadily, after he'd raced through Guthrie's life, coughing as though there was suddenly the dusty weathering of age in his voice, he was Bob Dylan.

# TEN

## THE STATE OF THINGS

My job for a few months was Bob Dylan as 2020 became in its own demanding, painful and hyper-anxious way horribly dramatic and memorable. It turned out to be the best job for me to have in a disordered world that was accelerating at the same rate as Dylan when he was changing the fastest, when he was at his most light-headed and dangerous, as if reality was continually reinventing itself. A devastating worldwide death toll kept increasing, time was becoming increasingly fluid and confusing, days were bleeding into weeks, weeks dissolving into each other, reality losing its grip on reality, and somehow this jumbled chronology suited where I was with my work, and his work, where thoughts were put together in any order, psychological order replacing chronological order.

He was always opening the door to a new future, often by heading backwards, determining his own chronology, his own internal weather, placing his songs in timeless settings, memories, ideas and assumptions existing side by side, the past and present, the living and the dead somehow coalescing and co-existing. Sometimes a song began with the epilogue. He was always describing the present, processing realms of disjointed data on the fly, editing everything down to an instantaneous now, his songs notable for their fragmentation, broken chronology, changing perspectives, shifts in tone and absent moments.

His work began again as *Rough and Rowdy Ways* was released, remaking his history in the way that he had remade the history of song, by keeping certain traditions alive not by preserving them but by embellishing, redirecting, even warping them. He changed history by offering new perspectives on it. Changing the past was one way of influencing the future.

The appearance of *Rough and Rowdy Ways* became yet another 'end' to the albums of Bob Dylan, and another way of beginning his discography; you can imagine a discography of Dylan albums that goes in an order not connected to the time when they were released, but organised to present a very different way of how Dylan went through his life, or through your own life. You can imagine *Rough and Rowdy Ways* as his first album, where he started out with a voice that sounded like it had been around for a long while one way or another, a voice that sounded exactly like he was more or less as third as old as America itself, the voice of sanity growing hoarse. You can go from there to where a final album is *Time Out of Mind*, or *John Wesley Harding*, or Bob Dylan Live 1975; The Rolling Thunder Revue, Bootleg Series Vol.5, or *The Basement Tapes*, or *Oh Mercy*, or, after all that, *Bob Dylan*, two ages meeting across the distance of time, a voice that starts old and ends old and in between the constant sound of recovery.

Everything can go in reverse; the songs find their own order, a continuous thread of revelation, a disorderly tangle of lines, long and short, weak and strong.

\*

As I worked from home, hours lost their meaning, which can happen either when you write a book or when you're in the middle of an extraordinary pandemic, both places where you find yourself stuck in a repetitive routine between crisis and boredom – I'm too exhausted to think about what happens on the next page, I'm staring at the same sentence for what seems like forever, I'm browsing Amazon for what could be hours as if that might help me, I have no idea what day it is, I have no idea where one day ends and the next day begins, I seem to have missed yesterday, I need to finish this week or something bad will happen. I would feel that way writing a book before living through the pandemic, and now as I had the same sensation writing this book, I would read about many others having the same experience, isolation, fear and the deadness of time, but because of the pandemic, not because they were writing a book.

As everyone lost their focus, not sure they could take the strain, I had found a temporary kind of sanctuary. I had a safe space even if nothing was necessarily safe when I got there. I could get lost inside Bob Dylan, inside his songworlds, mingle with all his characters, binge on his songs and his dreams, the stories he told and the stories that were told about him, monitor his trust of contrariness, the ways he manipulated our experience of time, how he had turned himself into a location, a place to get your bearings, to work out the distance between here and there and now and then. It was a good time to write about Bob Dylan, and how he set out not to change the world but to change people's understanding of what is going on in the world. Or maybe just change his own understanding. I was sad the writing, my job, the only travelling I was allowed to do, was coming to an end, but I got over the sadness by playing another Bob Dylan song, one of those that seemed to be playing on a loop inside my mind anyway, where he's singing 'back and forth in rhyme' again and again.

The variety in his life and songs filled in for a shocking lack of variety in the real world. If nothing seemed to be happening apart from the world losing the usual structures and routines that hold it together, I was there inside Dylan, where plenty was always happening. I could get away from things by busying myself with where I was in the writing, ready to go anywhere now that I couldn't in the real world, where it actually wasn't clear what was real. I decided that it would be good if Bob Dylan ended up as my job for the rest of my life, working out which song to save for last, as I stuck around to see his living story come to an end, and then worked up to my own end, one dream following another.

Dylan was also an interesting job to have in the middle of a pandemic that was happening during an election year in the USA, a fight for what kept being described as the 'soul of America', featuring constant convulsive battles between good and evil, us and them, superstition and science. A killer virus blended with political chaos, environmental catastrophe, racial strife. Thoughts, attention, politics, values, even identities were all at risk. Dylan as some form of mystical historian seemed to be interested in that so-called 'soul of America', the nature of good and evil, us-and-them, reality and unreality, and working out what that meant, if only to him, and sometimes it felt as though how the shattered world was reaching me, through the internet and television, was helping me navigate my way through Dylan. He had a universe inside his mind, and he'd never particularly thought that things should be easy to understand, even when he found a great melody and a series of irresistible rhymes.

The 24-hour news cycle became my constant companion as I got on with my job; I would play his songs over a constant parade of soundless images of a masked, burning, debating, rioting, murdering, endorsing, explaining, announcing, Zooming, seducing, crying, hoping, dying, marketing, suffering, forecasting, hurting, faking, campaigning nation pummelled by more and more information and even more disinformation. The connection was perfect between Dylan's visions of history, his decisions about the meaning of life, and the random collection of TV images, adverts, news flashes, presenters, replays piling up every hour vainly trying to maintain order. We were getting a chance to see the end of the world live on television, 2020 as the year of illusion, of the illusion of mass persuasion, instantly and endlessly analysed 2021 beginning as an unwanted, repetitive sequel, and Dylan had already anticipated the details of how reality was being replaced by fantasy, the hyper-creation of content, the recycling of time and how hard it is to hang on to any idea of 'normal'.

The long turn Dylan took after the mid-1990s towards an ending was also the long turn of America towards the end of the latest part of its history. It was definitely the fractured, frenetic end of the point in history that Dylan had occupied, a history that began during the Second World War, that began with cinema, teenagers and rock and roll, that began with civil rights protests, the death of a president and the Vietnam War, with the Beatles, double albums and 7-inch singles. He'd lived from the Japanese attack on America at Pearl Harbor to witnessing a sitting president's attack on America from Twitter where he tried to take over all of life, from the innocent early days of television as black and white enchantment to the relentless existence of television taking on an uncontrollable inhuman dimension. He'd kept up with the tempestuous changes, even as he was inevitably apart from the currents and crazes of social media, from the fashionable changes in musical styles, refusing to bend the knee to modern custom, continuing making the music he liked to hear because of when he was born, and what music originally got inside his mind.

As I worked, I listened to Dylan and watched TV as America unfolded in extremes and folded in on itself. This answered certain questions about why and how and when you listen to Bob Dylan – one of those many problems that there is when considering Dylan and his music, about where it fits into your world, a world, any world, how it is transformed into meaning. I listened to Dylan to get away from chaos, to understand chaos, to find out where America is, and how everyone there is doing what they think they're supposed to do.

The country wasn't just separated between the coasts and the middle territories, or the cities and the country, the suburban and the rural, old and young, the provincial and the international, it was in fact two countries laid over each other, each existing alongside and within the other two realities devastatingly juxtaposed. Dylan recorded and dug into these differences and observed them, both up close and personal and from a safe vantage point. His travels were within those different places far apart and on top of each other. His time on earth had existed inside a certain America, a location he found for himself which was the stage he performed on even as he existed outside America. He made you realise how a country is a place you only make up in your mind. Something you dream about and you sing about. It's not on any map, it's a story of places you've been and people you've met, full of songs, books, films and poems, a place where you don't have to live like anyone else.

Perhaps he was born out of his due place. Accident cast him amidst certain surroundings, but he always had a nostalgia for a place he'd never known. He was a stranger in his birthplace, the parks and streets and shops and schools of his childhood were just a place of passage. He felt his whole life an alien amongst kindred spirits and remained aloof from the only scenes he'd ever known. It was this sense of strangeness that sent him far and wide in the search for something permanent, to which he might attach himself. Perhaps some deep-rooted atavism urged him back to a land which his ancestors left in the dim beginnings of history.

And then – letting onto the page what is happening on the television as I write, like the writer who lets everything into their books as it happens around them, following the trail of an insect as it wanders along their desk – in the last few hours of my last day working on this particular task, 2020 lurched again, reality held on for dear life, and after days when time, which had already stopped, seemed to stop again, the results of the 2020 American presidential election were finally projected.

I couldn't finish the book until the winner was announced; whether you considered Donald Trump good or evil, sweet or sour, madman or a necessary disruption, four more years of his deadly, deeply disorientating performance art would move America further away from an America of Bob Dylan, threaten the absolute end of a period of history where there could be, even needed to be, a Dylan, with his kind of songs, consciousness and propensity for difficult surfaces, his interest in the tangle of language, his exclusive form of discourse, his faith in the continuity of human experience. More Trump at the centre of things, intoxicating believers with reeking lies, more enforced changes caused by Covid-19, more easily controlled, and erased, online ephemerality all suggested a rapid decaying of the world where Bob Dylan could exist and make some sort of sense, and therefore of the sort of world Bob Dylan represented.

Under Trump, context was flattened, language crumbled, and the 'nothing lasts forever' that Dylan had articulated with a sense of beauty and hope as well as grief and loss would be replaced with a crueller, lonelier 'nothing lasts forever', a dark ages he could see coming – because he could see into the past, which he knew needed to be surpassed, where fates and destinies and a world of polarities had been set in motion – but which he tried to outwit, jumping into the fray, dodging bullets, however distant and unconcerned he seemed, telling the truth and lying through his bardic hat, scaring himself with his own desert places, but doing the work he needed to do. All this would be reduced to obsolete romantic rot.

Trump's opponent Joe Biden, destined to be the oldest president ever elected, was younger than Dylan, and from the same world, where fair play could still stand up for itself as long as you played the game. During his campaign he made constant reference to one of his heroes, the Irish poet Seamus Heaney – who received the Nobel Prize in Literature in 1995, and who said he rhymed to see himself – Biden still believing in that kind of faith in thinking and hoping, in positive spiritual energy and music and delight. One candidate seeing the lively, living magic in words, one finding personal value and security in cutting words to shreds – one believing in Heaney saying that if you have the words, there's always a chance that you'll find the way forward, the other believing in using words to create shade and breed monsters.

It's a world before the time when Trump tortured people with language to get what he wanted, a world where Heaney knew that no poem or song or play can fully right a wrong 'inflicted and endured' but they are places where you can imagine new life, a hope for a great sea-change, where hope and history rhyme, where you can believe in miracles, cures and healing wells, that a further shore is reachable. You can walk on air against your better judgement. Biden's belief in Heaney is the belief that even when the hopes you started out with are dashed, hope has to be maintained.

Heaney would help anyone looking to come up with a manifesto proclaiming why a sensitive, probing imagination is a better thing for the world, that art finds the necessary metaphors by which a radically changing culture can be explained to its inhabitants, that it keeps ideals alive in a culture that does not yet realise them. 'A populace that is chloroformed day and night by TV stations like Fox News could do with an inoculation by poetry. Obviously, poetry can't be administered like an injection, but it does constitute a boost to the capacity for discrimination and resistance.'

Biden beat Trump – in one reality, where history makes no mistakes, setting up more unnerving clashes between us and them, between America and unAmerica – and if you believed in poets rather than sneers and snarls in uncivil war, the world seemed a little less stuck, a little less cold and lonely. Bob Dylan, born during the third term of the thirty-second president, Franklin D. Roosevelt, is still around on the battlefield after Joe Biden becomes the forty-sixth president, Kamala Harris becomes the first ever female and the first ever Black and Asian-American vice-president, and the Never Ending Tour may yet continue, with more voices to come.

And for those who felt relieved, however naively, that ageing Biden beat ageing Trump – as though that added up to young promise – perhaps there could be a wish in this possible new world that the forty-fifth president was made to listen again and again to something by Bob Dylan that conveyed in song the words of Bertrand Russell: 'The faculty of being acquainted with things other than itself is the main characteristic of a mind.' Which gives you a lot of songs to choose from.

The forty-fifth president, though, was only listening to his own voice, and believing in his own insular reality, as if eventually he could make everyone believe in the same thing. Those that did believe him didn't care if he was the real thing or not. They were comfortable arriving at a reality only to abandon it or exchange it for something that claimed to be another reality. Dylan had warned us about such darkness; the sense as in a nightmare of being involved in something both wildly improbable and relentlessly inevitable. This had to happen. Yet how could it have happened?

At this point, as my work is coming to an end, my final shift finishing, the television talks about 'America being back', and beside me on my desk are my notes, where I've worked out where I might go next in the book after Bob Dylan had read *Bound for Glory* for the first time, and everything started to make sense, like there was a light to see, a country to define, a mind to make up, wonder and majesty to investigate, fear and loathing to fight, defiance to maintain. America might be back, the healing has begun, but you'll still need hope, and you'll need it bad. Good luck with that. Good luck with finding the truth. And good luck with finding America.

I'd been listening a lot in my lockdown to Dylan's magnificent piece of writing 'Last Thoughts on Woody Guthrie', and I would have been anyway even if I hadn't been spending so much time in his demanding company. The 1963 prose-poem is one of the great consequences of him reading *Bound for Glory*, an extraordinary incorporation of his hero, a creative response to the book, a spellbinding transcendence of the influences, one of the great writings by one artist about another, about the impact their example has had on their thinking.

It is one of Dylan's most outrageously compelling performances, the definitive beginning of the momentum that took him to the Nobel Prize in Literature fifty-three years later, twenty-nine years after the Russian-American Joseph Brodsky, thirty-eight years after the Polish-American Isaac Bashevis Singer. If only for 'Last Thoughts on Woody Guthrie', there is no question the decision made sense and was completely legitimate; it's a poem, not a song, but with the rhythm of a song, and the emotions, already, of a lifetime. He uses the poem not so much to describe or define Guthrie or Guthrie's America, but to conceive his own country in his own mind, given clues how to do it by Guthrie, but with clues of his own. Dylan's last thoughts on Woody Guthrie are the last thoughts about the time Guthrie was alive, what happened to his dream of America, the one he made from art and emotions, how every time he wrote a song he changed who he was. Dylan changes a few times inside this one poem, from apprentice to master, searching for a dream, dreaming of a search.

He recited it in front of an audience of 900 at the Town Hall in New York on 12 April 1963, one of his first major concerts, feeling generous about the future when it felt like a promise not a threat. After his show, he returned to the stage and for the one and only time read a poem in public. He'd been asked for twenty-five words on 'what Woody Guthrie means to me' for a book about Guthrie, and he ended up writing nearly 1,700 over five pages. Less might be more, but more is grander.

He happened to have it in his pocket 'by accident' and he said he wanted to read it aloud, and the audience should roll along with him, the way Guthrie would sing about rolling along, and he recited it in a voice that might be another hint of a true, essential voice, an unfussy 'this is me' barely marked midwestern voice that occasionally materialises amongst all the 'I am other' voices. You can hear him breathe, to the edge of breath, take in some air, alive in the moment, each word cutting through the tension. The poem is coming alive in his head as he reads it, as though he's just thought of it, it's a surprise to him, but he knows it inside out. It's a poem about how great it is to be a writer, one word after another, after another, generating power, hugging his destiny. *Chronicles* begins here, *Tarantula* begins here, the sound of someone who has to write, to say what he sees and feels and loves and loses.

All his other voices build from this one, this low-key, natural speaking voice, stretching out a little as the pressure builds, pausing in unusual places, jumping from one idea to another, presenting his credentials. All of his songs are rooted inside this song that is not a song, where he strongly pushes against the pull of nostalgia even as he passes again and again through the past, memory as the mother of muses, refracting it through his present. All of his songs emerge from this great list of grievances and hopes and wishes and feelings and fears and treasures, risking going too far to find out how far one can go. All of his voices begin and end here, as he wonders as he mixes up words, is he mixed up too much, is he mixed up too hard? It's the voice-sound of a genius, not the genius presentation of a voice, or the pretend genius, because the occasion demanded he stand as himself, alone, as if he were at home, on his own, when he's most alive – which he kind of was, even in front of an audience beginning to realise that something was beginning to happen here, even if they didn't know what it was.

For a while, it was as private a moment as though he had been at home. It only existed in the memory of those who had heard him recite it. The recording Columbia made of the concert was stored away, perhaps because if the poem was included on a live album it might have an impact on Dylan's music career; the worldwide shadow-dancing weirdness of poetry was no way to promote a promising young singing entertainer. The first bootlegs only started to appear in 1970, the recording eventually appearing 'officially' on the Bootleg Series Vols 1–3 in 1991. In 1973, it was included in *Writings and Drawings*, one of those direct and indirect appearances Dylan was making as he slowly returned from somewhere and something before his 1974 Before the Flood tour, *Planet Waves* and *Blood on the Tracks*. You could read it, but not hear him speak it, but it's hearing him speak it that turns text on a page into a cosmic renaissance drama, a manifesto in rhythm, putting into words what cannot be put into words. He makes the whirling world stand still. As with his radio voice, which sounds separated from this voice by a thousand years and a million dreams, it is as though he is nothing but a voice.

The opening line about your head getting twisted and your mind growing numb is a line for 2020, when uncertainty and doubt gripped the planet. The poem is about what happens next, what happens now, how will he turn out, how will he find a role that fits in a world that never stops worrying him, it's about feeling left behind and losing control.

He speaks and breathes for the minutes it takes to travel through a life made out of thoughts and desires, the objects he remembers, the images from his dreams, through an America he likes to reason with, amongst mysteries, through a mind he'll spend years getting used to, being nobody but himself, clearly expressing mixed feelings, writing eternal graffiti in the heart of everyone who's listening. The song that is not a song has an opinion tucked away at the end, the opinion, and he may be right or wrong – and as he says this there's a little flare-up of his special sarcasm that doesn't belong inside this mantra – that the words have been heading towards.

Dylan without using music, open to the elements, comes to the conclusion that the power and mystery of music is what he worships. There are two choices, he says: the God you find in the church of your choice, or what you find in the Brooklyn State Hospital. God is in one, Woody Guthrie is in the other. You'll find both in the Grand Canyon at sunset, a sight to drive a saint to madness, a king to his knees, yet another opportunity to rest, and start the day again.

In a poem about hope and thinking for yourself, filled with hope and thinking, Dylan says out loud that where he finds the presence of God, or whatever you want to call it, is in music. Music is his religion. Music is a weapon. Whatever else he believed in, as he switched from faith to faith, or from faith to faithlessness, it was all set inside music, where you could do and be anything you wanted to be and you can get to the truth.

The last thoughts in 'Last Thoughts on Woody Guthrie' could have been written by the man who wrote *Bound for Glory*, but they were all his own work, part of how he created himself, out on his own, wherever he is, for much more than a moment.

# ELEVEN

## DISAPPEARING INTO HIMSELF

He carried *Bound for Glory* with him around Dinkytown like he used to carry his acoustic guitar around Hibbing, adjusted his accent to include a little Woody-style Oklahoma Okie which he let creep into his singing voice, tuning it into some unkempt folk, and completed a costume shift from James Dean rebel to Woody rustic – there's a natural segue from one rebel to another, as he adopted for his own purpose the appearance of the hobo, who inspired both fear and envy in people trapped in domestic routines. He learnt as many Guthrie songs as he could find. He became an unashamed self-styled Woody Guthrie jukebox.

Stealing some of the character and history of someone else seems in line with his understanding of what you can take from elsewhere to produce your own work. He steals a line here, a melody there, imitates this pose, that turn of phrase, so why not a whole persona? Some thought it was a kind of sickness way beyond teen fan quirkiness to be so infatuated with someone nearly thirty years older, even to try to be someone else, but he was just playing another role, freeing himself from his normal identity so he could see things with fresh eyes, and there was more to come.

We all take on a role until we find what we were born to do.

Or, he wasn't playing a role, he was just trying to be himself. He wasn't losing himself. He was seeing what fitted. It was a teenage phase, a little more convoluted, maybe a little more guileless, but in the end it was just a phase. Some at the time might have thought he was going to be some sort of Guthrie acolyte for years, but he knew he was just passing through. He would go beyond Guthrie in the way that he would go beyond himself, again and again, and he chose his influences well – being influenced by Woody Guthrie meant the last thing you'd want to end up doing is repeating yourself, even as you were always yourself.

He'd already been various others in his mind, a product of his vivid imagination, and this was just another performance, more or less the first to be made public. Starting to sound like Woody Guthrie meant he started to sound like Bob Dylan, and there were plenty of other voices and inspirations coming along for the ride into his early style – Lead Belly, Odetta, Ramblin' Jack Elliot. He'd immersed himself in the *Anthology of American Folk Music*, the bible of the new American folk scene, and knew all about the voices of Jimmie Rodgers, Bascom Lamar Lunsford and W. C. Handy that had influenced Guthrie. Through others we become ourselves.

After using some Guthrie, more difference, and more of the same (and many singers went much further in their worship of Dylan than Dylan did of Guthrie), once he had mastered the style he reached past it – beyond Baudelaire and the Beatles, beyond Frank O'Hara and Hank Williams – in much the same way as Shakespeare reached past Christopher Marlowe, even as Milton went beyond the King James Bible. Guthrie made him realise that to sing folk songs wasn't just a matter of singing neat arrangements nicely sourced – it took a whole lot of other work to be more than just a plain speaker, a straight talker, a discriminating collector, to just know the right chords and remember the words and melody. He needed to find out more. He took his excited obsession with Guthrie further and as though it was the obvious thing to do set out to get in touch with him, maybe needing to look him in the eye and feel a connection like he had with Buddy Holly. *Bound for Glory* was one of those books that knocked him out in such a way that when he was all done reading it, he wished the author was a terrific friend of his, and he could call him up on the phone whenever he wanted to.

Dylan's commitment to Guthrie was also because when he did track Guthrie down, encouraged initially by Diamond Dave, he found an extremely ill man, and as he followed in his footsteps – until they faded away and another path opened up – he was as much making sure Guthrie's songs and style didn't get forgotten as coldly studying him as a useful predecessor. Maybe that early preoccupation with death, where he sounded at twenty-one wearier and more woebegone than he would fifty years later, came from spending time with Woody Guthrie as he lived through his long, broken journey into silence.

An alcoholic prone to violence and paranoia, Guthrie had been diagnosed with Huntington's disease in 1952, having inherited it from his mother. The degenerative neurological disease destroys brain cells and leads to serious mood disorders, followed by uncoordinated and involuntary body movements, balance problems and dementia, with death usually occurring fifteen to twenty years after diagnosis. Guthrie would die in 1967 at fifty-five after a long and terrible illness.

Following years of confusions and vagrancy following his diagnosis that led to many arrests, he was hospitalised in Brooklyn, where in 1961 Dylan finally got to meet him, talk with him, visit him two or three times a week and sing him some of his own songs and some of Woody's. It's the first real audience for his songwriting, as if it all begins with entertaining a very sick hero.

Woody, slowly sinking, quietly listened to Bob sincerely singing his songs, his voice and manner modelled after him but not at all meekly, the whole future of his kind of close, urgent, resistance singing, his fiery force, filling his sad hospital room. He thought it sounded like a voice he could trust, although Bob could do with a little work on his singing. There was a kind of unspoken private ceremony witnessed by no-one where Guthrie deputised Dylan, giving him full authority to take on his mission.

There was no sense of where this mission would end up. There was no sense of how many changes there would be, how many voices Dylan would pass through over the next sixty years, and what he would end up doing with and to the art of the song influencing the past, rewriting its sources, colliding with the universe, making the folk go through so many changes until the dust was replaced by stardust, keeping up with the world and how the history of the world had changed. No sense of how, because of technology, his songs and voices would exist in many places, all at once, loss and transformation walking hand in hand.

The mission is a mystery that contains mysteries that Dylan turns into sound. The mission never loses sight of Guthrie, even as Dylan seems to have said farewell, one last time, thanks, and on I go – Guthrie's 'This Land is Your Land' was often the final track at the Rolling Thunder shows, his most experimental imagining of what his ideal tour would be, where he remembered his time in the hospital room with a stricken Guthrie not by repeating what he did but by electrically and psychically magnifying his spirit and modernising, even post-modernising, his music.

In 1992 a concert at Madison Square Garden celebrated Dylan's thirty-year Columbia recording career and featured Kris Kristofferson, Lou Reed, Stevie Wonder, Willie Nelson, Neil Young, Chrissie Hynde, George Harrison and Tom Petty singing Dylan songs. Bob's own brief appearance at this concert would include 'Song to Woody' – where a world is so ground down it looks like it's dying, and it's hardly been born – and a song high on its own fantastic fury that would cause Dylan himself to admit he had no idea where it came from, 'It's Alright, Ma (I'm Only Bleeding)' – with a sequel to the line from 'Song to Woody' where someone not being born is busy dying. Every voice he's ever used, from wise guy to wound down, sensible to manic, blues to crooner, rebel to weirdo, shiny new to the dark side of life can sing that line with just the right amount of urgency, as if something eternal has been accessed.

Guthrie gave him a card after their first meeting that said 'I ain't dead yet', and Dylan sent Diamond Dave a card that had a picture of Guthrie playing his guitar with the 'This machine kills fascists' label. In the card he said: 'Dear Dave, I met Woody. He likes my stuff – Bob.' Casual, like he'd just been hitchhiking, and somewhere between one place and the next he met a man named Woody Guthrie with some interesting stories to tell. That's exactly how it was, an alignment so perfect it's eerie, because some of all this was happening in dreamtime.

It's the idea of getting in touch with Guthrie that tugged Dylan out of the Midwest to New York. He shows up as though he arrives just as Guthrie, born to leave places, gets ready to make his New York exit, as he described it in *Bound for Glory*, as though the city was a peculiar, unnatural wilderness he could never get used to. Guthrie departs, on the road again, leaving a space to fill, and Dylan rolls into town, hungry for everything, and if he thought he'd been busy in Minneapolis, in between not going to classes, he hadn't seen anything yet.

It was a big leap for a young boy from a small town, even if he'd been feeling a little worldlier after a few trips to various cities and their music scenes, for real, or for not so real, for the purpose of padding out his biography, his past changing according to the route he followed. Building up his part, he imagined he'd been hanging out with characters with names like Sugar Butt Sam, Long Coat Lizzy and Slicker Fastblack, avoiding jail because the arresting sheriff was impressed to find a tramp reading Shakespeare, precariously hanging on to a rod under a train reading a pamphlet by Oscar Wilde.

He made himself part of an American gang of unconquerable adventurers, assorted oddballs and natural explorers, the kind ruined by routine, squatting on the straw-spread floor of a boxcar, riding in the dark for what seemed like years. As he rode and hiked, even if just in his own mind, he heard folk ballads, protest songs, hillbilly waltzes, country swing, pop standards and driving blues, and yearned for the fantastic promised land talked about in songs Pete Seeger sang like 'Big Rock Candy Mountain', a hobo's idea of paradise, where there are cigarette trees and hens lay soft boiled eggs.

Before Christmas 1960, driven by impatience, he told his

parents he was moving to New York, 'There's some oppor-
tunities out there for someone like me', and they didn't fully
understand that what he really meant is he was thinking about
making contact with an almost holy vocal American legend
losing the power of speech, and pretty soon he was starting to
tell people his parents were dead as he started splitting himself
into many different, false, identities. He'd got it all mapped out,
in his head, where he'd built a room for all his maps. There
were some folk clubs and coffee houses in Greenwich Village
that would suit his kind of music, a whole new movement he
might fit into, a few contacts to make. His dad understood all
about making contacts, about finding opportunity.

When Dylan did make it into those clubs and cafés, where
the serious-minded folk music that sets up the '60s was up and
fighting, they were filled with those who knew what they were
talking about, some pretty sniffy. A few wondered where this
wiry, raw-skinned character with a lot of nerve poking through
his nerves and neediness had come from. He'd gone out of his
way to look like he lived on the believe-it-or-not edge of isolation and emotional poverty, that he was tramping a perpetual
journey, as though he slept rough in parts of town that were a
little dangerous. He looked like he might have taken his walk
from Charlie Chaplin, gazed at strangers like he'd just strolled
out of a western legend, and everything else seemed stolen from
somewhere. Was there anyone actually there? Sang just like
Woody, dressed just like Woody, the Shakespeare in overalls,
knew one too many of Woody's songs. There were already a few
of those plying their trade as part of the scene. Did the world
really need one more? Who does he think he is? They weren't to
know that this newcomer playing mystery man hitting his guitar

strings harder than most had been given approval to spread truth to people by the only authority he needed approval from.

He wins some of them over, already skilled at embellishing his credentials, and finds himself at the centre of an exciting, cosmopolitan music scene buzzing with musicians, artists and poets, mixing and mating in all sorts of ways, collaborating and arguing about art and ideas. When he got to tell new friends about where he'd come from, his truth involved being pretty evasive. He was such a liar, he couldn't help it, and he was pretty hard to talk to. There were lots of stories about who he was, but he could never get them straight. Sometimes truths are so complicated it's exhausting to get them out in the right order. The question of a place of origin would loom forever, hazy and unresolved. You couldn't pin him down on anything; he'd already worked out that objection, evasion, joyous distrust and love of irony were signs of health, even signs of that authenticity that everyone was so keen on establishing.

Highway 61 or the Mississippi River don't take you to New York, except perhaps in old blues songs sung by those making up their own routes, but they did for Dylan, and the final ride that took him there, after a few hair-raising detours, definitely all in the mind, is Woody Guthrie. As Dylan finally made it into the great city, the most fatally fascinating in America, ringed with trash, equipped to handle strangers, a city that will even lend a child a sophisticated look, it didn't take him long to work out whether he belonged. There seemed to be some pollen of ideas floating in the air, which fertilises minds here and there which don't have direct contact.

He didn't see the city coming, and then suddenly he was there. He arrives again and again, in films, in articles, in blogs, in radio shows, in anniversaries, in interviews, in documentaries, in books, in this book, witnessed by me, in stories that make a case for knowing what had happened, and what happens next and when and where. He's arrived a million times before, always shrouded in vagueness, having left a trail of some sort, at the place he was always meant to be, and always meant to leave, his apprenticeship complete, as though one day it will all make sense, it will all be revealed, with a name he'd given himself, because what's in a name, and he always arrives as though for the very first time.

As he crosses the threshold, he sometimes sees his fabled future self, heading in the other direction, towards the western skies, not wanting to be trapped in the city that never sleeps, where big buildings hide the horizon and everything's for sale. It's where it all started but it makes no sense to him anymore. He needed to leave home to find his place but the city turned out to be another prison he needs to break out of, just like Woody when he went looking for salvation in that distant, imagined America where the land meets the sun, always at the other end of another all-night journey which might yet end somewhere dark. He goes to sleep in one place, wakes up in another, goes to sleep as one person, wakes up as another. He's bought a map, but he still gets side-tracked, there's someone out to get him wherever he happens to be, and he's got the blood of the land in his voice. In some places he visits nothing much changes. In other places everything changes.

He's coming and going, feeling like he's disappearing, changing form, never here and never now, keeping us guessing, sustaining himself during times of distress, walking towards and away from the lights, to and from 4th Street and Highway

61, between the Mississippi and Montague Street, between the North Country and the Gates of Eden, wondering where he is, watching himself make his moves, various, mobile and alone. There are hundreds of songs he's written curling around his head like rings of smoke, containing thousands of worlds, contained in rooms inside his mind.

At one point, near the beginning, after writing a few songs, as if that might be as far as things went, he signed a publishing contract in New York and received an advance of a hundred dollars against future royalties; at another point, after sixty years of making up another song, and another one, after becoming his songs, and counting the cost, he signed a contract with the Universal Music Publishing Group for his entire songwriting catalogue for an estimated $300 million. The songs that never ended turned into numbers that never ended. The songs that had entered a rarified zone, many beyond the passage of time, had also been given their own essential economic existence. He had no comment to make about the transaction. It didn't have anything to do with him. And whenever he tried to explain himself, he was out of time before he even began.

He's the space between what he'd like to be and what others made of him. Everyone wanted something different from him; they got to re-create him in their own minds. Was that me, he asks himself. God knows ... He's getting closer and closer to the end of the road, to coming to a conclusion, the unseen wind behind him. He's looking like he could do with a sleep, just to round things off, looking like he might have found a way to keep himself alive once he's gone.

Time once more to begin again, because of how things change.

# LO AND BEHOLD!

Iain MacGregor for commissioning and encouraging.

David Godwin and Philippa Sitters at DGA for negotiating and supporting.

All at Simon & Schuster for transforming the manuscript into a book especially my publisher Holly Harris and editor Kaiya Shang.

Jonathan Wadman (copy editor), Victoria Godden (proof-reader) and Sophia Akhtar (photos).

All those travellers, observers and thinkers before me who first reached the land and built on it.

The imagination of Elizabeth Levy.

Berlin correspondent; Madeleine Morley. On the phone; Carol Morley. French proverbs; Jayne Morley.

My mum and dad who gave me the middle name Robert, which I only now realise meant something.

# SELECTED ALBUM DISCOGRAPHY

Ladies and gentlemen, please welcome Columbia recording artist Bob Dylan.

## STUDIO ALBUMS

Bob Dylan (1962)

The Freewheelin' Bob Dylan (1963)

The Times They Are a-Changin' (1964)

Another Side of Bob Dylan (1964)

Bringing It All Back Home ((1965)

Highway 61 Revisited (1965)

Blonde on Blonde (1966)

John Wesley Harding (1967)

Nashville Skyline (1969)

Self Portrait (1970)

New Morning (1970)

Pat Garrett & Billy the Kid (1973)

Dylan (1974)

Planet Waves (1974)

Blood on the Tracks (1975)

The Basement Tapes (1975)

Desire (1976)

Street-Legal (1978)

Slow Train Coming (1979)

Saved (1980)

Shot of Love (1981)

Infidels (1983)

Empire Burlesque (1985)

Knocked Out Loaded (1986)

Down in the Groove (1988)

Oh Mercy (1990)

Under the Red Sky (1990)

Good as I Been to You (1992)

World Gone Wrong (1993)

Time Out of Mind (1997)

"Love and Theft" (2001)

Modern Times (2006)

Together Through Life (2009)

Christmas in the Heart (2009)

Tempest (2012)

Shadows in the Night (2015)

Fallen Angels (2016)

Triplicate (2017)

Rough and Rowdy Ways (2020)


## LIVE ALBUMS

Before the Flood (1974)

Hard Rain (1976)

Bob Dylan at Budokan (1979)

Real Live (1984)

Dylan & the Dead (1989)
MTV Unplugged (1995)
Live at the Gaslight 1962 (2005)
Live at Carnegie Hall 1963 (2005)
In Concert – Brandeis University 1963 (2011)


## THE BOOTLEG SERIES

The Bootleg Series Volumes 1-3 (Rare & Unreleased) 1961–
1991 (1991)

The Bootleg Series Vol. 4: Bob Dylan Live 1966, The "Royal
Albert Hall" concert (1998)

The Bootleg Series Vol. 5: Bob Dylan Live 1975, The Rolling
Thunder Revue (2002)

The Bootleg Series Vol. 6: Bob Dylan Live 1964, Concert at
Philharmonic Hall (2004)

The Bootleg Series Vol. 7: No Direction Home: The
Soundtrack (2005)

The Bootleg Series Vol. 8 : Tell Tale Signs Rare and Unreleased
1989–2006 (2008)

The Bootleg Series Vol. 9 : The Witmark Demos: 1962–
1964 (2010)

The Bootleg Series Vol. 10: Another Self Portrait (1969–
1971) (2013)

The Bootleg Series Vol. 11: The Basement Tapes Raw (2014)

The Bootleg Series Vol. 12: The Best of the Cutting Edge
1965–1966 (2015)

The Bootleg Series Vol. 13: Trouble No More 1979-1981 (2017)

The Bootleg Series Vol. 14: More Blood, More Tracks (2018)

The Bootleg Series Vol. 15 : Travelin' Thru, 1967-1969 (2019)

# BOB DYLAN AND HIS GRAMMY HISTORY

'Awards are a lot of headlights stapled to
your chest'
– Bob Dylan


## GRAMMY NOMINEE (2018)

Best Traditional Pop Vocal Album
For *Triplicate*


## GRAMMY NOMINEE (2017)

Best Traditional Pop Vocal Album
For *Fallen Angels*


## GRAMMY NOMINEE (2016)

Best Traditional Pop Vocal Album
For *Shadows in the Night*


## GRAMMY NOMINEE (2010)

Best Solo Rock Vocal Performance
For the song 'Beyond Here Lies Nothin''

### GRAMMY NOMINEE (2010)

Best Americana Album
For *Together Through Life*

### GRAMMY WINNER (2007)

Best Solo Rock Vocal Performance
For the song 'Someday Baby'

### GRAMMY WINNER (2007)

Best Contemporary Folk/Americana Album
For *Modern Times*

### GRAMMY NOMINEE (2007)

Best Rock Song
For 'Someday Baby'

### GRAMMY WINNER (2006)

Best Long Form Music Video
*No Direction Home: Bob Dylan* (2005)

## GRAMMY NOMINEE (2006)

Best Compilation Soundtrack Album for Motion Picture, Television or Other Visual Media
For *The Soundtrack – Bootleg Series, Vol. 7*

*No Direction Home: Bob Dylan* (2005)

## GRAMMY NOMINEE (2004)

Best Pop Collaboration with Vocals
For the song 'Gonna Change My Way of Thinking'
**Grammy [Nominee]** (2004)

## BEST MALE ROCK VOCAL PERFORMANCE

For the song 'Down in the Flood'

## GRAMMY WINNER (2002)

Best Contemporary Folk Album
For *"Love and Theft"*

## GRAMMY NOMINEE (2002)

Album of the Year
For *"Love and Theft"*

## GRAMMY NOMINEE (2002)

Best Male Rock Vocal Performance
For 'Honest With Me'


## GRAMMY NOMINEE (2001)

Best Song Written for a Motion Picture, Television or Other
Visual MediaFor 'Things Have Changed'
*Wonder Boys* (2000)


## GRAMMY NOMINEE (2001)

Best Male Rock Vocal Performance
For 'Things Have Changed'


## GRAMMY NOMINEE (1999)

Best Country Song
For 'To Make You Feel My Love'


## GRAMMY WINNER (1998)

Best Male Rock Vocal Performance
For 'Cold Irons Bound'


## GRAMMY WINNER (1998)

Album of the Year
For *Time Out of Mind*

## GRAMMY WINNER (1998)

Best Contemporary Folk Album
For *Time Out of Mind*

## GRAMMY NOMINEE (1996)

Best Contemporary Folk Album
For *MTV Unplugged*

## GRAMMY NOMINEE (1996)

Best Rock Song
For 'Dignity'

## GRAMMY NOMINEE (1996)

Best Male Rock Vocal Performance
For 'Knockin' on Heaven's Door'

## GRAMMY WINNER (1995)

Best Traditional Folk Album
For *World Gone Wrong*

## GRAMMY NOMINEE (1994)

Best Rock Performance by a Duo or Group with Vocal
For 'My Back Pages'

## GRAMMY NOMINEE (1994)

Best Contemporary Folk Album
For *Good as I Been to You*

## GRAMMY NOMINEE (1992)

Best Music Video, Short Form
For 'Series of Dreams' (1991)

## GRAMMY WINNER (1991)

Lifetime Achievement Award presented, by Jack Nicholson.

In his acceptance speech, Dylan acknowledged his father (who in turn had quoted a nineteenth century rabbi) as telling him that, even if one was defiled so much that one's parents turned away, 'God will always believe in your own ability to mend your own ways.'

## GRAMMY WINNER (1990)

Best Rock Performance by a Duo or Group with Vocal
For *Traveling Wilburys Vol. 1*

## GRAMMY NOMINEE (1990)

Album of the Year
For *Traveling Wilburys Vol. 1*

## GRAMMY NOMINEE (1989)

Best Traditional Folk Recording
For 'Pretty Boy Floyd'

## GRAMMY NOMINEE (1982)

Best Inspirational Performance
For *Shot of Love*

## GRAMMY NOMINEE (1981)

Best Inspirational Performance
For *Saved*

## GRAMMY WINNER (1980)

Best Rock Vocal Performance, Male
For 'Gotta Serve Somebody'

## GRAMMY NOMINEE (1974)

Album of Best Original Score Written for a Motion Picture or
a Television Special
*Pat Garrett & Billy the Kid* (1973)

## GRAMMY WINNER (1973) ALBUM OF THE YEAR

For *The Concert for Bangladesh*

## Grammy Nominee (1970)

Best Country Instrumental Performance
For 'Nashville Skyline Rag'

## Grammy Nominee (1969)

Best Folk Performance
For *John Wesley Harding*

## Grammy Nominee (1965)

Best Folk Recording
For 'The Times They Are a-Changin''

## Grammy Nominee (1963)

Best Folk Recording
For *Bob Dylan*

# INDEX

BD indicates Bob Dylan.

381